JADE

玉

Text and Photographs
Fred Ward

Editing
Charlotte Ward

3   In the Beginning
9   China and the Stone of Heaven
21   The Olmec, Maya, and Aztec
      in Mesoamerica
31   The Maori in New Zealand
37   Jade Today in Burma, China, Canada,
      New Zealand, Guatemala, Russia,
      Australia, and the United States
59   Buying and Caring for Jade
62   Global Jade Map

Burma's lavender jadeite is even rarer than green. This remarkable large showpiece is so elegant that the factory where it was carved asked to display it as the ideal blend of beauty, quality, and lapidary skill.

Shanghai Jade Carving Factory, Shanghai

IN THE
BEGINNING

J ade—say the magic word. Whisper it. *Jade*. Let its sound transport you to dreams of the Orient, to soft nights. Imagine a shadowed inn high in an isolated rain forest. Royal guests arriving by elephant. Luscious delicacies served on pure white stone. A beautiful woman. *Jade*. Wide tropical leaves backlit by morning sun. *Jade*. Green so rich and pure it brings spring into your heart. *Jade*.

Jade evokes exotic visions real, true, and deserved. To the Chinese for thousands of years jade was the *Stone of Heaven*. As you will see, they treasured jade beyond any other material. Europeans and Americans may desire diamonds or gold, but they do not revere either. The Chinese centered their culture around jade, exhibiting an impassioned love as old as China itself, one that transcended our present understanding.

But the story of jade is even more complex than that single historic relationship; for jade is global, its use ancient, and its position as a bridge between gems and minerals unique. Someone, somewhere, lost in the mists of time, realized that jade made a better tool than anything else ever had. We now know that the momentous discovery of jade as a tool took place more than 5,000 years ago, reflecting an instance of genius independently repeated later in a variety of other locations.

Today's industrialized societies can choose what will make the most effective tools, weapons, and art from a host of metals, plastics, glass, minerals, and other materials. Imagine living in prehistoric times when the options were limited to stone, wood, crystals, and other naturally occurring materials. Metals had not yet been worked when people first began using jade. Although it was a rock, because of its characteristics, jade conferred many of the benefits of metal. Even after humans moved into the Iron and Bronze Ages, their jade performed better as tools than did early metals, a situation that existed until people perfected alloys.

Reserved for royalty and the elite, white nephrite, the most valuable material throughout Chinese history, brings life to a great carving. This Warring States (475-221 B.C.) **ch'i**, *a ritual ax head, may be the best ever carved.*

National Palace Museum, Taipei

Having access to stones harder and tougher than the neighbors' produced distinct advantages. It is no surprise that the oldest jade artifacts seem to have been practical. Wherever jade occurred, early humans recognized its potential, fashioned it into tools and weapons, then ritualized its use by making symbolic pieces that usually reflected its initial utilitarian shapes. In a culture as old as China's, honoring any specific gem, metal, or stone for millennia resulted in a trove of utensils, ceremonial artifacts, and art, as well as myths and legends.

During a similar time period half a world away, European peoples capitalized on jade's special qualities. Around Lake Konstanz, in what is now Switzerland, a "stilt-house culture" developed on the edges of several local lakes. Between 3500 and 1800 B.C. a small Alpine group gathered pieces of both jadeite and nephrite—the two materials we know today as jade—mainly to fashion them into axes and adzes. London's Natural History Museum once printed a survey of prehistoric jade ax discoveries in Europe, documenting hundreds of jadeite and nephrite examples in the British Isles, France, Germany, Switzerland, Italy, and Yugoslavia.

Comparing Swiss and Chinese burial sites dating from about the same period reveals important differences in jade use. Whereas the Swiss stilt-house cultures apparently never progressed to ritualizing jade, even the oldest Chinese societies left relics that

Two of the most sacred objects in ancient China were often carved in nephrite jade, that culture's most precious material. A ts'ung (left) represented earth and a pi disc (right) symbolized heaven while it served as a conduit between heaven and earth. Both these superb examples are from the Western Zhou period, 1100-770 B.C.

National Palace Museum, Taipei

Honolulu Academy of Arts

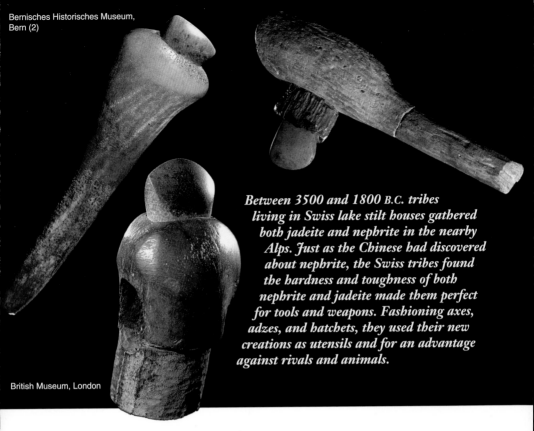

Between 3500 and 1800 B.C. tribes living in Swiss lake stilt houses gathered both jadeite and nephrite in the nearby Alps. Just as the Chinese had discovered about nephrite, the Swiss tribes found the hardness and toughness of both nephrite and jadeite made them perfect for tools and weapons. Fashioning axes, adzes, and hatchets, they used their new creations as utensils and for an advantage against rivals and animals.

included symbolic jade carvings. However early the Chinese formed jade tools, they apparently immediately began to honor the material by also carving it into their most precious possessions.

B y now you have noticed that two different names, *nephrite* and *jadeite*, refer to jade. This is the only instance in gemology where one word refers to two chemically different rocks. Through the resulting confusion, unscrupulous sellers take advantage of baffled buyers.

I deliberately use the word *rock* instead of *mineral* to classify jade. Rocks, like both jades, as well as lapis lazuli, charoite, and maw-sit-sit, are aggregates of one or more minerals. A mineral has a definite chemical composition and characteristic structure with consistent physical and optical properties. A rock is a collection of minerals. Although nephrite and jadeite are both hard and may be green, they differ from each other just as they differ from other green gems, such as emerald and peridot.

Historic accidents are largely responsible for applying one term— *jade*—to two different stones. By the time Spain conquered the New World, even though Europeans had shown a penchant for labeling all natural things, they had not yet classified the rocks so esteemed by the Chinese and vital to the Swiss stilt-house cultures. Within a few years after Columbus sailed, Spanish *conquistadores* adopted the native Mesoamerican custom of wearing local green rocks around the waist or carrying them in pockets to cure kidney disorders. Their name for the kidney cure, *piedra de ijada*—"stone of the

5

loins," stuck. When jade was transported back to Europe, its reputation spread to other countries. In France the phrase should have translated literally *pierre de l'ejade*, but in what may have been a printer's error, it appeared as *le jade*.

The Renaissance inspired a scientific revolution in Europe, and with it, Latin taxonomy. The Mesoamerican green rock, by then called *piedra de los riñones*— "stone of the kidneys"—became *lapis nephriticus*,

which translated to English as *nephrite*. So for a couple of centuries the word *nephrite* was used for the material we now know as *jadeite*.

As a result of early English, Spanish, and Portuguese trade, Europeans collected Chinese jade. In 1863 French scientist Alexis Damour noticed that some of the bright green jewelry and carvings arriving from China, which was made from Burma material, looked very different from ancient Chinese artifacts. Using new analytical tools, Damour observed two distinct compounds. He applied the already accepted word *nephrite* to old Chinese jade and created a name, *jadeite*, for the new Burmese material. Adding to the confusion, later analysis revealed that Mesoamerican jade, for which the word *nephrite* had been created, exhibited similar chemistry to Burma's jadeite. Even though China had never associated kidneys with jade, it was left with the Latin kidney connection. Unable to correct the linguistic and mineralogical tangle, scientists let both names and definitions stand. Consequently, the world has two jades.

Further complicating the saga, the Chinese have shifted their reverence from one rock to the other. China used to reserve creamy white nephrite for royal carvings. Today's Chinese seem to believe that only jadeite has great inherent value.

Nephrite, China's historic jade, is a silicate of calcium and magnesium, part of the amphibole group, which ranges from pure white (tremolite, absent of iron) to green (actinolite, colored by iron). In addition to chemistry, nephrite is defined by physical structure. It must have felted interlocking fibers (page 15), which give nephrite its unique resistance to breaking, thus making it the "toughest" natural material. Nephrite occurs in British Columbia (the largest commercial producer), Australia, New Zealand, Russia, South

Korea, Taiwan, Poland, South Africa, California, Alaska, Wyoming, Nevada, Washington state, and in small deposits in far western China. There, Uygur jade pickers walk the White Jade and Black Jade Rivers, looking for white pebbles, cobbles, and boulders, once prized by Chinese emperors. But nature doles out only a few hundred a year, keeping white nephrite one of the rarest materials of all time.

Jadeite, a silicate of sodium and aluminum, was the Maya's most precious possession. Chromium causes the vibrant green color. Jadeite's interlocking crystalline structure (page 15) gives a glassy polished look prized by rulers of the last Chinese dynasty and today's gem buyers. Burma (now called Myanmar), Guatemala, and Russia mine jadeite commercially. Japan, Switzerland, and California have small deposits.

A timeline helps to tell the story of both nephrite and jadeite (inside back cover). Artifacts show that the Chinese had a fully developed reverence for nephrite at least 5,000 years ago, perhaps preceded by 3,000 years of use. China traded for nephrite from a deposit in the western Kunlun Mountains to produce the finest stone carvings the world has ever seen. Between 3500 and 1800 B.C. prehistoric inhabitants throughout Europe made tools and weapons from both nephrite and jadeite. Beginning about 2000 B.C. the Olmec in Mesoamerica worked a jadeite deposit that served three cultures for 3,000 years. Following the Olmec, the Maya added significantly to jade art by carving their most precious religious and symbolic objects in jadeite until about A.D. 900. Then came the Aztec, who treasured jadeite until the Spanish overran them in the 1500s. Across the Pacific, after arriving in New Zealand around A.D. 1000, the Maori discovered nephrite, which played a pivotal role in their culture up to the 1800s. Only in the late 1700s did Burma begin to regularly export its jadeite to the world.

Found on the chest of a buried warrior in Nohmul, Belize, this jadeite Jester God bar pectoral (right) came from the Maya Early Classic period, A.D. 350-600.

New Zealand's Maori carved pekapeka (opposite, top), nephrite batlike figures.

Poised as if to speak, an animated depiction of a regal youth tops the A.D. 758 jadeite Mayan portrait jar from Tikal (opposite, bottom).

CHINA
AND THE
STONE OF HEAVEN

When people were new on the earth and prey to all the wild animals, the Storm God looked down from the heavens and took pity. With one hand he grasped the rainbow and with the other he forged it into jade axes. These he threw down for people to find. And so they did, and once discovering the axes, they guessed the origin of their precious gift, and thereafter called jade the stone of heaven.

A Chinese Legend

If jade is discarded and pearls destroyed, petty thieves will disappear, there being no valuables left to steal.

Dictionary from reign of
Emperor K'ang Hsi (A.D. 1662-1722)

Tradition has it that Confucius, China's best-known intellectual, was born after a unicorn delivered a jade tablet to his mother. The birth announcement bore an inscription calling the boy "a throneless king." Such was the Chinese regard for the perfection of jade that at times where we apply *gold* or *silver* as superlatives—such as "golden-toned," "streets paved with gold," or "silver-tongued"—the Chinese prefix *jade*, especially when referring to women. They call a beautiful woman "jade person," a woman's smooth skin "fragrant jade," her hands "jade bamboo shoots," her especially sweet singing voice "jade rich," and the death of one possessing those attributes "jade shattered." Poetically *jade* describes many other aspects of life. Gazing at a full moon, the Chinese admire a "jade plate"; when only a crescent remains, they cast their eyes toward a "jade hook" and toast it with wine cradled in a "jade boat."

Richard Gump started buying and collecting jade in China early in the 20th century. As he became famous for his San Francisco store, he wrote, "China built a civilization around the stone....[T]he use of jade is inseparably linked with the development of Chinese worship, court ceremonials, thought, and art...." I know of no historical parallel to China's relationship to nephrite. Even though the Spanish pillaged the New World, exterminating indigenous

One of China's revered jade forms, the ts'ung, *a tube of nephrite, symbolized earth. This richly-hued example dates from the Zhou period, 1027-222 B.C.*

National Museum, Singapore

cultures in their frenzied search for treasure, they never made gold and silver their *raison d'être*, their reason for being. The Chinese saying goes, "One can put a price on gold, but jade is priceless."

To the Chinese, nephrite jade transcended value, rarity, and beauty. No culture has ever assigned such a symbolic role to any other material. Only through the disc-shaped *pi* (pronounced "bee," page 4) could emperors speak directly to even greater powers, thus completing the cosmic link between heaven and earth. The origin of the *pi* form becomes clear when compared to the Chinese symbol for the sun, ⊙.

Pi discs may be plain, flat, and undecorated or filled with small raised circles, spirals, or other shapes. Ideally, the hole in the middle should be a fifth the diameter of the entire disk. Of all jade forms, the *pi*, as the symbol for heaven, was most significant.

At the highest levels of Chinese society jade played an integral part in everyday life. The first objects the emperor touched each morning were jade—most often white nephrite. Scholars were accorded the honor of using jade writing implements. Emperor Qianlong (r. 1736-1795) displayed perhaps the greatest veneration for jade as he assembled the empire's best craftsmen in his Beijing workshops. His devotion to the stone was so great that he decreed jade masters henceforth were to be referred to as "Sir," a distinct honor in the caste-conscious culture.

Gentlemen paced their lives by adjusting their gait so the jade pieces dangling from their belts tinkled a measured beat. Confucius, whose writings both reflected and established the essence of Chinese life, listed virtue, loyalty, intelligence, justice, humanity, and truth among the requisite jadelike characteristics gentlemen should aspire to. In the master's time to reward contests of skill, third place received an ivory scepter; second place won gold; only first place commanded jade.

Norma Lu Collection, Singapore

The Chinese excelled at designing jade carvings to contrast rich rind surface colors with underlying hues. Both these examples feature dragons, which the Chinese considered to be divine mythical creatures that brought ultimate good fortune. The carving opposite was most likely a sword hilt. Three dragons surround a glorious Sung Dynasty (A.D. 960-1279) jade drinking horn (right). Painstaking work on nephrite often took months or years, even with a treadle.

National Palace Museum, Taipei

Many fanciful stories but few firm facts enlighten us about the origins of jade use and jade carving. As in Egypt and other great archeological sites, scientists often collect the finest artifacts from the protective environment of tombs. Fortunately, Chinese culture expressed itself in nephrite, a material that does not rot or age, one that preserves history almost perfectly. Even though jade cannot be dated, accompanying burial relics can. Ritual jades almost as old as jade utensils indicate that the stone's earliest users honored nephrite's special qualities of beauty, hardness, and toughness.

Despite claims to the contrary, there appears to be little historical support for China's having had jade sources within its traditional borders. Of the millions of carvings over thousands of years almost all seem to have been shaped from imported nephrite from the Kunlun Mountains. For most of China's history that jade source was in Turkestan, an adjacent area that China often controlled but never owned until its border expansion after World War II (when it also enveloped Tibet). The Kunlun Mountains now lie within China's realm as part of Xinjiang Province (page 42).

One of the stops on the famed Silk Road, Hotan (formerly spelled Khotan) facilitated trade between Europe and Asia long before transoceanic commerce existed. At the edge of the great Taklimakan Desert near the confluence of the White Jade River (Yurungkax) and Black Jade River (Karakax), Hotan served as trading center, way-station, and location of the first Asian nephrite sighting by a European.

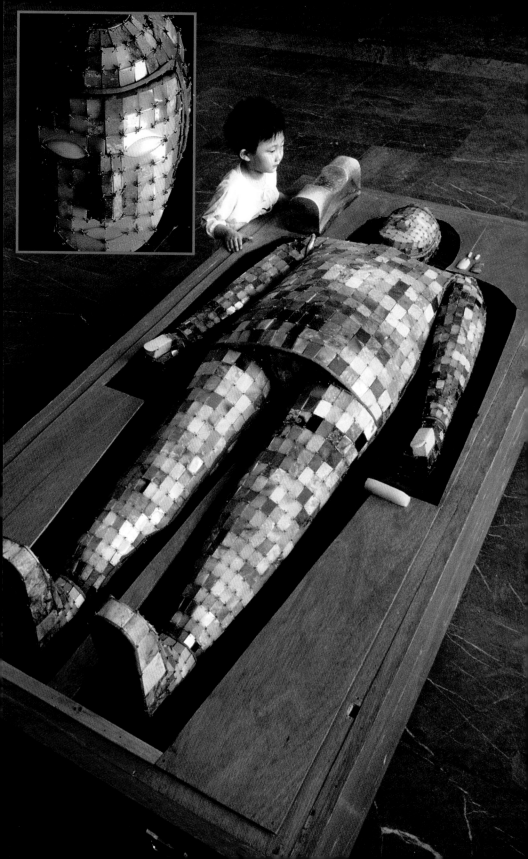

M arco Polo, the intrepid Italian adventurer, traveler, and writer, watched men pick small boulders from the area's two rivers. Afterwards he accompanied caravans transporting the stones to Beijing, where they "fetched great prices." Unfortunately, neither he nor any other European in 1272 knew enough about gems and minerals to identify the rocks properly as nephrite, which explains why he noted, in error, large numbers of "chalcedonies and jaspers." What Polo witnessed was the time-honored process of collecting jade, little changed in the 4,000 years before he arrived or in the intervening 700 years before I waded into those same waters to pluck out a few precious pebbles of my own.

No traditional jade mine exists in the Kunlun Mountains above Hotan. From time to time Uygur tribesmen as well as the Chinese government have tried to mine *in situ* deposits by heating cold boulders to coerce cracking. Although they have had little success, nature's seasons produce steadily, slowly feeding human need. Winter's expansion, contraction, and melting wash jade pebbles and boulders from cliffs and riverbanks into raging spring rivers, which tumble them downstream toward Hotan. Along the way Uygur "jade pickers" walk on the banks, or in the water when possible, looking for jade. A skilled picker with a donkey or a strong back can still make more money from jade in one or two months than from farming all year.

Far better than reality is the Chinese jade-collection myth. A long time ago, so the story goes, the local custom was to have young maidens disrobe and walk naked in the rivers by night. Because unclothed females (*yin*) naturally attract male (*yang*) jade, the girls had only to feel the nephrite pebbles rubbing against their bare feet and reach down to pick them up.

W e know the earliest Chinese found and honored nephrite, among the hardest substances and certainly the toughest available to them. Because it neither chipped nor flaked but kept a good edge, it made fine tools and weapons. But the most ancient examples are too small, too thin, and too delicately carved to have been practical. As meticulous as the Chinese were in keeping records and calendars, it seems the strangest of oversights that they omitted the origin of their use of jade, their most precious possession. The oldest records in China's vast written history include stories of carving nephrite jade and the special reverence and esteem with which it was held. I conjecture that jade use in China predated writing

Fit for a king and reserved for royalty, jade burial suits were used coincidentally in China (nephrite) and Mexico (jadeite). Only Chinese emperors merited gold wire to connect more than 2000 jade tiles. Lesser rulers, such as King Liu Yen, who died in A.D. 90, rated less noble metals (left).

Animal Magic

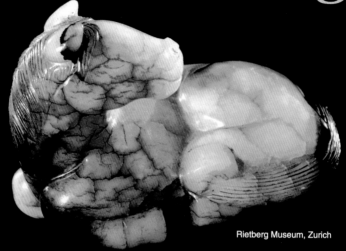

Chinese artists have expressed their understanding of animals with deeply sensitive nephrite carvings. A Ming Dynasty horse (A.D.1368-1644, above) has smiled through centuries. A similar Sung Dynasty horse (A.D. 960-1279, right) continues to slumber peacefully. Many Chinese carvings represent fantasies. A winged creature from the 18th century Qing Dynasty (A.D. 1644-1911, below) appears to have just alighted.

and that the Chinese recut their tools and weapons into ceremonial and ritual symbols, hence the Chinese have no record or cultural memory of a time without jade.

No matter where humans lived, they cycled through similar ages: the Paleolithic, when they chipped stones to form knives and ax heads and started using needles and harpoons; the Neolithic, when they refined stone and horn tools by grinding and polishing; then usually the Bronze and Iron Ages. The New Zealand Maori and the Mesoamerica Maya left jade tools older than their ritual jade carvings. Unlike other jade cultures, I have yet to see any Paleolithic jades from China. Even the earliest Chinese tools displayed in collections and museums were polished and often elaborately and beautifully decorated, suggesting ritual use. Because the Chinese capitalized on nephrite's metal-like characteristics, they may have bypassed or substantially shortened their Stone Age. No wonder they exalted jade.

Nephrite jade's position in Chinese religious services, ceremonies, burials, and mythology is unprecedented. From their legends it is clear the Chinese believed jade and people were intertwined from the beginning. For nearly four millennia of organized imperial court religious rites, which centered on obedience to heaven, jade played the pivotal role.

Despite the multimillennial relationship with nephrite, in A.D. 1784, quite late in Chinese history, an event of such magnitude occurred that the gem world still reels from its consequences. Among the cargoes that arrived in Beijing after a new trade agreement with Burma lay a material that tore the heart and soul of Chinese civilization from its nephrite roots. Once released, the brilliant temptress seduced an empire to abandon its past, luring it from its primal love with the folly of youth. It is a seduction that continues today.

The seductress was jadeite, in vibrant colors that captivated a court and then its people. This luscious upstart bedazzled China with lavenders, yellows, whites, rusts, and intense greens the likes of which no one had seen before. Burmese jadeite was everything nephrite was not—bright, shiny, even gaudy, a new stone for a new age. It remains the proverbial tail wagging the dog. The typical young cutter in China, the new upwardly-

Chemical differences distinguish nephrite from jadeite. Nephrite's toughness and subtle appearance result from its felted, fibrous composition (below, left). Jadeite's interlocked crystalline structure and its chemistry (below, right) produce intense colors and glassy finishes.

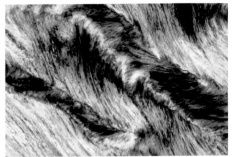

Nephrite thin-section photomicrograph, 200x

Jadeite thin-section photomicrograph, 100x

mobile Chinese consumer, the *nouveau-riche* Hong Kong gem dealer, and particularly the overseas Chinese and American jade buyers—now almost all believe that jadeite alone has value. By reducing nephrite to a souvenir-carving material, how tragically far from its illustrious past the world has let slip the Stone of Heaven.

Jadeite is without doubt a wonderful carving material and gem. Because it has all three requirements for gem status—beauty, durability, and rarity—it was destined for jewelry. Even though China admires lavender jadeite (cover), the second most valuable color, it prefers green. When green jadeite has top color and translucency, it is called "imperial" jade. Such green jadeite rivals the brilliance of emeralds and exceeds their price.

Almost instantly the Chinese extended their use of jadeite beyond rituals and religion. Overnight it became China's court favorite, a jade to wear, to show, to flaunt. Even though jadeite's popularity in jewelry cascaded through society, at first the Chinese retained nephrite for rituals. Then gradually they substituted jadeite for nephrite in new ceremonial objects until finally, with a civil war and the rise of communism, they dropped the ritual use of jade altogether.

More than a tinge of irony attends the capitulation of an egocentric insular culture like China's to an imported product from what it considered an insignificant neighbor worthy only of paying tribute. But capitulate it did, reserving the best, most beautiful green Burma jadeite for imperial and court use, much as white nephrite for millennia had been the perquisite of the court and the scholars.

Yü, the Chinese word for jade, once meant "a precious stone of great beauty." Picture three pierced pieces of jade threaded onto a vertical string. Remove the small dot or line on the bottom right to get the symbol meaning "one who rules." Represented by a pictograph believed to have originated in 2950 B.C., jade and ruler,

Burmese jadeite's arrival in the late 1700s transformed how China used and viewed jade. Bright green jadeite articles, such as the belt dangle and the praying mantis (opposite) and the tricolor tripod urn (left), captivated a new regal generation. Today most Asians and virtually all Westerners view jadeite as the jade of great value, completely reversing China's grand nephrite history. All three objects are from the Qing Dynasty (1644-1911).

Urn (left), The Baur Collection, Geneva;
Fob (top, opposite), National Palace Museum, Taipei

both intermediaries between heaven and earth, share a single sign of power. The Chinese never specifically limited the word *yü* to nephrite, the stone they most honored. Translators tell me *yü* now means "any hard, precious stone of great beauty." As appealing and innocent as this definition sounds, it opens the door to considerable abuse.

Although the Chinese had no jadeite when the word and symbol originated, today they use *yü* to refer to nephrite or jadeite. Often Chinese add "old" or "soft" to *yü* when referring to nephrite and "new" or "hard" when they mean jadeite. Such historic nuances and nonspecific adjectives are lost on most present-day buyers, leaving them sorely confused.

As Burma's jadeite supplies increased in the 1800s, thousands of carvings appeared. Soon jadeite animals, objects, and gems outshone nephrite. Disregarding China's 5,000-year nephrite history, in the past two centuries jadeite has achieved status as the country's preeminent stone and gem. It seems that no one objected to the culture's central substance being supplanted by a different material. Perhaps applying the term *yü* to both jades eased the transition. Initially the jadeite jewelry and carvings mimicked originals in nephrite, but with its unique qualities, soon the ingénue defined a role of its own. Carvers developed a jadeite style that remains basically unchanged today. Whether in China, Hong Kong, or other Asian factories, workers of Burmese jadeite typically form simple cabochons for rings, earrings, and pins, or carve pieces for bangles, pendants, or *objets d'art*.

Burma's jadeite green is unrivaled. Guatemala's jadeite, used by the Olmec, Maya, and Aztec in Mesoamerica for 3,000 years, occurs in a variety of colors, except for the most desirable intense green and lavender. Lavender, as well as multiple hues within a single piece, inspired China's carvers to experiment with new styles (page 16). Objects that would have looked subdued in nephrite, such as the bangles (page 19) and the praying mantis (below), glow electric in jadeite.

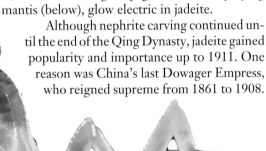

Although nephrite carving continued until the end of the Qing Dynasty, jadeite gained popularity and importance up to 1911. One reason was China's last Dowager Empress, who reigned supreme from 1861 to 1908.

The Baur Collection, Geneva

17

White Is Beautiful

A pair of large exquisite carvings illustrate how quickly Chinese artists mastered the new jadeite material imported from Burma. Walls with intricate patterns are only $1/16$-inch thick. Created during the Qing Dynasty (A.D. 1644-1911) using India's Mogul style, a teapot of unsurpassed delicacy illustrates utility soaring to the highest expression of artistry. Rubies, red spinels, and precise surface details complete the decoration of this breathtakingly-thin translucent treasure.

Lizzadro Museum of Lapidary Art, Elmhurst, Illinois

The Baur Collection, Geneva

Power hungry and greedy, a jade lover without equal, Tzu Hsi epitomized the stones' regal appeal. Through her period of controlling the empire, Tzu Hsi seemed to live for jadeite and nephrite. She entertained with all-jade settings—plates, cups, and chopsticks. She ordered her cape fringed with jade drops. She appeared wearing multiple jade rings, bracelets, and three-inch long fingernail protectors. Housing her personal jade collection required 3,000 boxes.

In their devotion to this gorgeous upstart, buyers who both love jade and want to emulate the last of China's emperors are willing to pay any price to wear imperial green. When emperors directed stone use, they could allocate jadeite with fabulous colors either to jewelry or to carvings. The world is richer because rulers loved jade and afforded the luxury of supporting artists to work a lifetime on only a few spectacular treasures. Fortunately, museums and collections display the best for us to see. Because the durable pieces rested undisturbed in tombs for thousands of years without deterioration, we now enjoy a priceless historic and artistic legacy.

Dragons and imperial-green jadeite—a match made in heaven. The Chinese dragon, or **Lung,** *symbolizes power and excellence, valor and boldness, heroism and perseverance, nobility and divinity. Rulers were believed to have descended from dragons, the angels of the Orient.*

The intense color of imperial-green jadeite immediately destined it for personal adornment. If carved today, the spheres at the top of the bangles would become half-million dollar cabs. Both the one-piece bangles and the above 3 ³/₄-inch-long belt hook are from the Qing Dynasty, A.D. *1644-1911.*

National Palace Museum, Taipei (2)

THE OLMEC, MAYA, & AZTEC IN MESOAMERICA

Hernán Cortés led a ragtag band of Spanish soldiers from Cuba to Mexico in 1519. First the fair-haired *conquistador* burned his ships to insure his unreliable "army" couldn't desert. Next he headed inland toward the Aztec capital of Tenochtitlan—now Mexico City—aiming to conquer Emperor Moctezuma and his empire. Audaciously, with more gall than sense, a few hundred Spaniards confronted the city of 300,000. They could not have known that Aztec myths had predicted the arrival of a fair-haired god from afar. So the native warriors greeted Cortés with some warmth. Feigning friendship, Cortés captured Moctezuma, thus beginning Spanish domination that enslaved the people, plundered the land, and almost eradicated the indigenous culture. When the Aztec grew alarmed at Spanish greed and passion for gold and silver, Moctezuma is said to have observed to his court, "Thank heaven they do not know about the *chalchihuites* (jades)."

Therein lies another tale of cultural clash. Nephrite that the Chinese loved beyond measure, most Europeans and Americans cast aside today as only souvenir-carving material. Jadeite that the Aztec, and the Maya before them, and the Olmec before them, honored as the most precious objects on earth, the Spanish *conquistadores* dismissed as green rocks.

Seeking a conciliatory gesture to avert impending conflict, Moctezuma told Cortés he wanted to present some very valuable stones for the Spanish king. Moctezuma supposedly exhorted, "These are *chalchihuites*, not to be given to anyone but your king. Each is worth two loads of gold." Cortés was not impressed, but he did at least send them toward Spain. Unfortunately the jades never arrived. French pirates hijacked the three treasure ships carrying them and precious metals. But the Aztec sense of value survives.

Occasionally jade carvings transcend a single culture. This jadeite portrait pectoral, from the Olmec Preclassic period (1000-600 B.C.), was later honored by the Maya and most likely worn by a Mayan ruler.

21

Moctezuma had sent a message much like Confucius: Gold has value; jade is priceless.

After Cortés placed Moctezuma under elegant but strict house arrest, the two continued daily discussions, even playing a native chesslike game, which ended with a gift exchange. One day the Aztec king presented Cortés with large gold and silver disks. Noting the Spaniard's obvious pleasure and in a desperate attempt to curry favor with the unenlightened infidels, Moctezuma promised that on the following day he would give the most precious gift of all. He offered Cortés three perfect jadeite beads, but, coveting gold and not beads, the *conquistador* was "bitterly disappointed."

Three grand conjectures attempt to explain how Mesoamericans came to work jade. I consider one to be outlandish, one farfetched, and one tantalizing. First, most detached from the truth are writers who propose that aliens built the long, straight "runways" on Peru's high plains and that jade knowledge came from space. Second, in his popular book *Kon-Tiki*, Thor Heyerdahl postulates that boat people from Polynesia settled South America. If so, his theory goes, they could have brought jade skills gained from other islands. But only New Zealand's Maori had jade skills, and it is apparent that the Maori are not related to South American natives.

Third, Mesoamerica's and China's historic and cultural relationships with jade did coincide in time, resulting in parallels too great to ignore. Were they coincidental or were they related? Some scholars wonder if the famous "land bridge" that twice allowed people to migrate by foot from Siberia to Alaska (and then to disperse throughout the Americas) also transported Chinese skill in working jade and devotion to its attributes. The 25,000 B.C. and 12,000 B.C. migration periods date long before any known Chinese association with jade. Still, I find striking similarities between Chinese jade history and what transpired in Mesoamerica.

National Museum, San Salvador, El Salvador

Whether worn by local royalty or incorporated as symbols into carvings, huge jadeite earflares were power symbols that announced the importance of their wearers.

Consider that the Maya (and sometimes the Aztec) assembled burial jades even more elaborate than China's. Mesoamericans arrayed their deceased royal personages in jade suits and masks (similar to the Chinese suit on page 12), jade head bands, jade hair tubes, jade wrist cuffs, jade necklaces, and ten jade rings. Surrounding them with personal jade objects (pages 6, 7, 22), they entombed their leaders in giant stone sarcophagi covered with jade.

Ponder these other coincidences between China and Mesoamerica. The Aztec named their brilliant green jadeite *quetzalitztli*, after their vibrantly-hued bird, the quetzal; in China the best green jadeite became *fei-ts'ui*, after the kingfisher's colorful feathers. And both the Maya and the Chinese shared beliefs of jade's extraordinary powers to heal the sick or injured, exorcise demons, prevent or delay body composition, and even bestow immortality.

The natives who had already populated what are now Mexico and Peru and the areas between discovered jadeite and mastered carving without the benefit of metals. The Olmec, who created the first culture in the Western Hemisphere, flourished on Mexico's Gulf Coast between 2000 B.C. and 900 B.C. Jade masters for more than a thousand years—during the same period when China's Hsia and Western Zhou Dynasties produced elegant nephrite *pi*, and *ts'ung* symbols—the Olmec carved unsurpassed human figures. Theirs are among the strongest representations of human faces ever sculpted in jade or any other material. Although less well known than the Maya and Aztec, the Olmec brought jade carving to a level that allowed later cultures to build on a solid artistic and technical base.

After the rapacious Spanish assault on native culture and religion, Indians withdrew so far from their roots that subsequent generations not only did not know how to carve jade but had no idea even where to find it. Because Mesoamerican jade carvings older than the Olmec do not exist, we assume the Olmec first discovered New World jadeite. Their sources were lost from the 1500s until the 1960s. As a result of some scientific sleuthing after World War II by William Foshag, Smithsonian's curator of geology, and archeologists in the 1960s (as well as a lucky jadeite find in 1957 by an American businessman), the search for Mesoamerican jadeite mines not only centered on Guatemala but on the Motagua Valley region. Then, with dogged determination, an American couple, Mary Lou and Jay Ridinger, discovered *in situ* jadeite boulders.

Earflares from National Museum of Archaeology and Ethnology, Guatemala City (top);
Pendant from Collection of Hernán Paez (right)

23

Faces Frozen In Time

These three portraits represented living rulers, preserved in their cultures' most precious material, jade. The mosaic funeral mask from Tikal (right) was buried about A.D. 527 and unearthed in 1963. The mask consists of a variety of green stones, but only the earflares test as jadeite.

The Olmec were master jadeite carvers. The elegant portrait pectoral (below), created between 1000-600 B.C., was so admired by the Maya that they made it theirs by adding inscriptions between A.D. 50-250.

Famous for beauty as well as informative details, the Teotihuacan jadeite plaque (opposite) depicts a regally dressed Mayan king on his stone throne. Carved by Maya between A.D. 600-800, the piece was later traded and moved to what is now central Mexico.

24

Exploration in the valley produced more surface occurrences in a variety of colors but no actual mine. Old Mayan work sites showed that small outdoor carving factories had operated in fixed locations for centuries. Today's "miners" still find small pieces of worked and unworked jadeite, as well as tools and pottery.

Then the Ridingers resolved another mystery—the source of the foamy blue-green jadeite favored by Olmec carvers and often found in Costa Rican graves (page 28). In 1987 they discovered the first such *in situ* boulder, thus proving that both the Olmec and Maya had mined jade in the Motagua Valley. The couple's next quest was to locate brilliant green jadeite such as researchers had found in tombs all over Central America, particularly in El Salvador and Belize. The absence of emerald-green or imperial-green jadeite after years of mining in the Motagua Valley region led to speculation that the Olmec had exhausted the original source or that another yet-undiscovered mine held the secret. During the 1980s the Ridingers found a few boulders with small bright green spots—but without imperial-green jadeite's translucency—leading them to believe that the most desirable of all the Mesoameri-

Dr. Guillermo Mata Collection

Wealthy Maya so treasured jadeite that they endured primitive inlays to make a fashion statement. Notice the beauty-notching in two teeth.

A silent 1500s Aztec rabbit nestles an eagle warrior between its protective legs. In the Aztec creation story, rabbits, eagle warriors, and pulque beer were all born on the same day.

Agape in anger or terror? We will never know. For more than 3,000 years the various cultures that flourished throughout Mesoamerica created mosaic jadeite masks, such as this dramatic Zapotec example (right).

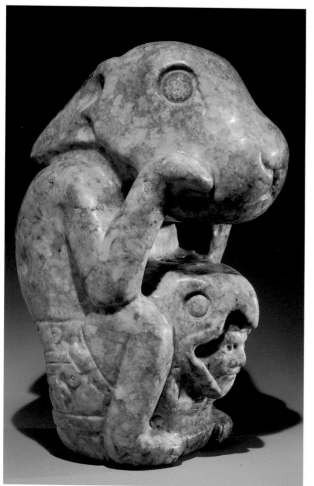

Dumbarton Oaks Research Library and Collections, Washington, D.C.

Mexican National Museum of Anthropology, Mexico City

can jadeite colors most likely originated in the Motagua Valley, although probably never in large quantities.

Finally, we understand why the Olmec and Maya produced so many beautiful jadeite carvings whereas the Aztec, even though they revered jade, made relatively few. Records indicate that the first two cultures had direct access to Guatemala's mining area; the Aztec apparently had to rely on southern tribes, who paid tribute in jade but kept their source secret. Based on jadeite colors and textures, we now believe that Guatemala's Motagua Valley region supplied most or all of the jade used throughout Mesoamerica for about 3,000 years. To date no one has found another jadeite source.

At some point around 100 B.C. to A.D. 100 the Olmec tradition ceased and Maya culture appears to have grown from Olmec roots. By A.D. 200 the Maya dominated Mesoamerica with one of the world's most advanced cultures. Their abstract reasoning, mathematical skills, 365-day calendar, sculptures, hieroglyphic writing, and architecture had no equal in feudal Europe. By the Late Classic Period, A.D. 600-900, an estimated two million Maya lived in what are often described as the world's most modern urban

Ax-gods, pendants with small figures atop stylized ax blades, are the most prevalent pre-Colombian jade artifacts found in Costa Rica. Although most authorities agree the jadeite came from far north in Guatemala, it is unclear whether the ax-gods arrived in Costa Rica as boulders, preforms, or carvings. What is clear is that between 300 B.C. and A.D. 500, when these ax-gods were carved, styles changed, beginning with the rear ax-god above, which is strikingly similar to ancient Chinese carvings, and ending with figures that encouraged alien visitor theories (above, front row right, and opposite far right).

Sometimes carvings appeared that seem to have no relationship to previous work, such as the double-snake and bird pendant (opposite, left) from the Atlantic Watershed area of Costa Rica, carved A.D. 300-700.

All ax-gods and snake/bird pendant (opposite) from Museum of Jade, San Jose, Costa Rica, except far left ax-god (above), Hernán Paez Collection; and second ax-god (above), Frederick Mayer Collection.

28

centers of the time. Although they had access to crystal gemstones, gold, and silver, the Maya, like the Chinese, made jade the focal point of their rituals, elevating it to the most important and precious material in their society.

The Maya also had what are for us some unpleasant ceremonial customs. Jade knives and bowls played central ritual roles in human sacrifices and bloodletting, which the Maya commonly practiced in multiples at important events. Contrary to their unwarranted reputation as placid natives, the Maya sought conflict as a means to capture prisoners. And in the civilization that followed, the ferocious and brutal Aztec expanded sacrificial offerings to such an extent that they had difficulty maintaining an inventory of victims to keep up with ritual demands.

In Mesoamerica today many substances carry "jade" or "jadeite" labels. Guatemala's insignificant nephrite finds are not sold locally. So anything marked *jade* in Central America ought to be jadeite, and certainly anything marked *jadeite* ought to be, because it is the proper name for a specific substance. Most geologists, gemologists, and appraisers strictly subscribe to correct nomenclature. But far too many archaeologists, curators, historians, grave robbers, and unscrupulous sellers lump any stone the Olmec, Maya, and Aztec carved under one convenient term, *jade*. Sometimes it is hard to differentiate carelessness from outright misrepresentation.

Kings were invariably buried with true jadeite, which proves that the original carvers knew the difference between jadeite and other stones, mainly by hardness and appearance. But workers cut the stones they had, and many of today's museum pieces contain mixtures of jadeite, diopside, albite, and numerous other materials. Jadeites are rocks, with widely varying compositions. Only when a piece is mainly composed of jadeite (the exact percentage is yet to be agreed upon by gemologists), should it be labeled *jadeite*. Other substances, such as serpentine or chloromelanite, should be accurately identified. At least they should not be misidentified as jade, though some academics recently have taken a strange stand by applying new terms like "cultural jade" and "social jade" to describe non-jadeite pre-Columbian carvings. The buying public needs to be aware of these inaccuracies.

The Maori in New Zealand

D awn neared on the cold waters. Chilled passengers huddled together in long double-hulled canoes, surely wondering whether this would be the day they died or the day they found land. Their first ritual act of the morning was to greet the great gods of the universe to seek divine assistance in their search for a new island. Sailing southwest by the stars, waiting for light, all watching for a shore, the crew of men, women, and children could not have known where they were, where they were going, or what they would find.

A thousand years have passed since the day the Maori arrived in New Zealand. By their language, culture, features, and legends we know they came from Polynesia but very little else. Their ancestors had migrated about 3,000 years before from Southeast Asia to islands south and east. Some offspring island-hopped across much of the South Pacific, ultimately to the Marquesas Islands. From the south a group moved northward to inhabit the Hawaiian Islands, then south again to Tahiti. Even though they made constant ocean forays, a thousand years had passed until about A.D. 1000 when they made their monumental move. They took to canoes, finding their way across the trackless and dangerous Pacific to the Cook Islands and New Zealand. With them they carried yams, taro, sweet potato, and other tropical fruits and vegetables. Instead of another warm paradise, they found a temperate rain forest, and on the South Island, glaciers, the Southern Alps, snow, ice, sleet, and for the first time in their lives, four distinct seasons. Their landfall provided a hidden blessing of monumental proportions. On the beaches and in the streambeds along a large section of the island's western coast, the Maori found nephrite jade, a treasure that eventually became, as retired director of the Southland Museum and Art Gallery Russell Beck says, "a pivotal part of the Maori way of life."

The significance of jade may be lost on today's readers. When the

*Best known of all Maori nephrite shapes, the **hei-tiki** figurine became the symbol of New Zealand's Maori. **Hei** means "to tie around the neck" and **tiki**, "human," "ancestor," or "the first person." This superb piece, from the early 1800s, was carried by various owners to India and England and was returned to New Zealand in 1948.*

Museum of New Zealand, *Te Papa Tongarewa*, Wellington

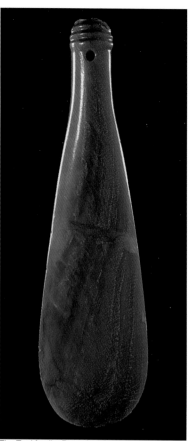

For the British and Americans, a mace is the symbol of power and authority. For New Zealand's Maori, of Polynesian heritage, a short (app. 16 inches) bat carved from local nephrite served that purpose. The mere *(pronounced "meer-ree"), originally used as a war club and jabbing weapon, evolved to symbolic duty. Often carved from a specific variety of New Zealand nephrite called* inanga, *a* mere *was hung from the wrist via a plaited flax cord threaded through a drill hole. This example, probably in use before Captain Cook arrived in 1769, displays all the desirable characteristics of the symbolic nephrite tool—rarity, beauty, and toughness.*

For the Maori, tattoos (opposite) represented substantially more than a fashion statement. Called moko, *they became a person's signature and a notice of status reserved for the elite, chiefs, and influential warriors. Patterns reflected nature, as do today's jade carvings.*

The Topi family, Ruapuke Island, New Zealand

Maori arrived in New Zealand, they were a stone-based people, and they remained so until Abel Tasman "discovered" them in 1642 and Captain James Cook "rediscovered" them and their islands in 1769. Before the Europeans came, the Maori had never seen metal. Aside from food and shelter, as Russell Beck told me, "jade provided the Maori with tools, weapons, ceremonial objects, and personal ornaments, the only stone in the world that could have served all those needs."

Nephrite jade most likely enabled the Maori to develop their culture in New Zealand. Harder and tougher than any metal the British later brought, nephrite did for the Maori what jade had already done for the Swiss stilt-house culture, the ancient Chinese, and the Olmec and Maya. With nephrite, the Maori possessed stone tools and weapons with metal-like properties. Jade blades hold sharp edges better than soft iron. Jade adzes became primary woodworking tools. Though the Maori were a relatively small group with common ancestry who arrived in several migratory waves, presumably from the same original home, they did battle with each other. Unlike most Native Americans who did not conceive of owning even a part of the earth, the Maori developed a land system. Disputes over territory and personal property provided suitable cause for frequent armed conflicts.

The Maori shaped jade jabbing clubs, called *mere*, wielded by leading warriors as weapons and later as symbols of chieftanship.

By the 15th century, jade work areas dotted several beaches on the South Island's west coast. Jade use became a fundamental part of Maori life. Some people specialized in collecting jade, others in carving. Because the North Island had no jade source, the South Islanders developed a jade trade. Like the Chinese and Maya, soon the Maori expanded making tools and weapons into crafting art, ornaments, and ritual objects (page 6). As the Maori remained without metal until Europeans arrived in 1769, their jade applications reflect the scope of their society. Basically they used jade as tools and weapons, and decorated both. Although they never achieved a written language, the Maori sense of design and workmanship surpassed other Polynesian groups. In the absence of contact with any other people, the Maori developed their own culture with jade, utilizing its properties of toughness, translucency, sound, color, and feel. They even heated nephrite to manipulate colors and hardness.

A chronicle of the *hei-tiki* (page 30), by far the best known of all Maori items of adornment, explains much of recent Maori jade history. Most likely of Polynesian origin in wood or bone, the figures are properly called *hei-tiki*, which means "human pendant." They depict a large-headed figure, either male or female, squatting with heels together and hands on thighs. The tilted head measures about half the height of the figure. The Maori refined the figure and defined its ultimate shape and style in jade.

But it appears the Maori had carved relatively few *hei-tiki* when Captain Cook arrived. Like foreign tourists today, the visiting crews fancied souvenirs, so the Maori complied by making so many to trade for British, French, and American metal objects that, according to Russell Beck, "They started to remanufacture their jade adzes into figures and still could not supply the demand." In the mid-1800s several European lapidaries in Dunedin, on the east coast of the South Island, went into making copies of *hei-tiki*, other pendants, and *mere*. They wholesaled their own non-Maori carvings to Maori on the North Island for reselling. The Maori then sold some to Anglo New Zealanders and others to overseas traders. As you might expect, various museums around the world now display the European-carved pieces as original Maori art.

By the end of the 1800s local Maori had so embraced British culture that they no longer carved jade in the traditional manner, but, ironically, they had already created a global demand for the one souvenir from New Zealand every visitor seemed to want. A hemisphere away the world's leading stone-carving town, Germany's Idar-Oberstein, filled the void. Between 1896 and 1914 four Idar families sold more than a million *hei-tiki* carved in Germany, far more than all the Maori had ever made in their thousand-year history. Hubert Dalheimer, whose grandfather imported enough New Zealand nephrite before World War I to last until the 1930s, told me his father had observed, "We never knew where all the figures were going, and then we started seeing our own work showing up in European museums as 'Maori *hei-tiki*.'"

No wonder the curators were confused. Today's tourists are still frustrated wondering what New Zealanders mean when they say "*greenstone*" instead of *nephrite* or *jade*. "Greenstone" is a translation of the Maori word *pounamu*, which refers to both nephrite and bowenite, a local translucent serpentine. This pairing of different materials continues the confusion. Then the government, in giving the Maori all rights to New Zealand *pounamu*, said the term includes nephrite, bowenite, *and* serpentine. Instead of simplifying jade nomenclature, these uses complicate it. So much for clarity.

Until the last two decades Anglo-New Zealanders did very little jade carving and the Maori even less. Local nephrite used to be worked mainly into trinkets for souvenir shops. Now everything has changed. Almost simultaneously several European-heritage sculptors emerged on both New Zealand's islands, transforming the quality, style, and public recognition of Kiwi carving. This revolutionary New Zealand band, at the forefront of the world's jade artists, has broken the barriers that once tied other jade carvers to Chinese, Maya, and Maori motifs. The Kiwis are redrawing the image of jade today (pages 50-51).

Today's world-class New Zealand carvings are done mainly by a small group of non-Maori Kiwis. Donn Salt has a global following for his masterful work (above). Most of the world's nephrite hei-tiki were carved between 1896 and 1914 by German craftsmen in Idar-Oberstein. More than a million went back to New Zealand for sale. Idar's Dieter Jerusalem (right) holds a tray of New Zealand jade carved by his great-uncles. Hubert Dalheimer (opposite, top) keeps his grandfather's tradition alive by filling new orders for old hei-tiki.

The Maori, like so many other indigenous people, began rediscovering their past in the 1980s and 90s. Just as natives pressed land issues in Canadian and U.S. courts and legislatures, so too did the Maori, who represent about 14 percent of New Zealand's 3.8 million people, seek redress from New Zealand for the land and culture they felt they had lost.

Maori activism targeted land and jade. Even though their ancestors had all but abandoned nephrite carving in the 1800s and only a few Maori expressed themselves in the medium, they sought control of the raw material and aimed to lock out local non-native miners.

At first the activism only slowed collection of nephrite boulders. But after a long and bitter battle, in 1997 the

national government acquiesced, agreeing to return almost all jade rights to the Ngai Tahu Maori tribe. They received ownership to nephrite in the Arahura River system, a main jade conduit, and wherever jade lay in their ancestral land, as well as to offshore seabeds. The name *Arahura* has significance to the Maori. It describes the action of "rising in the morning to seek the stone." Of relevance to anthropologists, both Tahiti and Cook Islands natives used the name *Arahura*.

The impact of New Zealand's decision has brought many costly and unexpected changes. Surprisingly, in November 2000 the Ngai Tahu placed a moratorium on commercial mining until a management plan is approved by the tribe. With the drying up of jade supplies (except for a few remaining leases and stockpiled boulders), carvers and dealers who prefer working with local material began importing foreign nephrite instead. Now many, if not most, New Zealand jade souvenirs and art pieces are carved from imported nephrite.

Hepi Maxwell, the best of a small new generation of Maori jade carvers, takes his inspiration from nature, as did the tattoo artists who preceded him. Many non-native New Zealanders call local nephrite "greenstone" instead of "jade," whereas Maori prefer their native word, "pounamu."

JADE TODAY

A Chinese salesman stood smiling behind the Hong Kong store counter, never wavering that his assumption was true. When I asked to look at his best jade, he produced a Burmese jadeite ring. I refined my query, asking to see nephrite carvings. "But," he said, "this is *real* jade." "So is nephrite," I replied. "Oh," he said, "are you looking for *soft* jade?" "No," I repeated, "I want to see good nephrite carvings." "Oh," he said again, "you want *old* jade." "No," I said for the third time, "I do not care if the carvings are old or new. What is your best?" "Ah, you want *precious* jade, our jadeite from Burma." So much for nephrite as the Chinese Stone of Heaven.

I see two markets continuing for both jades—jewelry and carving, with wide price variations. Imperial-green jadeite from Burma dominates jade jewelry. No other contemporary jade commands millions of dollars per piece. By comparison, Guatemala green, lavender, or black jadeite jewelry seldom surpasses $10,000. Both countries also produce carving material in more subdued, less desirable colors, but jewelry drives the jadeite market.

We have nephrite occupying the two extremes—the best and most expensive contemporary carvings and the worst souvenir trinkets. Following China's great tradition, most fine new jade art today is carved in nephrite, often by New Zealand and Canadian artists who are the remarkable exceptions that make today's nephrite market so exciting. As much as people from Alaska, Washington state, South Korea, Taiwan, etc. like their local jade, their nephrite continues to be used mainly in forgettable jewelry and carvings or sold to collectors as specimens.

There is more nephrite and jadeite available now than at any other time in history. New finds, greater mechanization of mines, better exploration techniques, and a greater number of people mining have created a jade revolution. In the following pages you will get a rare firsthand view of Burma's amazing jadeite deposit and the people who mine it. China's most distant province still produces some of the rare white nephrite once coveted by emperors. You will see why Canada and New Zealand are so important to today's artists, what Guatemala is doing after centuries of silence between the Spanish *conquistadores'* arrival and jadeite's rediscovery in the 1970s, and the surprising jade activities in Siberia, Australia, and California. Jade is enjoying an international renaissance.

Atop an elephant a Hong Kong gem store owner made his first buying trip to northern Burma's jadeite source in 1968. The boulders he bought supplied his shop for more than two decades with stones for jewelry, such as this gorgeous 5-carat imperial-green jadeite cabochon.

Burma's Jadeite

There's an old joke in the trade that people find gems in the worst places. Burma (now Myanmar) proves that sentiment. You might think that hundreds of years of successfully mining the world's richest jadeite deposit would have produced enough wealth to create nirvana for miners and residents. Alas, an oppressive military regime insures that only a few (of course, its own) retain the profits. Burma's political situation has been disastrous for so long that the country chokes under rampant inflation, closed universities, and economic stagnation. For jadeite (as well as rubies and sapphires) the dictatorship has meant unreliable business policies. The military exploits Burma's resources by forcefully becoming an unwelcome partner in most profitable ventures. Burma used to be Asia's rice bowl. With agriculture, oil, gems, and teak (as well as opium, heroin, and gold), it should be prosperous, as it was under thousands of years of kings and even under British colonial rule until after World War II. Instead, massive mismanagement has impoverished the nation.

The mining region, located several days north of Mandalay and cursed with a total lack of paved roads, is a living hell in both seasons, wet and dry. You name your misery by picking the time to travel. In the wet months movement solely in four-wheel vehicles is fitful at best, usually done in 100-yard spurts. At every turn, which comes often in the mountainous jungle, the mud ranges between ankle and waist deep. Vehicular traffic mires to a halt about half the time. The only available help comes from the nearby elephant

A small cottage industry in Mandalay fashions inexpensive jadeite for the local market. Amazingly, natural silica in native bamboo stalks provides enough abrasion to produce a high-quality jadeite polish. Burma finishes little of its fine jade. Instead, China cuts and carves the majority of Burma's rough material.

and his friendly *mahout*, with hand out for the US$10 fee per elephant pull. Slogging five miles a day seems like making good time. Gasping in the dry season, although you can move through the ankle- to knee-deep brown dust, you can't see where you're going or speak without wheezing.

What prize justifies such miserable traveling conditions? Jadeite, of course, from the world's biggest and most valuable jadeite mine, Hpakangyi. A cross between a huge open-pit cooper mine and a dust bowl, Hpakangyi is written in superlatives. It mines the most jadeite anywhere. Its material is worth more than that mined anywhere else, and, with 10,000 workers in the hole daily, it uses more people than any other jade operation. Men dig almost all the jadeite by hand and with jackhammers. The tons of rocky debris they produce are removed from the gigantic mine on human backs, mainly womens', who make less than two pennies to lug a heavy double basket load from the deep hole up long steep slopes.

Upper Burma's productive jadeite mining area extends approximately 15 by 20 miles, with Hpakan, the town, and Hpakangyi, the mine, as its core. All but one of the numerous smaller mines occur in alluvial deposits, which means the jadeite formed somewhere else and washed to its current location. At a primary deposit, such as Tawmaw, jadeite formed where it now lies. Balanced on rafts in the middle of the Uru River, coworkers bob madly, working bicycle pumps to supply air to enterprising divers feeling their way along the murky bottom hoping to pick up smooth round jade river rocks.

More than 10,000 coolies toil daily at the world's largest jadeite mine, Hpakangyi, in northern Burma. For carrying out the rock and gravel debris, they earn about 1 $\frac{1}{2}$ cents a round trip. No wonder smuggling is endemic in a town where canned drinks cost $1 and beer $2. These jadeite cabs atop a flashlight were offered for US$100.

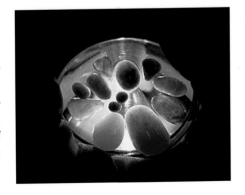

This Hpakan street seller offers a typical jadeite cobble, sliced to reveal its desirable color. Teams of diggers work on small leases outside the main mine, then market what they find in town. **Hte Long Sein** *jadeite (right), a new discovery north of Hpakan, has great green color but lacks Burma's traditional jadeite translucency.*

Most of Burma's jadeite—and its rubies, sapphires, teak, and heroin—reaches the outside world via the black market. If given a choice, smuggling small, lightweight gemstones has more appeal than smuggling trees and boulders. Then too, Burmese jadeite is no ordinary rock. Such enormous profits await those who successfully travel by foot, truck, or mule train to Thailand or China that the black-market game attracts many players. China and Hong Kong cut almost all Burma's jadeite—the majority is carried out illegally; the minority is sold at the semiannual government emporium in Rangoon.

There is a small internal market for Burma's jadeite. Whether the material comes from workers smuggling out a few boulders from the mines around Hpakan or from the numerous tiny operations with two to six people digging or from the Uru River swimmers, there is some jade to sell openly. Every evening boys move through Hpakan's jade market offering cobbles and the hope of hidden treasure. A larger market operates daily on the streets of Mandalay, where people sell both jade rough and polished cabs. Several small cutting operations attached to local homes in these two towns supply some of the internal demand for inexpensive carvings and gems.

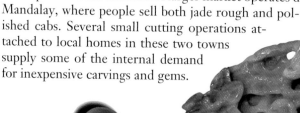

adeite necklace (above) and cabochons (below and opposite), Mason-Kay

The ultimate Chinese gem gamble is buying jadeite boulders, sold either sliced or "windowed" to whet buyers' appetites. I have seen boulders sell at auction in Rangoon (and illegally in Chiang Mai, Thailand) for over a million dollars apiece, with no more than a polished inch of green peeking through one edge. What lies beneath is anyone's guess. Green spots within boulders are cut as cabs; large areas without marketable gem color are carved. Many gamblers lose big. Some win.

Seldom does a gem material have only one source and one market. However, at the pinnacle of jadeite pricing, only Burmese jadeite is considered by the trade to have great value, and Asians are almost the exclusive customers for premier quality. Prices skyrocket with rarity, and bright translucent cabs in Burma's top green and lavender jadeite qualify as some of the rarest gems known. (For the inquisitive, trace amounts of chromium cause the green color; iron causes lavender). Demand for large, fine material follows Asia's economic upswings; successful businessmen spend big money on themselves and the women in their lives. Burma jadeite stands without competition as the most desirable gemstone in Asia, especially for people of Chinese heritage no matter where they live.

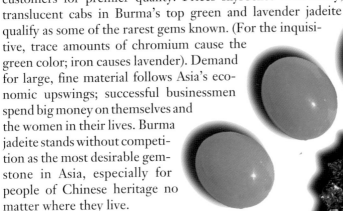

Jadeite carving (left) and ring (right);
Mogok International Pte. Ltd., Singapore

41

China's Nephrite

Paradoxes abound concerning the source of white nephrite jade, the most valuable commodity in the empire throughout most of Chinese history. The Imperial Court long kept secret its main source for white and green nephrite, the Kunlun Mountains south of Hotan, more than 2000 miles from Beijing. The Chinese only infrequently exerted direct control over Turkestan, a desert area outside its far western border. China often treated the region as a tribute state until the Mao's communist government overran it in the 1950s.

Native Uygur tribesmen still pick up each boulder by hand, retrieving only a ton or so of white nephrite annually and from 10 to sometimes 40 tons of green and near-black nephrite. But China cannot begin to supply its numerous jade industries with domestically-produced material. No other

Nephrite jade from China's far western desert border area is not actually mined—it is collected. In the Kunlun Mountains, each spring thaw rushes enough water through the White Jade and Black Jade Rivers (above) to extract jade pebbles and boulders from the banks and sweep them downstream toward Hotan, a stop on the old Silk Road. After the spring melts pass, the river beds revert to sandy gulches. Jade pickers (right), farmers with an eye good enough to separate nephrite from other rocks and a back strong enough to walk the banks and carry boulders downhill for days, can make a year's salary in a month or two.

white nephrite has the historic significance or the soft creamy appearance and texture of that from the Kunlun Mountains. This beautiful material, which China's emperors reserved for court use, has always been in short supply.

Russia's white nephrite appears yellowish by comparison and South Korea's white nephrite is tinged with pale green. Crystalline white jadeite from either Burma or Guatemala has a harder look and feel than Kunlun's subtle "oily" nephrite. Now, unlike in those periods when India bought nephrite directly from Hotan, only the Chinese government can legally buy Kunlun jade. To keep its factories busy, China also imports massive amounts—hundreds of tons a year of Burmese jadeite and British Columbian nephrite—and mines dozens of other cutable rocks, minerals, and jade from other locations within its own borders.

In the past few years China made a concerted effort to find domestic jade. More than three dozen sites—mainly in Xingiang and Qinghai provinces—are listed as promising; but so far nothing found equals traditional nephrite producers in color or quantity. The new sites appear not to have been mined in the past because their output does not match the look and feel of historic jades. Only one or two of the recent discoveries are said to produce

China operates its only government jade-buying station in Hotan. Once a week the government's manager conducts an outdoor viewing of what the local Uygur tribesmen have collected. Walking up and down their jade-filled mats, the manager marks each boulder he wants for the price he sets. The remainder of the nephrite is left to the pickers, supposedly for their own use, because the government is the only legal jade buyer. The purchased material is stacked in a secure shed (above) until it can be transported to various carving factories to the east.

More than 1500 workers toil in China's largest stone-carving factory in Beijing, utilizing dozens of materials including jadeite and nephrite.

jadeite, although I have yet to see samples.

Toward the end of China's 5,000-year-imperial history between 1911 and the conclusion of World War II, a great jade-carving tradition almost died. Chairman Mao and his communist regime later opened a number of "jade-carving factories," not to rekindle the country's ancient heritage but to install foreign currency profit centers.

Few of the new "jade" factories carved any jade at all, and none carved only jade. Most worked with agate, quartz, soapstone, serpentine, chrysoprase, and numerous other stones China either mined or imported. When the government did distribute jade for carving, it was usually jadeite from Burma not nephrite from the Kunlun Mountains. Later, as sales increased, China contracted with British Columbia's Kirk Makepeace, the world's largest nephrite producer, for more than 200 tons of jade annually. After they disconnected from their own nephrite heritage, the Chinese rarely sought jade for artistic, symbolic, religious, or ritual objects. Disregarding their reverence in ages past, they relegated luxurious nephrite to inexpensive

In an attempt to pacify local tribes and develop its western border areas, China builds factories and trains workers. In distant Xinjiang Province, site of the country's only jade sources, teenagers learn to carve nephrite.

Of the 40 or so stone-carving factories in China, Yangzhou, on the east coast, does most of the best jade work. Its 370 carvers use diamond-tipped electric drills to cut stone blocks marked by the factory's designer.

Even though the Yangzhou factory has electricity and power tools, it maintains eight foot treadles as a bridge to its cultural jade past so artists can produce several traditional pieces annually. A 43-year-old female carver spent four months hand-fashioning the mythical beast (below) from a White Jade River nephrite cobble.

beads, jewelry, and souvenir carvings, particularly a bear with a fish in its mouth. Strangely, these figures have become the most popular Chinese carvings ever made from Canadian nephrite.

China's current involvement with jade is mixed, the result of a socialist system where bureaucrats and entrepreneurs instead of emperors or artists make decisions. Young students with the best grades move upward through high schools and universities. Dropouts who fail the all-important routine school tests are assigned to factories that pay a dollar or two a day. Stone factories, like other government enterprises, receive new workers from a pool of youths without the skills, intellect, or motivation to pass academic tests. Jade carving, most honored of all arts and crafts in ancient China, has fallen into the hands of underachievers for whom it is more a job than a passion. Without access to raw materials, tools, and a market, gifted carvers have little choice but to fill orders on assembly lines instead of taking creative risks for aesthetic satisfaction.

Remarkably, on a floor with a hundred other carvers, a few excel as artists, producing extraordinary work they do not own and cannot sell. They remain cogs in the greater China industrial wheel. At the moment, the grand historic unsurpassed Chinese jade tradition fades, languishing for better days.

Fred Ward collection

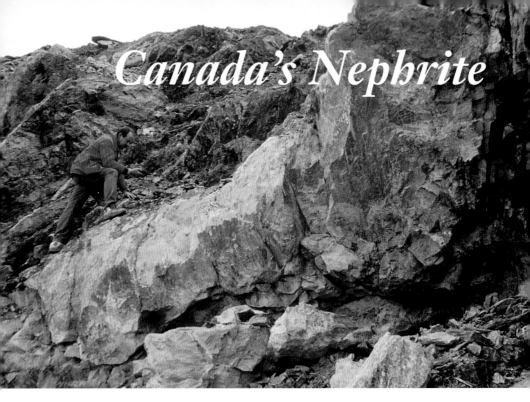

Canada's Nephrite

For thousands of years China and Central America produced most of the world's jade. During the 1970s and 80s every aspect of nephrite jade mining and marketing changed as Canada's British Columbia forever altered the perception and reality of jade consumption. Behind this amazing renaissance for nephrite has been the equally amazing success of one young Canadian who recast a business centered on construction material and tiles to one directed toward the gem and jade-carving market. A series of fortuitous conditions coalesced to make Canada, British Columbia, and Kirk Makepeace the dominant forces in nephrite. Kirk does not look, act, or talk like a tycoon. Nevertheless, he controls the world's nephrite jade markets by annually mining 300 tons or more of salable rough in a short two- to three-month season.

Kirk bought and consolidated leases until he controlled all three of the major Canadian nephrite deposits—first Ogden Mountain, which he is not currently mining; then Kutcho, the biggest volume producer; and finally Polar, phenomenally successful because of the color and translucency of its boulders. Polar is the only nephrite with a recognizable brand name.

British Columbia's Kirk Makepeace, above on a shelf of Polar Jade, dominates the world nephrite market. He mines more jade than any other person, or any country. Polar Jade all comes from the side of a single mountain near the Yukon border (opposite, bottom). Canada's Lyle Sopel, one of the world's premier carvers, uses British Columbian jade for his popular animal sculptures (left). American artist Elizabeth Beunaiche created a dramatic dragon pendant utilizing translucent B.C. nephrite (opposite, top).

Lyle Sopel

As China and Taiwan cab or carve most of the world's jade, they have become the biggest annual buyers of Canada's nephrite. Every October at the end of the mining season a steady stream of international customers spreads out over Kirk's field to note and mark the boulders they want, but once their packed crates of jade reach Hong Kong, mainland China, and Taiwan, Canada's nephrite is almost never again identified by origin. When next seen, Kirk's boulders have been transformed into Asian products—sculptures, jewelry, cabs, and beads—cut, carved, and marketed in the Orient.

Now that Taiwan, New Zealand, Australia, and the U.S. produce so little nephrite, Canada—actually Kirk Makepeace—determines the annual supply and price. Before he first mined Polar in 1995, British Columbia produced traditional nephrite in seemingly unlimited amounts. Then one remarkable mountaintop in a province punctuated by thousands of mountain peaks surprised jade users with the hardest, greenest, most translucent nephrite ever found—inspiring luminous artful carvings and jewelry as well. Though not quite a rival for Burma's jadeite, still, Polar turned the nephrite market topsy-turvy. In comparison, other attractive B.C. nephrite that had sold easily the year before suddenly looked less interesting to overseas buyers. Everyone wanted Polar, and Kirk went into overdrive to produce it. He now spends most of his season at the Polar site, searching for the elusive glowing boulders.

Elizabeth Beunaiche

Fortune struck big in July 2001. Directly under the spot where I had stood to make the photograph on page 46, the miners uncovered the largest, most valuable, most stunning Polar boulder yet seen. Weighing in at almost 18 tons, the jolly green giant proved too big to move, so the workers had to slice it right at the mine (half the original is seen above). The two faces revealed all green, all Polar, of fine quality all the way out to its thin rind. What do you do with such a gift? "I'm going to let the world decide," says Kirk. "I named this one *Polar Pride*, and I'm not going to cut it any further. Instead I'll auction it this way, as a wonder of nature. It's an icon that I expect to see as a museum piece, a monument, a symbol; the world's best green nephrite boulder ever."

Canada's jade artists were first to adopt Polar for carvings. Now that China has had several years of experience with the new material and other artists have seen the results, look for major moves to Polar for new carvings.

Despite the obvious need for heavy equipment to move multiton jade boulders from their spectacular setting, much of the daily work extracting Polar Jade from its mountain home is done by hand. Far more jade is left on the ground at Polar and nearby Kutcho mines than is transported to Vancouver for sale to the world. Boulders with natural cracks or fissures are encouraged with sledges, wedges, and saws to separate for easier transport. Because of Polar's latitude, 59 degrees north, Kirk can mine 14 hours in daylight.

48

Creative artists see many creatures within Canada's nephrite boulders. Each uses vision and skill to coax delicate lines from a hard, tough material. Elizabeth Beunaiche is best known for her exquisite equine carvings, such as Teddy, a powerful study of a real draft horse.

Deborah Wilson, one of Canada's finest jade carvers, works her magic into fluid designs that capture the essence of her subjects, in this case an octopus.

All of Canada's creatures are fair game in the skilled hands of Lyle Sopel. His wizardry captures bears, otters, dolphins, eagles, and ducks, freezing them in time and stone.

Photo by Brian Beaugureau   Elizabeth Beunaiche

Deborah Wilson

Lyle Sopel

New Zealand's Innovative Nephrite Carvers

New Zealand's artists produce some of the best contemporary nephrite carvings. Hepi Maxwell, the only Maori represented here, lives in harmony with nature, relying on organic themes to link his Maori past to today's art scene. From the world's toughest, most difficult-to-carve material, Ian Boustridge, a master of the medium, elicits delicate swirls and native forms (page 51) inspired by his island home.

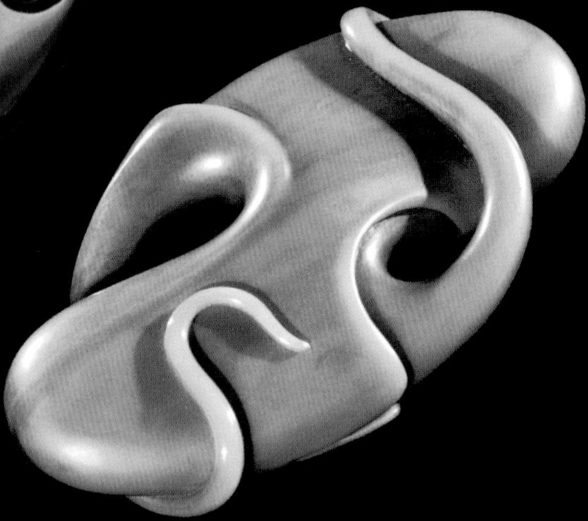

Hepi Maxwell

Donn Salt works local nephrite with impeccable skill, coaxing from his imagination avant-garde pieces in great demand by tourists and local collectors.

Donn Salt (2)

New Zealand's new breed of jade carvers stands alone for their individual styles and skills. Almost all who enter the field as artists are young and non-native. Having long since left animal and hei-tiki figures that mire others in mediocrity, the inspired carvers expand jade design with impeccable technique. Only the best of the Canadian artists match the New Zealanders, with their innovative concepts and flawless finishes. Unlike jade carvers in China, Hong Kong, and Taiwan, who mainly repeat traditional forms, Kiwe carvers are sculpting a new page in the glorious nephrite jade history.

Donn Salt

Ian Boustridge (3)

51

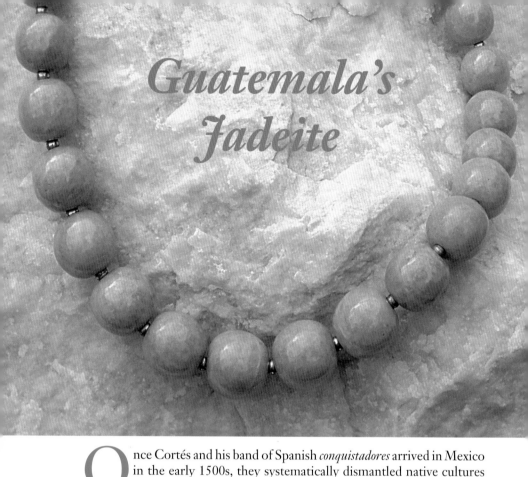

Guatemala's Jadeite

Once Cortés and his band of Spanish *conquistadores* arrived in Mexico in the early 1500s, they systematically dismantled native cultures and expropriated their treasures. One result of Spanish decimation was that each native society, which for several thousand years had centered much of their ritual life on jade, subsequently lost contact and involvement with the precious stone. Although the Mesoamerican material was jadeite, not nephrite, China's historic stone, Mesoamerican cultures paralleled China's in their devotion to and use of jade.

Mesoamerica owes much of its current success with jadeite to archaeologist Mary Lou Ridinger and her husband Jay Ridinger. In the 1970s this American couple set out to locate the source of Central America's jadeite, forgotten by the natives for four centuries. Using information from geologists, mineralogists, and archaeologists, they explored the most likely location for jadeite, the Motagua River Valley region. When they discovered jade boulders and even original Maya mining tools, they began

a 25-year project to resurrect ancient traditions. Their initial discovery motivated them to open their first store in Antigua. They hired and trained workers to design, carve, fabricate, promote, and sell a huge variety of jadeite jewelry and objects to foreign tourists who frequented the colonial town with its many quaint homes and shops.

Although a number of firms have tried to copy their success, Jades, S.A. remains the largest jadeite operation in Central America. It markets a wide selection of replicas handmade by today's Mayan descendants using only Guatemalan jadeite, the same material once treasured and revered by priests and rulers. To its credit, and in a practice all too rare, Jades, S.A. clearly marks replicas as such. First-generation Guatemalan carvers are just beginning to realize the impact local jadeite had on their ancestors.

By the early 1980s the Ridingers had worked three quarries and picked up stream boulders in a remote valley area covering more than 4,000 acres. Almost all their initial discoveries were commercial-grade greens and some black and white jadeites that supplied their retail needs. Through those years their mining luck continued as they regularly uncovered new jadeite colors apparently unseen by the Maya. In addition to green and very dark material came light gray and white—and then a rich creamy ebony the Ridingers dubbed "Maya Black" (right). That was followed in 1987 by one of the strangest jades ever found, a beautiful black-based gem laced with flecks of gold, silver, platinum, pyrite, nickel, and cadmium (page 54). It is unique.

Jades, S.A. in Antigua, Guatemala, replicates Maya artifacts using jadeite found in the Motagua Valley. Native craftsmen trained in the company's factory have revitalized jade carving, lost by Maya descendants from the 1500s, when Spain conquered Central America, until 1975, when the Ridingers rediscovered jadeite in Guatemala.

The original Jaguar Warrior mosaic mask (top left), apparently worn as a pendant, dates from the Maya Late Classic period, A.D. 600-900. The original Jade Dancer Plaque (above), from Early Classic period, A.D. 200-600, was unearthed in a Tikal tomb.

All jadeite products by Jades, S.A., Antigua

Reminiscent of the glowing sky in Van Gogh's *Starry Night*, the celestial jadeite became "Galactic Gold."

Also in 1987's second quarry came the first boulders that actually matched some of the jade that had been used by the great Olmec carvers. The relics, illustrated by the photographs in this book (pages 20-29), are almost all green or blue-green. Finding what the Ridingers called "Olmec Blue," thought to have been exhausted, strongly suggested that the Olmec had also mined their jade in what is now Guatemala. As the Ridingers continued searching, in 1998 they uncovered a colorful medley of jadeite in hues never before seen in Mesoamerica (page 52 and the color chart on page 63). They called them "mint," "apple," "Maya Imperial," "lilac," "blue," "pink," "yellow," "coffee," and "charcoal."

No other Central American jade source has since been identified. Recently-mined boulders match the color and patterns of major native artifacts. So it seems likely that Guatemala has been Mesoamerica's jade source for more than 2000 years. Within Guatemala almost all jadeite discoveries have been in the Motagua River Valley area.

Only three countries produce jadeite commercially. It might seem that their materials would look similar. As a matter of fact, the jadeites differ significantly in color, texture, and translucency. Burma jadeite sets the standard with its translucent saturated lavender and emerald-like imperial-green. Guatemala's jadeite has a tendency to look granular, mottled, and opaque, but it displays a broader color range in muted tones. As you can see on the next page, Russian jadeite falls somewhere between. Its green can be intense, a much deeper tone than any jadeite from Guatemala or Burma, but the material is so dark that to be effective, it must be cut extremely thin (page 55). Russian jadeite usually contains black spots. Fortunately, each country's jade has its own unique color, texture, and pattern appeal. Such variety also produces price ranges for every taste and pocketbook.

Carving,
John Hull;
Cabs & jewelry, Jades, S.A.

54

Russian Jade

Unlike other jade cultures with thousands of years of usage, Russians apparently had little relationship with jade until an early 1800s nephrite discovery. Two markets have emerged for the lovely green material. China was first to recognize Russian nephrite's potential. Using Russian jade purchased between 1820 and 1911, Chinese carvers fashioned some of the finest large bowls, platters, and urns ever made. Then came the phenomenal relationship between the last three czars and the House of Fabergé (1855-1917), which produced extraordinary pieces in precious metals, crystal gems, and nephrite for the czars and their families (below).

Deborah Wilson

Russia's best jadeite occurs in multiple deposits in the Polar Urals. Unfortunately, because harsh weather permits only two to three months of mining annually, so far no one has been able to fund the effort. Both jadeite and nephrite occur in eastern Siberia near Lake Baikal. Nephrite production includes green and a creamy-white popular with carvers. Almost all Russian jadeite loses its origin after being sold to Hong Kong, where it passes into the market as Burmese.

Alexander Sekerin (2)

It is easier to find nephrite boulders in Siberia's roadless wilderness (left) than it is to get them to market. Frigid winter conditions limit mining to no more than three summer months. White and creamy nephrite (top left and above) from a variety of Russian sources always has ready buyers. Russian jadeite (top right), a late find, is most often sold in China as Burmese. Fabergé created the best-known Russian nephrite carvings ever between 1872 and 1917, such as this small jade-and-enamel watering can.

55

Cowell, Australia is the site of the world's most underused fine-quality nephrite deposit. Shuttled from owner to owner for decades, it has never been properly developed. The tragedy is that it contains some of the best black nephrite ever found, but buying any is almost impossible. Located at the end of a mountain of iron ore, Cowell's boulders have the highest iron content of any jade. Exposure to air causes the huge boulders to oxidize. Imagine how tantalizing it is for a collector to stand among great rusty monoliths, knowing that each one contains a creamy rich black interior.

America's most unusual jade mine is underwater. Diver and sculptor Don Wobber (below) collects nephrite boulders washed from the cliffs at Jade Cove, California. Diving alone with scuba gear, he descends 40 feet or more into the cold Pacific waters. Floating ton-sized boulders with multiple inner tubes, Don tows his treasures to shore, hoists them onto trucks, and later carves them into free-form pieces of ocean art (below) or lightly polishes them into collectible boulder specimens.

Jade Buddha

One morning Bangkok Abbot Phra Yanaviriyajan (below) awakened to the revelation that the jade boulder he sought from an earlier vision was waiting for him in Vancouver. Unknown to him, jade miner Kirk Makepeace had just purchased a massive 70,000-pound nephrite giant from a gold miner and cut it into thirds for moving. The abbot arrived just in time to see a newspaper photo of Kirk's car-sized jade boulders. Sensing his destiny, he sought out Kirk and touched the boulder that fulfilled his dream. After raising $350,000, and hiring Italian marble artists, he brought Kirk and assistant Tony Ritter (right) to Thailand to polish it, then built a glass temple. Now seated in the temple's rotunda (below), at seven-tons the world's largest true Jade Buddha gazes serenely down on Thailand's tourists and devotees.

BUYING AND CARING

Buying either nephrite or jadeite is more challenging than acquiring almost any other gemstone. Both jades are chameleons, occurring in hues from white to black and most shades between, as well as in scores of patterns. Most people cannot visually differentiate jadeite and nephrite from hundreds of rocks that have been misidentified as jade. Testing is the only answer. Readily available specific gravity, refractive index, and spectro-scope readings are usually sufficient to identify jade, but sometimes a sophisticated lab test is needed.

Consumers should note that confusion, deception, and fraud are common with both stones, occasionally accidental, but too often deliberate. Be cautious when buying expensive pieces or dealing with people who are difficult to revisit. Unlike most crystal gem dealers, who accurately inform you whether a red jewel is a ruby, garnet, spinel, or tourmaline, most folks selling rocks will happily tell you that their tables are filled with jade even when they have few, if any, real nephrite or jadeite specimens. For someone who loves jade as I do, nothing is more maddening or counterproductive.

Of course jade can be tested for an accurate identification. But many sellers do not want to pay for lab reports, and some do not want to know that their merchandise is valueless. Every gem show I visit has more jade lookalikes than real jade, a common practice in the U.S. West and China. I stopped counting the number of stones from California, Arizona, Idaho, Nevada, Wyoming, and Washington sent to me as jade that turned out to be worthless rocks.

Jade artifacts are in another league; they are not for casual impulse buying. Potential buyers need either to become an expert or to hire one. Be sure to deal with people who have serious jade knowledge.

Artifact age, material, color, and style affect prices greatly. Remember, a gem lab can determine what the stone is, but not its age.

Burma still produces small quantities of brilliant imperial-green jadeite, such as once captivated Chinese royalty. The material's high price destines it for use in jewelry. Fine jadeite typically is cut into cabochons for rings or carved, such as "Bat on Mountain," which is set in platinum with 8 carats of diamonds.

Estimating a period when an artifact was carved can only be arrived at by testing associated tomb relics or consulting a specialist, both of which services cost.

Jewelry, beads, and souvenir carvings make up the majority of jade products offered to the public. The first thing you will notice about jade jewelry is the phenomenal price difference between jadeite and nephrite. Jadeite has become one of the world's most expensive gems, with auction sales topping $9 million for a 27-bead necklace and $1.74 million for a 35.78mm cabochon. Of course many fine jadeite pieces sell for $1000 to $100,000; they are always more expensive than comparable nephrite items. Does that mean that nephrite is underpriced? For good color and quality, such as the best Polar Jade, probably so. Does this mean that jadeite is overpriced? No. Little first-rate material is found each year, and more than enough buyers wait to pay dearly for the privilege of owning it.

Enhancing gems is as old as time. Nephrite is almost never treated except for waxing. Dyeing jadeite has escalated during the last two decades from an annoyance to a major problem. Earlier coloring consisted of dunking cabs and carvings into hot food dyes, which faded over time. The next treatment development complicated jadeite buying enormously. Three new names appeared: "A," "B," and "C" jade. "A" jade is defined as natural

Neil
Hanna

New Zealand's Neil Hanna combined Australian black nephrite with his local green nephrite into a ceremonial fish hook (above).

Problems seldom arise with name artists, who proudly and accurately identify their jade. Not so in Hong Kong's outdoor "jade" market, where vendors offer tourists dozens of jade substitutes, such as serpentine, quartz, chalcedony, idocrase, or any green rock. Much of the green and lavender material is "B" and "C" jadeite, both polymer impregnated and dyed. Many new pieces are treated to look old. Bargains are hard to identify. Buyers would do well to be observant, knowledgeable, and very cautious.

Elizabeth Beunaiche

untreated material (except that a waxed surface is acceptable). "B" jade is polymer impregnated. The process begins with a hot bath in strong acid to bleach spots and stains, but acid bleaching also alters jadeite's internal structure lessening its durability. Next the polymer (a plasticlike substance) is forced inside the jadeite to hold it together, make it more translucent, and give it a shine. This coating is often difficult to detect without the use of a fairly expensive infrared spectroscope. "C" jade is "B" jade with added dye to produce a polymer-impregnated piece with green or lavender dyes, or both.

Caring for both natural jades is simple. Because both jadeite and nephrite are hard, durable, and resistant to most chemicals, they are likely to be the strongest part of your jewelry. You can wash them with soap and water or detergents, or you can use an ultrasonic or steam cleaner. If you notice either jade becoming dull, you can have it rewaxed. "B" and "C" jadeites are not as durable and should not be subjected to chemicals, detergents, or ultrasonics. Use only soap and water with them.

Both untreated jades are usually trouble-free possessions, already tens of millions of years old, that will provide you with decades of pleasure and wear. With jade's unsurpassed history, beauty, and allure, nephrite and jadeite can add new dimensions to your collection.

Nephrite (above in a carved horsehead necklace of Wyoming jade) and jadeite (right in a Burmese lavender pendant), are among the most durable gems. Both respond well to ultrasonic cleaning or washing with soap and warm water.

Nephrite and jadeite are harder than most steel. Jade will be one of the hardest components of your jewelry. It can scratch your gold, platinum, and silver; it is likely to be scratched only by harder crystal gemstones, such as diamonds, rubies, sapphires, and emeralds. For safety, store individual jewelry pieces in separate bags.

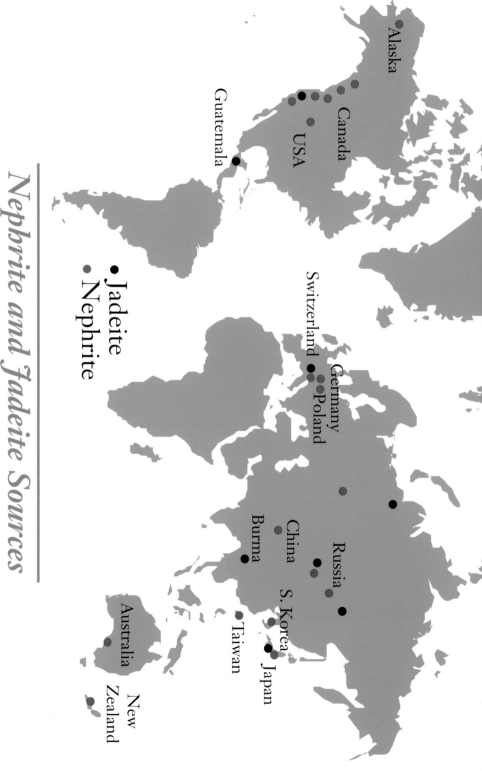

Nephrite and Jadeite Sources

- Jadeite
- Nephrite

Alaska

Canada

USA

Guatemala

Switzerland

Germany
Poland

Russia

Burma

China

S. Korea

Taiwan

Japan

Australia

New
Zealand

Burma Jadeite Colors

Guatemala Jadeite Colors

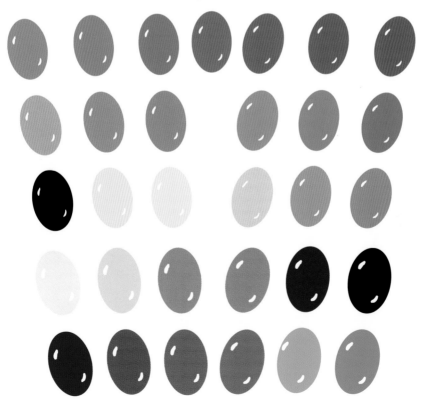

Fred Ward at British Columbia's picturesque Polar Jade Mine

Glamour, intrigue, romance, the quest for treasure—these are all vital aspects of humankind's eternal search and love for gemstones. As long as people have roamed the globe, they have placed extraordinary value on the earth's incredible gifts from land and sea.

Jade is the ninth in a series of gem books written, photographed, designed, and published by Fred Ward. Each book, *Rubies & Sapphires*, *Emeralds*, *Diamonds*, *Diamonds* (in Russian), *Opals*, *Pearls*, *Gem Care*, *Jades of Mesoamerica*, and *Jade* is part of a 24-year global search into the history, geology, lore, and sources of these priceless treasures. He personally has visited the sites and artifacts displayed here to provide the most authentic and timely information available in the field. Fred Ward's original articles on these topics, except opals, first appeared in *National Geographic* Magazine.

Mr. Ward, a Graduate Gemologist (GIA) and a respected authority on gems and gemology, is in great demand as a speaker to professional and private groups. Also he conducts gem searches for clients looking for unusual or unique treasures.

Mr. Ward designed *Jade* using Adobe PageMaker and Janson typefaces on a Mac G4 computer. It was printed by S & S Graphics in Laurel, MD.

Fred Ward at Burma's huge Hpakangyi jadeite mine

Hawai'i

Wildlife Viewing Guide

Written by Jeanne L. Clark

A multi-agency project developed in cooperation
with Watchable Wildlife, Inc.

ADVENTURE PUBLICATIONS, INC.
Cambridge, Minnesota

Hawai'i Wildlife Viewing Guide
Copyright 2006 by Watchable Wildlife, Inc.
Published by Adventure Publications, Inc.
820 Cleveland St. S
Cambridge, MN 55008
1-800-678-7006
www.adventurepublications.net
All rights reserved
Printed in China
ISBN-13: 978-1-59193-126-3
ISBN-10: 1-59193-126-6

ABOUT WATCHABLE WILDLIFE, INC.

Watchable Wildlife Inc. is an independent 501c-3 nonprofit working with communities and state and federal wildlife agencies to promote sustainable wildlife viewing programs. Our mission is simple:

"TO HELP COMMUNITIES AND WILDLIFE PROSPER"

We work towards accomplishing this mission with our partners by focusing our efforts in three areas: our annual conference, publications like this Hawai'i Wildlife Viewing Guide and on the ground projects.

Our annual Watchable Wildlife Conference is the nation's best vehicle for presenting new ideas. It also serves as an international forum for training and recognizing the works of professionals in the field of wildlife viewing. Watchable Wildlife Inc. works hands-on with conservation-minded partners on projects around the world to develop safe, satisfying and sustainable wildlife viewing.

Our Viewing Guide Series is a continent-wide effort to meet the needs of North America's growing wildlife viewing public. We hope these guides encourage people to observe wildlife in natural settings and will provide them with information on where to go, when to go and what to expect when they get there. We believe the presence of well-managed wildlife viewing sites will have positive social and economic impacts on nearby communities.

We want wildlife viewing to be fun. However we also believe it should be an economically viable resource for the host community, as well as a tool for preserving the area's natural resources. In the larger context, we want people to learn about wildlife, to care about it and learn ways that they can help to protect and conserve it. We conduct workshops to help community leaders better understand the importance of protecting these wild and scenic areas. For more information about Watchable Wildlife Inc. and our projects, visit us at www.watchablewildlife.org.

Thank you for your support through the purchase of this guide and remember to respect the wildlife you're viewing and the community you are visiting.

Yours truly,

James Mallman
President, Watchable Wildlife, Inc.
www.watchablewildlife.com

Brown road signs with the binoculars logo let travelers know that they're in a great spot to see some wildlife! These uniform signs are officially approved by the National Department of Transportation and are one example of the programs sponsored by Watchable Wildlife, Inc.

Table of Contents

INTRODUCTION

About Watchable Wildlife, Inc. 3

Hawai'i Watchable Wildlife Steering Committee 6

Hawai'i Watchable Wildlife Sponsors 7

About this Guide 9

Your Guide to Hawai'i's Amazing Wildlife 9

Wild Hawai'i 10

Arrive Prepared 16

Watching Hawai'i's Wildlife 21

Wildlife at a Glance (charts) 26

Amenities at a Glance (charts) 28

How to Use This Guide 30

Sample Page 31

SITES

Kaua'i - The Garden Isle 32

Hā'ena State Park 34

Nā Pali Coast State Wilderness Park 38

Kīlauea Point National Wildlife Refuge 43

Po'ipū Beach Park 48

Kōke'e State Park 53

O'ahu - The Gathering Place 58

Diamond Head State Monument 60

Hanauma Bay Nature Preserve 65

Hālona Blowhole 70

Makapu'u Point State Wayside 72

Hāmākua Marsh Wildlife Sanctuary 76

Waimea Valley Audubon Center 80

Ka'ena Point Natural Area Reserve 85

Maui - The Valley Island 90

Kanahā Pond Wildlife Sanctuary 92

Haleakalā National Park: Summit Area 96

Polipoli Springs State Recreation Area and Kula Forest Reserve 100
Wai'ānapanapa State Park 104
Haleakalā National Park: Kīpahulu Area 108
Keālia Pond National Wildlife Refuge 113
Molokini Crater 118
Hawaiian Islands Humpback Whale National Marine Sanctuary 123
Mākena State Park 128

Lana'i & Moloka'i - The Pineapple & The Friendly Islands 132
Mānele-Hulopo'e Bays 134

Hawai'i - The Big Island 138
Kahalu'u Beach Park 140
Kealakekua Bay State Historical Park 144
Pu'uhonua o Hōnaunau National Historic Park 149
Manukā State Wayside and Natural Area Reserve 154
Hawai'i Volcanoes National Park: Chain of Craters Road 159
Wailoa River State Recreation Area 164
Kīpuka Pu'u Huluhulu 166
Kalōpā State Park 170
Kaloko-Honokōhau National Historic Park 175

The Hawai'i Watchable Wildlife Program is guided by a steering committee that includes representatives of the primary conservation organizations and governmental agencies involved in wildlife and wildlands conservation, education and tourism in Hawai'i. The steering committee works under the umbrella of the national organization, Watchable Wildlife, Inc., a nonprofit organization that began the national wildlife viewing program in 1990 and supports state wildlife viewing programs nationwide. Watchable Wildlife, Inc. is the publisher of the Hawai'i Wildlife Viewing Guide and other state wildlife viewing guides.

This guide is the result of the vision and hard work of a group of dedicated individuals and organizations working on the steering committee. Their commitment of money, time and expertise has resulted in a book unlike any other. Every site that is featured has been carefully reviewed and selected by the committee to ensure that Hawai'i's natural resources are protected from harm while providing visitors the best possible wildlife viewing experience. In addition to this guide, the steering committee has other joint projects; revenues from book sales, along with grants and other contributions, will help fund future wildlife viewing projects in Hawai'i. You can track their progress at www.HawaiiWildlife.org.

Thanks to the following organizations and individuals:

Committee Chair: Ray Tabata

Hawai'i Audubon Society: Wendy Johnson

Hawai'i Ecotourism Association: Annette Kaohelaulii

Hawaii Tourism Authority: Robbie Kane

NOAA Fisheries: Trevor Spradlin, Chris Yates, Tamra Faris, Margaret Akamine

NOAA Hawaiian Islands Humpback Whale National Marine Sanctuary: Naomi McIntosh

National Park Service: Bryan Harry

State of Hawai'i: Department of Land and Natural Resources: Randy Honebrink, Jeffrey Walters, Jolie Wanger, Deborah Ward, Martha Yent

State of Hawai'i: Department of Transportation: Bryan Kimura, Michael Shishido

The Nature Conservancy of Hawai'i: Sam Gon

U.S. Fish and Wildlife Service: Bob Dieli, Barbara Maxfield

Marjorie Ziegler (Conservation Council for Hawai'i) and Sharon Reilly

Project Staff

Project Manager: Bob Garrison, Nature Tourism Planning (www.naturetourismplanning.com)

Steering Committee Chair: Ray Tabata

Author: Jeanne L. Clark

Administration: Ruth Uemura

Marketing/Promotions: Karen Killebrew

Hawaiian Language Editor: Diane Paloma

Fund Administrator: Jim Mallman, Watchable Wildlife, Inc.

National Oceanic and Atmospheric Administration

The National Oceanic and Atmospheric Administration (NOAA) conducts research and gathers data about the global oceans, atmosphere, space and sun, and applies this knowledge to science and service that touch the lives of all Americans. NOAA, an agency of the U.S. Department of Commerce, is dedicated to enhancing economic security and national safety through research to better understand atmospheric and climate variability and to manage wisely our nation's coastal and marine resources. www.noaa.gov.

NOAA's National Marine Fisheries Service (NOAA Fisheries Service) is dedicated to protecting and preserving our nation's living marine resources and their habitat through scientific research, management, education and enforcement. The agency is responsible for implementing several marine conservation laws, including the Marine Mammal Protection Act, Endangered Species Act and Magnuson-Stevens Fishery Conservation and Management Act. NOAA Fisheries Service provides effective stewardship of marine and protected resources for the benefit of the nation, supporting coastal communities that depend upon them and helping to provide safe and healthy seafood to consumers and recreational opportunities for the American public. www.nmfs.noaa.gov.

NOAA's National Ocean Service manages the National Marine Sanctuaries Program and works cooperatively with the public to protect sanctuaries while allowing compatible recreational and commercial activities. The program enhances public awareness of our marine resources and marine heritage through scientific research, monitoring, exploration, educational programs and outreach. The National Marine Sanctuary Program serves as the trustee for a system of 14 marine protected areas, encompassing more than 150,000 square miles of marine and Great Lakes waters from Washington State to the Florida Keys and from Lake Huron to American Samoa. The system includes 13 national marine sanctuaries including the Hawaiian Islands Humpback Whale National Marine Sanctuary and the Northwestern Hawaiian Islands Coral Reef Ecosystem Reserve, which is being considered for sanctuary status. www.sanctuaries.nos.noaa.gov

Hawaii Tourism Authority

The Hawaii Tourism Authority (HTA) was established by the Hawai'i Legislature in 1998 as the overall tourism agency for the State of Hawai'i. HTA formulates short- and long-range tourism policy; develops and implements the state's tourism marketing plan and efforts; administers programs and activities that foster and sustain a healthy tourism industry for the state; develops and monitors coordination of the Tourism Strategic Plan; and coordinates tourism-related research, planning, development and promotional activities with the public and private sectors. By 2015, tourism in Hawai'i will honor Hawai'i 's people and heritage; value and perpetuate Hawai'i's natural and cultural resources; engender mutual respect among all stakeholders; support a vital and sustain-

able economy; and provide a unique, memorable and enriching visitor experience. HTA hopes to raise the awareness of all stakeholders about the responsible use of natural resources by "encouraging environmental stewardship and the efficient use of resources by educating all stakeholders" and by "providing accurate and responsible information to visitors."
www.hawaii.gov/tourism/

The Nature Conservancy

The mission of The Nature Conservancy is to preserve the plants, animals and natural communities that represent the diversity of life on Earth by protecting the lands and waters they need to survive. This project moves toward that mission by helping build a constituency of educated, concerned people that help support protection and management of native wildlife. http://nature.org.

Whale and Dolphin Conservation Society

The Whale and Dolphin Conservation Society is the global voice for the protection of whales, dolphins and their environment. It works to reduce and ultimately eliminate the threats to whales, dolphins and porpoises and raise awareness of these remarkable animals and the need to protect them in their natural environment. These objectives are achieved through a mix of campaigning, research, education, awareness-raising and representing the interests of whales and dolphins at national and international forums. www.wdcs.org

U.S. Fish and Wildlife Service

The mission of the U.S. Fish & Wildlife Service (Service) is working with others to conserve, protect and enhance fish, wildlife and plants and their habitats for the continuing benefit of the American people. The Service manages 19 National Wildlife Refuges in the Hawaiian Islands and on U.S. Territories and Possessions in the Pacific. These terrestrial and marine habitats conserve and protect more than 7,000 species—including migratory seabirds and shorebirds, waterbirds, forest birds, bats, fishes, plants, invertebrates and marine mammals—many of which are found nowhere else on earth. More than 26 percent of America's threatened and endangered plant and animal species live within this region, more than in any other state in the union.
www.fws.gov

Department of Land and Natural Resources

The state of Hawai'i is mandated to conserve and protect Hawai'i's natural beauty and all natural resources, including land, water, air, minerals and energy sources, and to promote the development and utilization of these resources in a manner consistent with their conservation, for the benefit of present and future generations. All public natural resources are held in trust by the State of Hawai'i for the benefit of the people. The Department of Land and Natural Resources' mission, as the state's land management agency, is to manage, administer and exercise control over public lands, the water resources, ocean waters, navigable streams, coastal areas (excluding commercial harbor areas), minerals and all other interests therein. As part of this mission, the department manages and administers the state parks, historical sites, forests, forest reserves, aquatic life, aquatic life sanctuaries, public fishing areas, boating, ocean recreation, coastal programs, wildlife, wildlife sanctuaries, game management areas, public hunting areas, natural area reserves and other functions assigned by law.

State of Hawai'i Department of Transportation: Highways Division

The mission of the Highways Division is to provide a safe, efficient and accessible highway system through the utilization of available resources in the maintenance, enhancement and support of land transportation facilities.

ABOUT THIS GUIDE

The purpose of the Hawai'i Wildlife Viewing Guide is to highlight some of the best wildlife viewing experiences across the state. The guide is unique because it was produced by the Hawai'i steering committee, made up of sponsoring and supporting organizations throughout the state. The committee includes many of the agencies and organizations that manage the destinations featured in the guide.

The Hawai'i Wildlife Viewing Guide is coordinated by the nonprofit organization Watchable Wildlife, Inc. The purpose of Watchable Wildlife, Inc. is to help communities and wildlife prosper. The proceeds from the sales of these guides will help fund Watchable Wildlife programs throughout the country and in Hawai'i. A significant portion of the proceeds from this guide will be returned to the Hawai'i steering committee. The committee will be able to use the royalties from guide sales to develop interpretive and educational displays, improve the infrastructure of viewing sites and initiate other activities aimed at enhancing the wildlife viewing experience.

YOUR GUIDE TO HAWAI'I'S AMAZING WILDLIFE

Hawai'i packs amazing diversity into a handful of small islands that offer numerous opportunities for you and your family to connect with nature.

The Hawai'i Wildlife Viewing Guide provides information, resources and contacts for planning your visit. The site profiles offer important details regarding the best times of year and even times of day to visit to maximize your viewing experiences. Many sites were considered when developing the guide and some were not included. Even though these sites offer great wildlife viewing, the wildlife might be imperiled or sensitive to disturbance. The infrastructure of the site may not be adequate to accommodate numerous visitors.

The Hawai'i Wildlife Viewing Guide focuses on wildlife, but showcases many sites that are known for their outstanding scenery, cultural values or water-oriented recreation. Visits to even a few sites on an island can expose you to some huge gatherings of seabirds, remarkable scenes of migrating whales, up close views of rare forest birds or incredible underwater vistas of coral gardens and colorful fish.

Kalalua Valley - Kaua'i

Wild Hawai'i

Hawai'i, one of the nation's favorite vacation destinations, is well known for its relaxed lifestyle, translucent turquoise waters, spectacular sunsets and stunning shorelines and beaches. It is also a place rich with wildlife viewing opportunities. Visitors come from around the world to snorkel and watch Hawai'i's colorful reef fish, see humpback whales breaching or spyhopping and observe birds found nowhere else on earth. No matter which island you visit, you will find wildlife viewing experiences that are minutes away and easy to combine with other activities.

The Hawaiian Islands are frequently described with superlatives: the bluest water, the best snorkeling, the most beautiful tropical vistas.... Hawai'i's natural attributes are world-class: Hawai'i claims the tallest and most massive island volcanoes, it has the tallest sea cliffs in the world and includes the only tropical islands with habitat that extends into the alpine zone.

Much of Hawai'i's flora and fauna is unique. Volcanic development, isolation and people have all played a crucial role in shaping these exceptional resources. A prime focus of this guide is to acquaint you with wild Hawai'i: its wildlife and habitats and their importance to Native Hawaiians, island residents and visitors alike.

Island Development and Isolation

Stand on any shore within this island paradise and you will be struck by a feeling of isolation. The Hawaiian Islands are located 2,500 miles from the nearest continent, close to the middle of the Pacific Ocean. These islands form the most isolated inhabited landmass in the world. This remoteness has had a profound effect on Hawaiian flora and fauna. Whether the pioneering plants or animals arrived by the wind or sea, many species have evolved into new forms because of the Hawaiian Islands' isolation—not only from the rest of the world, but also from each other.

- Seventy to eighty million years ago, a deep hot spot in the Pacific Ocean floor gushed molten magma that gradually built this chain of islands. Hawai'i, the youngest island at the south end of the chain, is less than one-half-million years old, and the volcanoes that formed it are still spewing lava. In fact, Lō'ihi, a steamvent volcano, is creating a still-submerged island southeast of the Big Island. Hawai'i and Maui are young, uneroded islands with sloping landscapes and limited reef development. By contrast, at the northern end of the main Hawaiian Islands, Kaua'i was formed over six million years ago. Older islands that have been buffeted by wind and sea have steeper vertical cliffs and more well-developed reef systems.

These differences in island development and age are reflected in the types of wildlife and habitats that you'll see. In this limited geographic space, you can see much of the variation in climate and habitat that you see on the planet Earth. The islands receive from 8 to over 400 inches of annual rainfall and temperatures vary from sweltering desert-like heat to freezing. You can move from wet and dry habitats at sea level to alpine environments, and from flat terrain to vertical cliffs. The Hawaiian Islands have all ten soil types classified by the U.S. Department of Agriculture and more habitat types in one small area than any other spot on earth. According to scientists of the U.S. Forest Service, a large country, such as Brazil, has eleven recognized life zones; the tiny Hawaiian Islands support twenty-seven.

silversword

Plant and Wildlife Evolution

Hawai'i's unique volcanic development and its isolation from the rest of the world have made the islands an evolutionary treasure house. The Hawaiian Islands are home to more than 10,000 species of plants and wildlife. More than ninety percent of these species are endemic, which means they occur naturally in only this one place. In fact, the requirements of some species are so specific that they are found on just one island, such as the 'anianiau, a native forest bird on Kaua'i, or the wēkiu bug on the summit of Mauna Kea.

 More than ninety percent of the species in the Hawaiian Islands are endemic, which means they occur naturally in only this one place.

Endemic plants and wildlife have been evolving for millions of years on these isolated specks of land bounded by miles of ocean. Before humans arrived in Hawai'i, the only types of plants and wildlife that reached the islands were those dispersed by the wind or ocean currents. Plant spores and seeds had to be light enough to float in air or on water, survive submersion in salt water or make it through a bird's digestive system. Only a relatively small number of species could even reach these remote islands.

Weary birds navigating the aerial highways discovered this welcome landfall; some were blown here and became residents while others were migratory, returning only to nest. Spiders, dragonflies and other invertebrates rode the wind to these lava outposts. Marine species, such as monk seals and sea turtles, swam to these secluded beaches, staying to rest and have their young.

Early colonists that managed to find their way to these remote islands and survive gradually evolved as they adapted to the islands' broad range of habitat conditions. When these first plant and wildlife settlers branched out into a wide variety of species—each uniquely adapted to specific niches—they demonstrated a process called adaptive radiation. This explosive evolutionary process likely occurred because of Hawai'i's benign tropical environment, its tremendous variety of environmental conditions and the low rate of new introductions. In one genera of lobeliads for example, 35 different species evolved from a single ancestor. Among forest birds, the 'amakihi has differentiated into three different races: the Hawai'i race is the brightest; the Kaua'i race is the largest; and 'amakihi on O'ahu all have two bold wingbars instead of one faint wingbar.

What does the process of adaptive radiation mean when it comes to Hawaiian plants and wildlife viewing? Many species that are considered common and easy to see in the Hawaiian Islands simply don't exist elsewhere.

Once they were discovered by people, these isolated Hawaiian Islands and their pristine evolutionary processes changed forever. Early Hawaiians developed a strong relationship with the native plants and wildlife, weaving them into their mythology and daily lives. However, as more people came to Hawai'i, they introduced a myriad of non-native species—from orchids to eucalyptus trees and from cats and pigs to mongooses—that competed with and often replaced native species. Some introduced species, such as mosquitoes, carry diseases that pose a serious threat to native birds. People also valued plants and animals, using them for food, jewelry, ornamentation or tools, practices that placed further pressure on their populations.

stocky hawkfish

Wildlife and Hawaiian Culture

Early Polynesians sailing in voyaging canoes first found these islands by chance, much like the landing of a spider or a seed pod on these distant shores. These first settlers brought many plants and animals from their homeland. The number of introductions increased with the arrival of Europeans. Often, these non-native species competed better than those that had been evolving in isolation on the Hawaiian Islands, driving some native plant and animal species to extinction.

As you visit the islands, you will often hear about and see the strong ties among Hawaiians, the land and its creatures—relationships that continue today. For some families, a specific animal, such as a turtle, owl or shark, is an 'aumakua, or a physical manifestation of an ancestral spirit. Often, the sites associated with these animals are sacred to people of that area, requiring added sensitivity while you are viewing. Because wild animals and the earth they inhabit are an intimate part of Hawaiian culture, it is important to show respect for them and Hawaiian cultural sites when you visit.

At Wai'ānapanapa State Park on Maui, for example, the beautiful pools are a tourist attraction. 'Ōpae 'ula, a red shrimp living in these pools, are tied to a traditional story about the murder of an important princess. Even today, the appearance of red shrimp at the pools evokes this story.

If you visit Hāmākua Marsh Wildlife Sanctuary on O'ahu you might see the Hawaiian moorhen, or 'alae 'ula. This waterbird has a loud, distinctive voice, symbolic of the respected voice of the chief whose convincing explanations might sway the opinions of those who are gathered. Often, the chief who offers the most compelling argument is even referred to as the 'alae.

Animals have also provided richly for native people. Their meat served as food, and their shells, bones and skin were used for tools and decoration. The bright red, yellow and black feathers of forest birds figure prominently in traditional capes, helmets, standards and other items. Often, only royalty could possess these prized feathers and they selected specialists to collect them. These learned people, often called kahuna, spent much time studying animal habits and their behavior. They felt responsible for these animals and had a sophisticated relationship with them.

Hawaiian lore is filled with traditional sayings, songs and stories that refer to native wildlife. For example, if someone wants to honor a person that they view as respectable, they might say "kaha ka 'io i ka mālie" or "the hawk soars in the calm sky." Just as a calm sky accentuates the beauty and power of a soaring hawk, a respected person is likewise honored by this comparison.

 'Āina is the Hawaiian word for land and means both that which nourishes and that which consumes.

Native Hawaiians view animals as family or ancestors. In Hawaiian mythology, humans are the last living things that were created. They are the youngest siblings. The land is the chief and the people are the servants, charged with the responsibility of caring for the land. 'Āina is the Hawaiian word for land and means both that which nourishes and that which consumes. The land and its creatures require sustenance and it is the responsibility, or kuleana, of people to nourish the land so it can, in turn, provide for peoples' needs. This is the foundation of the Hawaiian culture, and for conservation and stewardship vital in this island paradise today.

Modern Threats and Conservation

The pristine ecosystems that once flourished on the Hawaiian Islands now exist mostly in remote areas or small protected pockets. In the last 200 years, agriculture, fire, development, urbanization and the introduction of many non-native plant and animal species have had a significant impact on native fauna and flora. Today, Hawai'i accounts for only 0.2 percent of the land area in the United States but claims 75 percent of its plant and bird extinctions. Of the 150 natural communities present today, 85 are critically endangered. Over half of the original Hawaiian landscape has been converted or changed.

Most areas below 1,500 feet in elevation are largely transformed landscapes covered with non-native plants that no longer support once common species. At many sites, some of the most prominent wildlife is no longer native at all, but introduced species that have become exceedingly common, such as the myna, cardinal, sparrow, finch, canary, chukar and quail. You can enjoy seeing these birds throughout the islands, but you should know that they may have displaced native species.

Introduced cats, dogs, mongooses, pigs and rats have wreaked havoc on native ground-nesting birds, eggs and fledglings. Rats have even learned to climb trees high in the forest to devour the eggs of forest nesting birds. Mongooses, cats, dogs and pigs have driven the nēnē, a goose once common in lower elevations, to sub-alpine mountain tops.

 Too many visitors, or visitors who don't follow viewing ethics, can place so much pressure on animals that they will abandon traditional nesting areas.

When early Hawaiians cleared the land for their taro fields, they used flooding methods that actually expanded waterbird habitat. Today, natural wetlands have been so heavily drained for development that these wetlands, and the wildlife they sustained, are often imperiled.

The beauty, tranquility and rich wildlife experiences that have drawn visitors to the islands for decades have changed in response to development and, in some cases, overvisitation. Popular beaches can be overrun with visitors who crowd snorkeling areas and feed fish, try to swim with dolphins, get their boat close to breaching whales or take their children's photographs sitting atop resting sea turtles. One of the best places to see wildlife is often their nesting areas. Too many visitors, or visitors who don't follow viewing ethics, can place so much pressure on animals that they will abandon traditional nesting areas. The Hawaiian moorhen, for example, is very shy; it will leave a well-used nesting area if there is too much human presence.

traditional taro field - Moloka'i

If one of the reasons you are visiting sites featured in this guide is to enjoy some of Hawai'i's unique and visible wildlife:

- Select a tour operator who shows regard for conservation measures.

- Familiarize yourself with laws protecting wildlife and follow ethical standards for viewing.

- Understand that laws protect a unique natural legacy and Hawaiian cultural traditions—and can help to make your wildlife viewing experience a positive one. They are also vital for Native Hawaiians, who rely on Hawai'i's plants and wildlife for both subsistence and cultural sustenance.

- Read the wildlife viewing tips on pages 21–25, which are designed to enhance your viewing experience while ensuring wildlife conservation.

While you visit, do your part to tread gently on the land and make time to learn about some of the important conservation programs being developed today. Volunteers are removing exotic vegetation and planting native plants to restore native ecosystems at places such as Hakalau Forest National Wildlife Refuge on Hawaii. Children get involved with marsh cleanup at Hāmākua Marsh on O'ahu. Botanical gardens are preserving ailing or disappearing plant species at places such as Waimea Valley Audubon Center on O'ahu. And a variety of agencies and not-for-profit organizations are cooperating to reintroduce imperiled wildlife species or restore vital habitats on every island. Through this guide they hope to introduce you to some outstanding wildlife viewing experiences and the complementary—and essential—wildlife viewing ethics needed to protect Hawai'i's rich wildlife heritage.

humpback whale

Time Your Visit

There are peak tourist seasons when you can expect to see more people at popular attractions, usually during the summer vacation season and the Christmas/New Year's vacation period. No matter what the season, try to visit wildlife viewing areas in the morning when crowds are lighter.

There are also peak seasons for viewing wildlife. Each site profile provides information regarding the best times of year and best times of day to view specific wildlife species. While you can spot a green sea turtle or spinner dolphin in some areas throughout the day, shorebirds may be more visible in the mornings and evenings when it is cool, or when the tide is low. Learning about the natural history of the species that particularly interest you can help you plan your trip and maximize your viewing experience.

Check the Weather

You should expect extremes in weather on the islands. It can be in the 80s, sunny and breezy on the beach, and 40 degrees cooler, foggy, with near gale force winds on the top of a mountain. Depending where you are, rainfall ranges from 8 to 400 inches a year on the islands. It can rain several times a day at places such as Princeville on Kaua'i or in Hilo on the island of Hawai'i. Mornings can be calm and afternoons may be windy. While the water is fairly stable at 75 to 82 degrees, it can feel much warmer or cooler, depending on the air temperature. The climate affects the feeding and resting habitats of some species, such as birds, which may be more active during the cooler parts of the day.

Check Tidal Tables

If you plan on snorkeling or swimming at the beach, you may want to check the local tide tables to determine the best time to visit coastal areas. You can find them at dive shops or at several websites, such as www.co-ops.nos.noaa.gov/tides05/tab2wc3.html#167.

→ Dress Appropriately

While bathing suits, shorts, T-shirts and sandals are the foundation of the laid-back Hawaiian "dress code," plan on bringing layers if visiting a site at a higher altitude. Pack a sweatshirt and bring a light rain jacket. Wear sturdy walking shoes if you plan to hike on any trails, especially those with lava. The Hawaiian sun is very hot, so protect your head with a hat that provides ample shade for your face, neck and ears.

Carry Fluids

The predictable tradewinds that cool Hawaiian beach communities make it easy to forget that the breeze and exercise can leave you dehydrated. Bring water and drink plenty of fluids while outdoors.

Bring Sun Block and Mosquito Repellent

Many visitors have had a vacation spoiled because of sunburn. The cooling tradewinds may make you forget how easy it is to become sunburned. Clothing is available that is permeated with products which provide protection from ultraviolet rays. Hat and sunglasses are other essential items. Use a sunblock lotion—one that is waterproof if you plan to be in the water—and reapply it regularly. The same is true for insect repellents. If you don't wish to use a repellent, wear long-sleeved shirts and long pants.

Choose a Good Tour Operator

Many visitors and residents experience nature and wildlife by guided tour. Local island publications advertise a wide range of boat and land tours. Since so many species play an important role in Hawaiian culture, be sure the tour also includes information about Hawaiian history, culture and lore.

How do you choose a good tour operator? Here are some simple guidelines to help you make a selection.

KEEP IN MIND...

- **Look for operators that show responsibility toward the environment.**
  Some offer "ecotours," but be forewarned that the use of the term in a brochure doesn't mean they abide by the tenets of sustainable tourism. A legitimate ecotour is an environmentally sensitive way to experience nature. Ecotours should benefit the local community and preserve the natural and cultural resources you will be enjoying. To learn more about environmentally sensitive travel, contact the Hawai'i Ecotourism Association at www.hawaiiecotourism.org.

- **Evaluate the materials provided before you go on your trip.**
  Responsible operators should suggest codes of conduct that are appropriate for the site being visited and the culture. They should provide thorough background information about the wildlife, site, culture and other aspects of the experience. They should suggest suitable clothing or equipment and make it clear what they are providing. They should have provisions for health and safety.

- **Ask whether they have a trained naturalist on the tour—someone who is knowledgeable about the site, wildlife and culture.**
  Your experience will be enriched if you can learn accurate, timely and relevant information about the animals you are viewing. Ask if guides and binoculars are provided. If there are non-English-speaking people in your group, ask what languages are spoken and if foreign language publications exist.

- **Look for evidence that the tour operation conforms to laws and policies that protect wildlife and the environment.**
  Check their advertisements to see how they promote the experience. They should follow these rules and inform guests of rules that will affect the experience. They should also be courteous toward other operators and their guests.

Extend Your View with Binoculars

Many views of marine mammals and small forest birds will be distant. Binoculars will considerably enrich your viewing experience, so consider bringing them with you. Binoculars that are between seven and ten power will be suitable. (The power is first number identified on the binoculars, such as 7 x 35, indicating these are seven power). Full-sized binoculars tend to offer a better field of view but compact binoculars are easier to carry. Try out a number of styles before you buy.

Invest in Nature Guides

You'll often see snorkelers wearing a white plastic card dangling from their wrist. Most dive shops sell these waterproof fish identification cards to help you determine what you're seeing. Local bookstores also sell a variety of nature guides about fish, marine species, birds and other wildlife. Part of the fun of viewing wildlife is learning the names of species and aspects of their natural history. Leave some extra room in your suitcase and consider purchasing a book about local wildlife while you are in the islands.

Consider Other Supplies

Most people bring cameras so they can capture memories of their Hawai'i visit. You can purchase one-time-use cameras at any grocery store and many even carry one-time-use underwater cameras. Consider bringing a day pack or fanny pack to carry water, guides and other supplies. Bring a flashlight if you plan to visit any caves or do night walks to see the volcanoes.

Be Courteous

Some sites can become crowded, so try to be tolerant and respect the needs of other visitors. Be sensitive about the privacy of residents when searching for parking at urban sites. Whether you are on a paved trail or a path passing through a rocky lava field, please remain on the trail and be a "zero impact traveler." Take only memories and leave no trace of your visit.

Get Help from Local Visitors Bureaus

The Hawai'i Visitors and Convention Bureau offers a wealth of travel and tourism tips to aid in planning your island vacation. The Bureau and its island chapters, along with a handful of destination area marketing organizations, can offer recommendations for lodging, food and a full range of activities. Every profile includes contact information for the closest tourism organization. If you stop by one of their offices or call, they can provide brochures, adventure guides and other publications. Start with the Hawai'i Visitors and Convention Bureau, 1-800-464-2924, www.gohawaii.com.

Renting Snorkeling Equipment

Snorkeling is something you can enjoy on every island. You can easily rent snorkeling equipment from a variety of outlets conveniently located near snorkeling areas and in towns. Most rent by the day or may give a reduced rate if you rent multiple days. If you're a novice, you'll find several sites that have easy entries and snorkeling conditions, as well as great tropical fish. Be sure to read pages 21–25 for tips about underwater fish viewing and snorkeling etiquette. The shop can also provide diving/snorkeling conditions and give advice about where to go on a given day.

Accessibility for Those with Disabilities

A number of sites featured in this guide offer trails, boardwalks and other facilities that are accessible to those with disabilities. A few offer shuttle transportation as well. If you are challenged by uneven or sloped terrain, or have sight or hearing deficiencies, or other special needs, be sure to call in advance to determine if the site can accommodate your needs.

KEEP IN MIND...

There are probably natural areas where you live. If you are moved by nature during your Hawaiian trip, make time to get involved in your community's projects when you return home. Volunteer. Join a conservation organization. Get your children involved. Taking a hike, planting a tree or helping with a cleanup project will expand your understanding of nature, lighten your spirit, enrich family ties and most important, help preserve the world's wildlife for future generations.

SAFETY FIRST

Water Safety

Hawai'i's famous surf provides great recreation opportunities—and potential risks. Unfortunately, drownings regularly occur on the islands, often because people have ignored safety precautions. Wind-driven currents and dangerous rip currents can make ocean activities dangerous. Although the surf may be calm, even periods of low tide can pose hazards because at these times, swimmers and snorkelers are exposed to shallow reefs. When in or near the ocean, follow any warnings and regulations at sites suggesting that you avoid specific areas under high surf conditions. Avoid staying in the water during storms. Remember, unless otherwise posted, lifeguards are not on duty at many Hawaiian beaches: Enjoy the water but pay attention!

Flash Flooding

Areas that receive hundreds of inches of precipitation per year can receive a huge volume of rain in one storm. Flash flooding is common at many Hawaiian rivers and streams. If it is raining or has recently rained, pay attention as you hike across streams or drive on roads adjacent to them.

lava field - Hawai'i Volcanoes National Park

Things that Bite, Scratch and Sting

They are underwater, in the air and underfoot.... Corals, sea urchins, jellyfish and a variety of biting bugs, from mosquitoes to centipedes, can turn a fun time into a painful one. Snorkelers should be careful around coral, which can scratch and cause minor infections, and avoid sea urchins, which have needle-sharp spines. Box jellyfish invade the nearshore waters one week to ten days after a full moon. You should avoid going in the water during these times and check for posted beach warnings signs. There are many other organisms in the ocean that sting, but you can prevent injury if you look and do not touch.

Be aware that some streams and other freshwater bodies may support leptospirosis, a waterborne bacteria that can cause illness in humans. To prevent infection, avoid entering freshwater bodies if you have open cuts or scrapes. And do not drink the water.

The lava rock underfoot on all of the islands looks mean—and it is. Keep your sandals for the beach and wear heavy-soled shoes for travel over lava rocks.

Vehicle Safety

Like any major resort destination, this island paradise is not without crime. Break-ins occur regularly, especially at remote areas, usually by people who are watching as you prepare to leave the car. Be sure to lock your car and do not leave any valuables, such as money, jewelry or expensive cameras, in the car or trunk.

It is not necessary to have a 4WD vehicle to visit any of these featured sites, unless you are plan to use unpaved roads. Exercise caution if you must drive off of paved roads; the lava can be perilous to vehicle tires and road services may be very far away. Always stay on designated roadways because your vehicle can disturb sensitive habitats and the wildlife species they support.

It can rain several times a day on the windward sides of islands, such as Kaua'i or Hawai'i. Please remember that roads can become slippery when wet, especially unpaved roads.

nēnē

TIPS FOR YOU, PROTECTION FOR THEM

Wildlife viewing in Hawaiʻi offers you the opportunity to view some of the most unusual and rare animals found in the United States. Many of these species are threatened or endangered due to habitat loss and non-native species that out-compete them. Whether on land or in the sea, many of Hawaiʻi's native birds, marine mammals and sea turtles struggle to survive so you must use extreme care when viewing these remarkable and protected animals.

This guide features some of the best sites to view native wildlife and habitats on each island. But finding a destination is only the beginning. The following tips are designed to help you be a successful and responsible observer, and to protect wildlife from harm or disturbance. In some cases, viewing guidelines are backed by state and federal laws.

 Wildlife viewing in Hawaiʻi is different. Unlike other states on the mainland, where you might be able to see a few dozen species of wildlife on any excursion, in Hawaiʻi—on a good day—you are more likely to see three or four native species. The exception is in the water, where the diversity of nearshore fish species offers snorkelers and divers the opportunity to see a multitude of fish of every imaginable size, shape and color.

General Viewing Guidelines

Look in the right place at the right time. Many species live in very specific habitats, such as high elevation rain forests or coral reefs. Some may be unique or endemic to specific islands. In addition, the time of day or season are important factors to consider when looking for wildlife. Generally, animals are most active in the early morning and late afternoon. Seasonal migration periods are also key times to look for some birds and marine mammals, such as humpback whales.

Learn before you go. Read about the wildlife, viewing sites and local regulations to get the most from your viewing experience. When you arrive, stop at the visitor center, talk with residents and hire local guides to increase your chances of seeing wildlife.

Keep your distance. Wild animals are sensitive to human disturbance. Resist the temptation to move too near to them. Use binoculars, spotting scopes and zoom lenses to get a closer view. If an animal changes its behavior—if it stops feeding, raises its head sharply, appears nervous or aggressive, changes its direction of travel, exhibits a broken wing or circles repeatedly—move away slowly. Maintain your distance from nests, rookeries and resting areas.

Look, but don't touch. Wildlife may approach you, but resist the temptation to reach out and touch any animal. If a wild animal comes toward you, stay calm and try to back away. If the animal appears sick or injured, contact the local authorities for advice. An animal that is sick or injured is already vulnerable and may be more likely to bite if it feels threatened or afraid.

Do not feed or attract wildlife. Feeding or attracting wildlife with food, decoys, sound or light disrupts normal feeding cycles, may cause sickness or death from unnatural or contaminated food items and habituates animals to people. Habituated animals are more vulnerable to injury and can become aggressive if they are taught to expect food from people.

Help others. Speak up if you notice other viewers or tour operators behaving in a way that disturbs the wildlife or other viewers, or impacts sensitive habitats. Be friendly, respectful and discrete when approaching others. When operating a boat, lead by example and reduce your speed in areas frequented by marine wildlife, anchor properly and encourage others to do the same. Violations of the law should be reported to local authorities.

Respect the rights of other people. Many people enjoy Hawai'i's public parks and beaches. Always seek permission to enter private lands and abide by all no trespassing signs. Be considerate when parking in and walking through urban neighborhoods.

Lend a hand with trash removal. Human garbage is one of the greatest threats to wildlife. Carry a trash bag with you and pick up litter found along the trail, shore and in the water. Plastic bags, floating debris and monofilament line pose the greatest risk to marine wildlife.

Land-based Viewing Tips

Here are a few tips for making your wildlife viewing on land more successful.

Look for flowering native plants. Hawai'i's native wildlife has evolved to take advantage of the diverse native plants on the islands. Flowering native trees and shrubs are magnets for colorful honeycreepers and butterflies.

Listen for the calls of birds. Dense tropical forests can make birdwatching a challenge. Listen for calls and songs to help you locate the bird.

Find a high spot and sit awhile. One of the best techniques for wildlife viewing is to find a spot that overlooks a valley or bay. Watch for movements in the water or treetops, then switch to binoculars for a close-up view.

KEEP IN MIND...

Clean your shoes after the hike. Seeds from invasive plant species are often transported to other sites in the tread or on the soles of muddy shoes.

Water-based Viewing Tips

Never chase or harass marine wildlife. Following a wild animal that is trying to escape is dangerous. Never completely surround the animal, trap an animal between a vessel and shore, block its escape route or come between mother and young. When viewing from a boat, operate at slow speed or put the engine in neutral until the animal moves away. Move parallel to the swimming animals. Avoid approaching head-on or from behind and separating individuals from a group. If you are operating a non-motorized vessel, emit periodic and gentle noise to make wildlife aware of your presence.

Let resting animals be. Some marine animals, such as monk seals and green sea turtles, leave the water or are exposed at low tide as part of their natural life cycle. This is normal behavior and typically does not indicate illness or distress. Young animals that appear to be orphaned may actually be under the watchful eye of a nearby parent. If possible, try to stay at least 50 yards away from animals on the beach and farther back if young are present. If it is not possible to keep a safe distance of 50 yards because of the type of terrain, avoid sudden and abrupt movements to minimize the risk of disturbance.

Know your abilities before entering the water. Ocean conditions can vary from hour to hour, so be aware of the weather and water conditions before entering. Always stay with a buddy and wear personal flotation devices when kayaking.

KEEP IN MIND...

If you are operating a motor boat in Hawaiian waters, visit the NOAA Fisheries website for more details on safe boating practices around marine mammals and sea turtles at www.nmfs.noaa.gov/prot_res/MMWatch/hawaii.htm.

spinner dolphin

Whales and Dolphins

Humpback whales are present in the winter months and dolphins occur year-round. When looking for cetaceans, scan the ocean without binoculars to search for their spouts as they rise to the surface to breathe. Once you see spouts, switch to binoculars and sight along their path for a closer view.

The best viewing is often from shore with binoculars, where an elevated view allows you a broader and more stable vantage point. Water-based viewing is best done with a reputable commercial tour operator who is sensitive to the animals' need for space. Mothers and their young are the most vulnerable to disturbance and injury so use extreme caution when young are present.

Whales and dolphins in U.S. waters are protected by the Marine Mammal Protection Act. Some species, such as humpback whales, are also protected by the Endangered Species Act and Hawai'i state law. Humpback whales in Hawai'i are afforded additional protection under the National Marine Sanctuaries Act. See pages 125 and 147 for more natural history information about humpback whales and spinner dolphins.

KEEP IN MIND...

Federal regulations prohibit vessels and people from approaching humpback whales closer than 100 yards by water or 1,000 feet by air. Federal guidelines further recommend that vessels and people remain at least 50 yards from spinner dolphins and other species of small cetaceans to avoid illegal harass-ment of the animals. Please refrain from trying to swim with the dolphins as this can disturb them, which is illegal under the Marine Mammal Protection Act. Under Marine Mammal Protection Act regulations, feeding or attempting to feed marine mammals is also illegal.

Hawaiian monk seal

Hawaiian Monk Seals

Your best chance of seeing monk seals is when they are resting on shore. They tend to haul out on sandy beaches or shallow rocky reefs, so look for their distinctive dark forms along the shore.

Monk seals in U.S. waters are protected by the Marine Mammal Protection Act, Endangered Species Act and Hawai'i state law. They are one of the most endangered marine mammals in the United States. Seals are vulnerable to canine diseases, so keep pets well away from beaches where seals are known to rest. See page 51 for more natural history information about the monk seal.

KEEP IN MIND...

Federal guidelines recommend staying at least 50 yards away from the seals whether they are resting on shore or swimming. As with other species of marine mammals, it is illegal to harass, feed or to attempt to feed monk seals.

green sea turtle

Sea Turtles

Green sea turtles are fairly common throughout the Hawaiian Islands. They are attracted to shallow shelves of lava or coral reefs where they feed on algae or limu. From shore, watch the nearshore waters for the turtles as they surface to breathe, swim in the surf and feed on the bottom. Green sea turtles also regularly come ashore to warm in the sun (a behavior known as basking).

Keep your distance from sea turtles resting on land. If you are in a vessel, avoid paddling, swimming, snorkeling or diving near a swimming turtle. Back off further if your presence is disturbing the turtle. Limit your viewing time to 30 minutes. See page 177 for more natural history information about the green sea turtle.

KEEP IN MIND...

Sea turtles are protected by the Endangered Species Act and Hawai'i state law, so it is illegal to disturb them. Do not touch, ride, feed or otherwise disturb sea turtles on land or in the water. For more information about Marine Wildlife Viewing Guidelines, go to www.nmfs.noaa.gov/pr/MMWatch/hawaii.htm

Fish and Coral Reefs

The best snorkeling and diving occurs around rocky areas and coral heads where reef fish have places to hide from predators. Sandy beaches generally have poor visibility and limited diversity of habitats, so head for rocky headlands or outcrops for the best viewing.

No peas please! Feeding fish frozen peas or any other food can cause illness or death and disrupt natural fish populations. Do not attempt to touch fish or any marine life. In shallow water, avoid stepping on or touching coral heads by entering the water at a sandy location and floating above the coral. See pages 67 and 151 for more natural history information about reef fish.

ornate butterflyfish

'apapene

Birds

No matter where you are viewing, start by using your eyes to watch for movements and your ears to listen for calls. Once you spot a bird, switch to binoculars to get a close-up view.

Ground-nesting seabirds are the most vulnerable to disturbance. In areas where Laysan albatrosses and wedge-tailed shearwaters nest, stay on designated trails and well back from nest sites. All nesting birds are sensitive to disturbance so if you spot a nest, back away from the area. See pages 46, 55, 83, 87, 115 and 161 for more natural history information about Hawaiian birds.

Wildlife at a Glance

Do you want to increase the likelihood of seeing a particular species? Try the chart below. Although many of these species can be found in every site, these places are the most likely sites to see these species.

	coral reef/fish	whales	dolphins	seals	turtles	bats	exotic birds	seabirds	shorebirds	wetland birds	forest birds	raptors
KAUA'I												
Hā'ena SP pg. 34	X	X	X	X	X		X	X	X			
Nā Pali Coast State Wilderness Park pg. 38	X	X	X	X	X	X	X	X	X			
Kīlauea Point NWR pg. 43		X	X	X	X			X	X	X		
Po'ipū Beach Park pg. 48	X			X	X		X		X			
Kōke'e SP pg. 53							X	X			X	X
O'AHU												
Diamond Head State Monument pg. 60		X					X	X				
Hanauma Bay Nature Preserve pg. 65	X				X		X	X				
Hālona Blowhole pg. 70		X	X		X		X	X				
Makapu'u Point State Wayside pg. 72		X	X				X	X				
Hāmākua Marsh Wildlife Sanctuary pg. 76									X	X		
Waimea Valley Audubon Center pg. 80							X		X	X		
Ka'ena Point NAR pg. 85	X			X	X		X	X				
MAUI												
Kanahā Pond Wildlife Sanctuary pg. 92							X		X	X		
Haleakalā NP: Summit Area pg. 96							X	X	X		X	X
Polipoli Springs SRA/Kula Forest Reserve pg. 100							X				X	
Wai'ānapanapa SP pg. 104		X	X		X		X	X	X			
Haleakalā NP: Kīpahulu Area pg. 108		X	X		X		X	X	X	X		
Keālia Pond NWR pg. 113		X			X		X		X	X		
Molokini Crater pg. 118	X	X			X			X				
Hawaiian Islands Humpback Whale NMS pg. 123		X	X									
Mākena SP pg. 128	X	X			X		X		X	X		

	coral reef/fish	whales	dolphins	seals	turtles	bats	exotic birds	seabirds	shorebirds	wetland birds	forest birds	raptors
LANAʻI & MOLOKAʻI												
Mānele-Hulopoʻe Bays pg. 134	X	X	X		X							
HAWAIʻI												
Kahaluʻu Beach Park pg. 140	X				X		X					
Kealakekua Bay SHP pg. 144	X	X	X					X			X	
Puʻuhonua o Hōnaunau NHP pg. 149	X	X	X		X	X	X		X			
Manukā State Wayside/NAR pg. 154							X	X			X	
Hawaiʻi Volcanoes NP pg. 159		X	X				X	X	X	X	X	X
Wailoa River SRA pg. 164							X		X	X	X	
Kīpuka Puʻu Huluhulu pg. 166											X	X
Kalōpā SP pg. 170						X	X			X	X	X
Kaloko-Honokōhau NHP pg. 175	X				X		X			X	X	

nēnē

Amenities at a Glance

Here's a quick look at what resources and amenities are available at which sites.

Site	boardwalks	trails	lookout/viewing platform	interpretive signs	visitor center	brochure	book/gift store	restroom	food	drinking water	picnic area	bus accessible	overnight lodging	campground	lifeguard
KAUA'I															
Hā'ena SP pg. 34		X	X					X	X						
Nā Pali Coast State Wilderness Park pg. 38		X	X	X				X						X	
Kīlauea Point NWR pg. 43			X	X	X	X	X	X		X					
Po'ipū Beach Park pg. 48			X					X	X	X	X	X			X
Kōke'e SP pg. 53	X	X	X	X	X	X	X	X	X	X	X	X	X	X	X
O'AHU															
Diamond Head State Monument pg. 60		X	X	X		X		X	X	X	X	X			
Hanauma Bay Nature Preserve pg. 65	X	X	X	X	X	X	X	X	X	X	X	X			X
Hālona Blowhole pg. 70			X									X			
Makapu'u Point State Wayside pg. 72		X	X	X											
Hāmākua Marsh Wildlife Sanctuary pg. 76			X												
Waimea Valley Audubon Center pg. 80		X		X	X	X	X	X	X	X	X	X			X
Ka'ena Point NAR pg. 85		X	X	X											
MAUI															
Kanahā Pond Wildlife Sanctuary pg. 92			X			X						X			
Haleakalā NP: Summit Area pg. 96		X	X	X	X	X	X	X	X	X	X	X		X	
Polipoli Springs SRA/Kula Forest Reserve pg. 100		X						X			X		X		
Wai'ānapanapa SP pg. 104		X						X			X	X	X	X	
Haleakalā NP: Kīpahulu Area pg. 108		X	X	X	X	X		X			X	X		X	
Keālia Pond NWR pg. 113	X	X	X	X											
Molokini Crater pg. 118															
Hawaiian Islands Humpback Whale NMS pg. 123			X	X	X	X		X			X	X			
Mākena SP pg. 128								X			X				

28

	boardwalks	trails	lookout/viewing platform	interpretive signs	visitor center	brochure	book/gift store	restroom	food	drinking water	picnic area	bus accessible	overnight lodging	campground	lifeguard
LANA'I & MOLOKA'I															
Mānele-Hulopo'e Bays pg. 134		X	X					X		X	X				
HAWAI'I															
Kahalu'u Beach Park pg. 140	X	X	X					X	X	X	X	X			X
Kealakekua Bay SHP pg. 144			X					X		X	X				
Pu'uhonua o Hōnaunau NHP pg. 149	X	X	X	X	X	X	X	X		X	X	X			
Manukā State Wayside/NAR pg. 154	X		X					X		X	X	X		X	
Hawai'i Volcanoes NP pg. 159	X	X	X	X	X	X	X	X	X	X	X	X	X	X	
Wailoa River SRA pg. 164								X		X	X	X			
Kīpuka Pu'u Huluhulu pg. 166		X	X					X	X		X				
Kalōpā SP pg. 170	X		X		X			X		X	X	X		X	
Kaloko-Honokōhau NHP pg. 175	X		X	X	X	X	X	X				X			

Hanauma Bay

The sites on each island are presented in a sequential driving loop. Each island sequence starts from the major city that will most likely be your point of arrival. There are three types of sites that you'll encounter.

The "premier," or most significant sites, are the places you'll want to consider visiting if you have only a limited time on the island. Their site narratives run for six pages.

The next level is "regional" sites. These are important sites that may be located farther from populated areas, requiring more of a time commitment for viewing. In some cases, the types of wildlife species that might be seen are more limited. Regional site narratives run four pages.

The "local" sites are normally in a significant urban or suburban location and may offer only seasonal viewing opportunities, such as whale watching. They are often small and have limited parking. Please do not be quick to discount these sites because they are located near businesses or residences. Many are magnets for wildlife and offer surprisingly good wildlife viewing experiences. Local site narratives are two pages long.

As you glance through the pages of this guide, you will notice that each site narrative follows the same format. This should make it easy for you to compare sites and find important information.

Sprinkled throughout the book are "Species Notes," featuring more than a dozen highlighted species with illustrations by noted Hawaiian artist Patrick Ching. His art captures common or interesting species that you should see during your visit.

There is information about Hawaiian culture throughout the guide. Native Hawaiians have had a long presence on the islands and a reverent association with native plants and wildlife. These relationships are discussed throughout the guide. Many of the featured sites include important temples (heiau), sacred rocks or other aspects of Hawaiian culture.

For at-a-glance information about where to find particular species or facilities, refer to the charts on pages 26–29. The charts follow the island and site order that you'll find in the rest of the guide.

Waimea Canyon

The site name is often the most common name attributed to the site. All of these sites are managed by one or more organizations or entities. It is not always possible to reflect these multiple ownerships or managers in the site name.

BACKGROUND: Offers an historical perspective and sometimes includes important cultural information.

DESCRIPTION: Mentions some of the key sights and wildlife experiences at the site.

WILDLIFE TO WATCH: Gives specific information about the species you might expect to see, the best seasons for viewing and your chances of seeing them. Some natural history information is also provided.

VIEWING TIPS: Suggests where to see the species and ways to improve your chances of seeing them.

Site Notes Gives information about the sites, such as the existence or length of trails, the recommended minimum amount of time for visiting the site, parking or entry fees or other specific tips.

Hours Gives hours the site is open to the public. Opening and closing times are subject to change, so call ahead to verify hours.

Nearby Services Provides names of the closest places that offer gas, food and lodging. The name, telephone number and website address for the local visitors' bureau is listed to help you with trip-related needs. Every island publishes free tourist magazines readily available at hotels and grocery stores that provide a wealth of information about lodging, recreation and other activities.

Special Tips Discusses safety information or warnings. Gives suggestions or reminders about what to bring.

Contact Information Provides the site manager's address and telephone number. Note that not all sites have a local office and telephone number; sometimes the state or island office for the agency is listed. Whenever possible, a website address is provided.

Map shows the exact location of the site and the best way to reach it while driving. In a few cases, written directions are provided to complement the map.

The facility icons show you at a glance the types of amenities that are available at the site.

Kaua'i - The Garden Isle

ISLAND FLOWER
mokihana berry

The Garden Isle is known for its miles of white sand beaches, misty rain forests and dramatic scenery. It is a place shaped by moisture, or the lack of it. In Kaua'i's windward mountains, hundreds of inches of rain fall annually and feed countless waterfalls on the steep Nā Pali cliffs, recharge the rich wetlands of Hanalei Valley and flood taro fields that have been farmed for centuries.

As storm clouds pass over Mount Wai'ale'ale, Kaua'i's highest peak, they dump 300 to 500 inches of rain each year. The moisture charges the Alaka'i Swamp, a remote, rainswept haven for forest birds and plant species, some of which are found only in this secluded sanctuary. The clouds continue over the leeward side, scudding past remarkably arid terrain chiseled by wind, water and time to form Kaua'i's own "Grand Canyon of the Pacific," Waimea Canyon.

Kaua'i is like two islands: a tropical world and an arid one, each supporting unique plants and wildlife. Many native habitats, temples (heiau) and cultural sites are protected in the island's national wildlife refuges, parks and other conservation areas. Among them is the National Tropical Botanical Garden, which was created by the U.S. Congress to preserve Kaua'i's unusual native flora.

This diversity in habitats yields some of the richest and most varied wildlife viewing opportunities in Hawai'i. At Kīlauea Point National Wildlife Refuge you can stand just a few feet away from nesting seabirds. Look seaward and you may see green sea turtles (honu), humpback whales (koholā) during winter and maybe even a monk seal ('īlio holo i ka uaua). At Kōke'e State Park and the Alaka'i Swamp you can see more native forest birds than any other place in Hawai'i. At Po'ipū Beach Park you will find underwater coral gardens with brightly colored tropical fish, as well as excellent opportunities to see monk seals.

Near many wetlands and streams you may see non-native cattle egrets, native Hawaiian coots ('alae ke'oke'o) and other ground-nesting water-birds that have managed to survive because Kaua'i has no mongooses, an introduced predator that decimates ground-nesting birds. Fallow fields may produce views of black francolin and red junglefowl (moa), the first bird brought to Hawai'i by the Polynesians. At ponds and reservoirs you may see wintering diving ducks, such as scaup and ringnecks (hakō). And you can occasionally enjoy views of unusual birds for the area, from the greater necklaced laughing-thrush to the western meadowlark.

'anianiau

Hā'ena State Park

Coastal views and great snorkeling at the end of the road

BACKGROUND

The parking area at Hā'ena State Park is always full for a good reason: this 65-acre Park at the end of the winding Kūhiō Highway is the gateway to the majestic Nā Pali coast. The Park offers a little of everything a visitor might want: scenic 2,000-foot spires that flank the wave-battered coast, snorkeling at a picturesque white sand beach, the chance to spot seabirds and spinner dolphins (nai'a), an opportunity to view an ancient temple (heiau) and a hula platform that is still used by hula schools. Hawaiian legends place the goddess Pele at this platform located west of Kē'ē Beach, where she assumed the form of a beautiful young woman to dance with Lohi'au, a handsome Kaua'i chief.

DESCRIPTION

Begin your stay at Hā'ena State Park by finding the Kalalau trailhead and read the interpretive panel about the Nā Pali coast. Then walk a short distance on the trail to the first coastal overlook. The green-mantled cliffs seem to plunge vertically into the turquoise surf, a scene that is repeated like a visual echo as far as the eye can see. Watch for white-tailed tropicbirds (koa'e kea) soaring beside the cliffs, so easy to identify with their long white tails. Return to the trailhead and settle down at Kē'ē Beach, where a network of coral reefs provides excellent snorkeling throughout the summer.

After you've cooled off, continue walking around the point and watch for spinner dolphins and green sea turtles (honu) close to shore. When you reach Limahuli Stream, return back along the beach. You may see mynas, cardinals, doves and other non-native birds on the way. Be sure to visit the wet caves along the road to the parking area; these former sea caves, partially filled with water, can be dangerous, so swimming is not allowed. Across the road from the caves you'll find a restored taro field. If it hasn't rained to cool you off, try another round of snorkeling at Kē'ē Beach.

WILDLIFE TO WATCH

You will see some wildlife during your visit but you should be prepared to enjoy the other Park attributes. **Monk seals** ('īlio holo i ka uaua) and **green sea turtles** make occasional appearances on the beach, but do not approach them. Snorkelers will be treated to views of many reef fish throughout the year. **Wrasse** (hīnālea) are colorful fish known for their speed. The **unicorn fish** (kala) is named for the horn protruding from its forehead while the goatfish (weke) is named for the two barbels on its chin. You're also likely to see bright yellow **butter-**

flyfish (lauwiliwili) and the **convict tang** (manini), which is named for its conspicuous stripes. Non-native resident birds, such as **doves**, **sparrows**, **cardinals** and **mynas**, are often near the parking area. Throughout the year you should see **brown noddies** (noio) near the cliffs at Kē'ē Beach. **Ruddy turnstones** ('akekeke) seek this isolated coast from fall through spring and are fairly common in flocks along the shore. Watch for their signature behavior of flipping over rocks while searching for crabs. The **wandering tattler** ('ūlili), a small grayish shorebird, is also a common winter resident. You may see them at Limahuli Stream, where they often dunk their heads entirely underwater as they probe for insect larvae. They commonly call "too-li-li-li," which probably gave rise to their Hawaiian name, 'ūlili. You may also spot **spinner dolphins** and **white-tailed tropicbirds**.

VIEWING TIPS

Wildlife numbers are limited here and viewing opportunities may be unreliable. Try to arrive well before 10 AM to increase your chances of seeing wildlife before the beach and trail get crowded. You will also enjoy better snorkeling if you beat the crowd. Views of birds, dolphins and sea turtles may be distant, so bring binoculars. Don't be dismayed if the wildlife viewing is light because the scenery is unparalleled.

As you leave (or enter) the Park, consider making a stop at Limahuli Gardens, located just before the Park entrance. Though not part of the State Park, the gardens offer an excellent opportunity to see and learn about many native plants used by Hawaiians. The entrance fee buys you a self-guided trail experience past taro fields and through a picturesque valley encircled by towering cliffs. You should see non-native birds in the shrubs and tree canopy, and a variety of native damselflies and dragonflies (pinao) around flooded taro fields.

Site Notes Park in the designated lot located before the end of the road.

Hours Open during daylight hours

Nearby Services Gas, food and lodging are available at Hanalei or Princeville. For more information, contact the Kaua'i Visitors Bureau, (808) 245-3971, www.kauaidiscovery.com.

Special Tips The Park is often crowded by 10 AM. The parking area has recently been repaved. It is narrow, congested and parking spaces are limited. The beach is subject to heavy surf during the winter, a time when snorkeling and swimming are not safe. There are no lifeguards on duty. Please show respect at the hula platform and Kauluapaoa Heiau, a sacred cultural site, and refrain from climbing on them.

Contact Information Department of Land and Natural Resources, Division of State Parks, 3060 'Eiwa St., Room 306, Līhu'e, HI, 96766, (808) 274-3444, www.hawaii.gov/dlnr/dsp

white-tailed tropicbird

KAUA'I • *Hā'ena State Park*

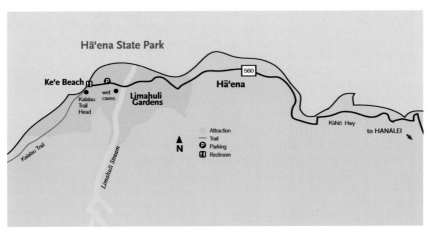

Hā'ena State Park

Ke'e Beach

Kalalau
Trail
Head

wet
caves

Limahuli
Gardens

560

Hā'ena

Kalalau Trail

Limahuli Stream

Kūhiō Hwy

to HANALEI

Attraction
Trail
Parking
Restroom

N

BACKGROUND

It feels like a place that time has forgotten. Its beauty and rugged grandeur are nearly mystic. Nā Pali, "the cliffs," stand like fluted sentinels 3,000 feet tall with their rocky bases gnawed by battering waves. Waterfalls gush down the cliffs year-round, their silvery trails always visible. Abundant rainfall in the area close to Hāʻena State Park has created a lush carpet of green vegetation that softens the craggy volcanic rock. This is one of the most remote places on the island and the wildlife abounds here, from seabirds and sea mammals to non-native birds, nēnē and bats.

The 6,150-acre Park is rich in history. The rock-lined agricultural terraces built into the lower slopes and valley floors were used to grow taro by the early Hawaiians. Two hundred acres of cultivated land in Kalalau supported one of Kauaʻi's largest populations prior to pre-contact settlement in 1778. Coffee was grown here in the late 1800s and clumps of coffee shrubs still remain. In 1893, a young Hawaiian with leprosy and his wife hid in Kalalau, evading attempts by the authorities to remove them, even when they fired a cannon. During the 1900s, many non-native plants and fruit trees were introduced, along with an increasing population of feral goats. The isolated area was a haven for hippies during the 1960s, who stayed until the area was designated a Wilderness Park in the late 1970s. Today, the Park belongs to the wildlife and visitors who make the effort to hike along this wild and remote coastline.

DESCRIPTION

Nā Pali Coast State Wilderness Park feels like one of the most remote places on earth and is difficult to reach. There are three ways to see this Park: by hiking its rigorous trails, viewing it from a helicopter or seeing it from an ocean boat tour. A day-long boat tour can reveal the secrets of this isolated paradise–without steep and strenuous hiking. Several boat tours offer hikes to cultural sites and snorkeling at the reef of Nuʻalolo Kai. A boat tour will also help you avoid the crowds attempting to find parking at popular Hāʻena State Park, the gateway to the Nā Pali Coast.

If you're fit and you enjoy hiking, you won't be disappointed. You can follow the same route as early Hawaiians along the Kalalau Trail, which covers 11 miles from Hāʻena State Park to Kalalau Beach. You can also do a 2-mile, one-way walk along the same trail from Hāʻena State Park (Kēʻē Beach) to Hanakāpīʻai Beach.

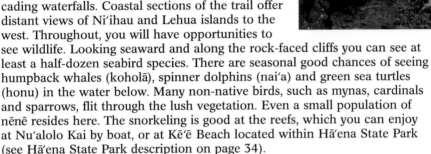

Trails in Hanakāpīʻai, Hanakoa and Kalalau Valleys meander past agricultural terraces and cascading waterfalls. Coastal sections of the trail offer distant views of Niʻihau and Lehua islands to the west. Throughout, you will have opportunities to see wildlife. Looking seaward and along the rock-faced cliffs you can see at least a half-dozen seabird species. There are seasonal good chances of seeing humpback whales (koholā), spinner dolphins (naiʻa) and green sea turtles (honu) in the water below. Many non-native birds, such as mynas, cardinals and sparrows, flit through the lush vegetation. Even a small population of nēnē resides here. The snorkeling is good at the reefs, which you can enjoy at Nuʻalolo Kai by boat, or at Kēʻē Beach located within Hāʻena State Park (see Hāʻena State Park description on page 34).

WILDLIFE TO WATCH

The seabird viewing can be excellent for some species. **White-tailed tropicbirds** (koaʻe kea) are always present and easy to spot against the green vegetation; **great frigatebirds** (ʻiwa) are common. Also abundant are **brown noddies** (noio kōhā), which have a sleek, dark brown body, a white head cap and a wedge-shaped tail. **Black noddies** (noio) nest from May to August in the cliff faces and shubbery. If you spot a nesting colony, you may see the nodding between adults that is responsible for their name. In spring and summer, you may even see a few **red-footed** and **brown boobies** (ʻā) flying on updrafts near the cliffs. Look for **Pacific golden-plovers** (kōlea) on vegetated slopes in the winter. As you glance seaward, watch anytime of year for **spinner dolphins** and **green sea turtles** cresting through the waves. There are good chances you may see **monk seals** (ʻīlio holo i ka uaua) draped over the rocks below. This is a good spot to see **humpback whales** during winter and spring. You may also spot **mynas**, **nēnē** and **Hawaiian hoary bats**.

VIEWING TIPS

In most cases the views are distant, so bring binoculars or a spotting scope. The easiest way to see the site is from a boat. If you take a boat tour, be sure to select an operator with a naturalist on board who will focus on wildlife viewing as part of the experience.

Site Notes   Parking, restrooms and interpretive signs for Nā Pali Coast State Wilderness Park are located at Hāʻena State Park. The area is congested and parking spaces are very limited. This is where the trailhead for the Kalalau Trail is located. Permits are required from State Parks to camp or hike beyond Hanakāpī'ai or to make boat landings at designated sites. Self-composting toilets are located at Hanakāpī'ai, Hanakoa, Kalalau and Nu'alolo Kai. Allow a full day to explore this remote site.

Hours Open during daylight hours

Nearby Services Gas, food and lodging are available at Hanalei and Princeville. Most boat trips depart from Port Allen in Hanapepe and Kīkīaola Small Boat Harbor, between Waimea and Kekaha. For more information, contact the Kaua'i Visitors Bureau, (808) 245-3971, www.kauaidiscovery.com.

Special Tips If you hike, sturdy hiking boots are required; do not attempt to hike in sandals or beach shoes. The trails are steep, rough and difficult. Frequent rain makes the trails slippery. Hikers must come prepared with water, food, sunscreen and other necessities. Hikers may encounter goat hunters when using trails into the backcountry of Hanakoa, Kalalau and Miloli'i.

Contact Information Department of Land and Natural Resources, Division of State Parks, 3060 'Eiwa St., Room 306, Līhu'e, HI 96766, (808) 274-3444, www.hawaii.gov/dlnr/dsp

Hawaiian monk seal

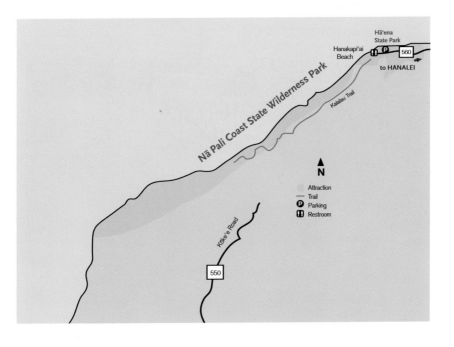

Hā'ena
State Park

Hanakapi'ai
Beach

to HANALEI

560

Nā Pali Coast State Wilderness Park

Kalalau Trail

N

Attraction
Trail
Parking
Restroom

Koke'e Road

550

Kīlauea Point National Wildlife Refuge

Famous light station yields outstanding views of seabirds

red-footed booby

BACKGROUND

Rugged cliffs that plunge into the ocean, spectacular coastal views, a historical lighthouse and the chance to see seabirds, nēnē and marine mammals combine to make Kīlauea Point a premier destination. At times, you can watch seabirds that are literally just a few feet away.

This site may only be a few hundred acres, but it is one of the most heavily visited areas on Kaua'i and has among the highest visitation in the National Wildlife Refuge System. While this sounds as if it could be crowded, impersonal and disturbing to wildlife, it isn't, thanks to concerted management efforts by the Refuge. Access to the site is regulated.

A small paved overlook perched above and outside of the Refuge gate gives visitors a panoramic view of Kīlauea Point, the lighthouse and many seabirds in flight. Most visitors stop here before proceeding onto the Refuge. As you enter the Refuge, watch for endangered nēnē grazing and resting in the grassy areas. Hawai'i's state bird is making a comeback at protected areas such as Kīlauea Point.

DESCRIPTION

Most people stop at the Visitor Center to take in the excellent interpretive displays about Hawaiian habitats and wildlife. The bookstore at the center is managed by the Kīlauea Point Natural History Association; proceeds help support Refuge programs. From the Visitor Center, it is a 300-yard walk to the lighthouse, a white sentinel with a large Fresnel lens that helped passing boats avoid the rugged coast for more than 60 years before it was retired in 1976. Knowledgeable staff and volunteers are on hand to talk about the lighthouse; to provide insight into wildlife activity visible through spotting scopes, binoculars or on a big-screen T.V.; and to help you identify some of the seabirds riding the gusty air currents around the Point. Some of the vegetation you pass on the way to the lighthouse has been planted as part of a restoration program to bring back native coastal plants, such as naupaka, 'ilima and Hawaiian spurge ('akoko).

The real show at Kīlauea Point is provided by seabirds, which are there year-round. Marine wildlife species make frequent, though seasonal, appearances.

WILDLIFE TO WATCH

There are few places in Hawai'i that offer such superb seabird viewing opportunities. Minutes after leaving the Visitor Center, you may see **red-footed boobies** ('ā), **Laysan albatrosses** (mōlī), **great frigatebirds** ('iwa) and both **red-tailed** (koa'e 'ula) and **white-tailed** (koa'e kea) **tropicbirds** with their long, elegant tails. The boobies are the most visible of the seabirds, nesting and roosting on trees and shrubs on the slopes of Crater Hill. You can see booby chicks from April through July. The red-tailed tropicbirds are unmistakable with their white, gull-sized bodies and long, red tail streamers. They often celebrate their courtship with clamorous aerial displays. Both white- and red-tailed tropicbirds are present from spring through fall. During the same seasons, look for burrows used by **wedge-tailed shearwaters** ('ua'u kani) as they nest and raise their downy young along the trail to the lighthouse.

The Laysan albatross's reappearance at Kīlauea Point in the late 1970s was big news. The species had been missing from Kaua'i for over a thousand years. Today, the conditions are so perfect at Kīlauea Point that these large birds nest in greater and greater numbers, treating visitors to elaborate courtship displays that include bill clapping, sky-pointing and bowing. Most pairs mate for life. Albatrosses can be seen at Kīlauea Point from November through July. Another species making a comeback at the Refuge is the nēnē. Reintroduced to this protected site in 1991, the endangered species is thriving. While nēnē can be seen year-round, families with goslings are plentiful from November through March.

Humpback whales (koholā) may swim close to the Point during January, February and March, and **spinner dolphins** (nai'a) may be seen during spring and early summer. **Green sea turtles** (honu) surf through the surge zone. **Monk seals** ('īlio holo i ka uaua), on the other hand, are much less common, but Kīlauea Point is one of only a few places in the main Hawaiian Islands where you might see them. Look for them draped over the rocks of the offshore island or in the cove east of the lighthouse.

VIEWING TIPS

You don't have to work hard to see seabirds. They regularly fly back and forth to nests and roosts; some of the shearwaters use burrows that are next to the paved pathway to the lighthouse. You will see a number of seabird species throughout the year. Since many nest, there are good to excellent chances of seeing activity from spring through fall. Stay on paved areas to avoid trampling burrows. If you take time to watch other visitors or the volunteers, they will cue you to the presence of an interesting bird, or whale, dolphin, monk seal and turtle sightings. Just follow their gaze! There are binoculars and mounted spotting scopes to help extend your views, but often the birds fly close enough to see the glint in their eyes.

Hanalei National Wildlife Refuge

Where can you see cascading waterfalls and a mosaic of wetlands dotted with waterbirds, all embraced by the graceful arch of a rainbow? Just seven miles from Kīlauea Point.

After you leave Kīlauea Point, drive north on the Kūhiō Highway toward Princeville. On your left, just before Princeville, a newly developed Hanalei Valley overlook (scheduled to open by 2007) will provide distant, but excellent, views of wetlands, taro fields and waterbirds. It showcases the Hanalei Valley with its marshes and wetland agriculture, the mountains of north Kaua'i and Hanalei Bay. This well-placed overlook is on Hanalei National Wildlife Refuge.

Hawaiian waterbirds have nested in the valley for thousands of years and remain in fair numbers today. The valley is home to the endangered nēnē and all four endangered waterbirds—the Hawaiian stilt (ae'o), Hawaiian coot ('alae ke'oke'o), Hawaiian moorhen ('alae 'ula) and Hawaiian duck (koloa). You may spot a northern pintail (koloa māpu) or northern shoveler (koloa mohā) on the ponds, while the shallows and mudflats attract Pacific golden-plovers (kōlea), sanderlings (hunakai) and ruddy turnstones ('akekeke) in winter. These species, especially those that nest, are benefiting from the Refuge's work to remove or exclude non-native animals, an effort that is also helping to retain the exceptional ecological value of the valley.

The new overlook will include restrooms, interpretive signs and a visitor center/bookstore. The overlook is the best way to see Hanalei National Wildlife Refuge. The road through the Refuge is narrow, and the wetlands and taro fields are not open to the public.

S P E C I E S   N O T E S

Nēnē

Hawai'i's state bird, the nēnē (Hawaiian goose), is easily identified by its black head and nape and contrasting buff-colored cheek and neck. Its long neck is lined with dark furrows. Its resemblance to the Canada goose is not just a case of similar markings; genetic studies suggest a shared ancestor.

The nēnē looks like a waterfowl species you would expect to find in a marsh. The birds do inhabit Hawaiian wetlands, but the reduced webbing on their feet suggests they also have adapted to terrestrial life in non-wetland areas. Nēnē extended their range to upland grasslands and lava flows before the introduction of mammalian predators.

During the last century, however, nēnē were nearly exterminated because of hunting pressure, habitat loss and the introduction of non-native predatory species, such as the mongoose, and non-native browsers, such as goats, which eat the nēnē's forage.

A few nēnē populations are rebounding because of aggressive captive breeding initiated in 1949, reintroduction programs that began in 1960 and vigilant predator control. Today, the statewide/worldwide population of this endangered bird is only about 1,300, down from an estimated 25,000 in the mid-1800s.

Despite these low numbers, nēnē are surprisingly visible at a number of protected sites. You can still see them on the Big Island at Hawai'i Volcanoes National Park, sometimes near parking areas or on lawns bordering buildings near the Kīlauea Military Camp on Crater Rim Drive. Nēnē have been reintroduced to Kaua'i, Maui and Moloka'i. Nēnē can be aggressive during breeding season (October to February), so keep your distance.

This bird has importance in Hawaiian cultural history. Many place names include "nēnē," such as Pu'unēnē (nēnē hill). Unele is the Hawaiian word for honk, and the word nele means to live in a state of poverty. The nēnē's honk is very plaintive, almost as if it was complaining about a sorry state of being. So if someone is called a nēnē or makes the honking sound of the nēnē, it has come to mean that the person is poor or in some way lacking.

See pages 21–25 for ethical viewing tips.

Site Notes Kīlauea Point is one of the best places in the Hawaiian Islands to see seabirds, nēnē, turtles and marine mammals because they are so close and accessible. This is a perfect site for those who want their viewing to be easy or who have difficulty walking. The Refuge operates motorized carts for those who need help getting to and from the lighthouse.

Hours 10 AM–4 PM daily, except federal holidays

Nearby Services Gas and food are available in Kīlauea. Lodging is available in Princeville, Hanalei or Kapa'a. For more information, contact the Kaua'i Visitors Bureau, (808) 245-3971, www.kauaidiscovery.com.

Special Tips Seasonally, parking spaces may be limited between 10:30 AM and noon. To avoid waiting, plan your visit for later in the day. You may bring drinking water to the Refuge, but food and other beverages are not allowed.

Contact Information Kīlauea Point National Wildlife Refuge, P.O. Box 1128, Kīlauea, HI 96754, (808) 828-1413, www.kilaueapoint.com

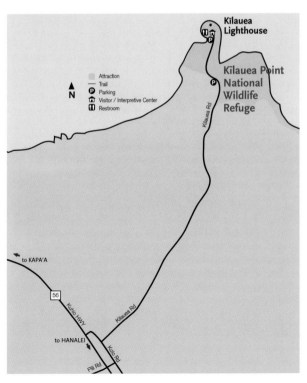

BACKGROUND

Warm, moisture-laden tradewinds reach the north coast of Kaua'i, dropping much of their moisture as rain to create lush rain forests, charge streams and rivers, and fill cascades and waterfalls that define Hawai'i's wettest island. By the time the storm clouds pass over the peaks of Wai'ale'ale in the center of Kaua'i and reach the south, or leeward side, the moisture is largely gone. Dry conditions and sunshine are the norm at Po'ipū Beach, making it a popular destination for visitors who just want to sun, swim, snorkel or surf without the prospect of frequent rainstorms and high humidity. The groomed Park at Po'ipū Beach rounds out the perfect conditions for families and others who don't want to rough it: grassy, shaded picnic areas, restrooms and changing rooms and a great vantage point to watch for seabirds, green sea turtles (honu) and monk seals ('īlio holo i ka uaua) that frequent the area.

DESCRIPTION

Miles of sandy beaches and dunes, cliff-lined shores, a blowhole and the Pacific in hues from turquoise to azure create some of the most beautiful scenery in Kaua'i. Po'ipū Beach, named for its "crashing" waves, is a water lover's dream. Add lifeguards on duty and the site becomes a perfect area for people unused to ocean conditions and snorkeling to gain confidence and skill in exploring Hawai'i's underwater reefs. With little effort and an easy entry you can enjoy limited snorkeling opportunities among the shallow reefs. The sandy bay to the west offers excellent snorkeling. Look up while you're snorkeling and you may spot green sea turtles stretching their heads above water to breathe. Many seabirds ply the coastal waters during spring, including large groups of wedge-tailed shearwaters ('ua'u kani). And at anytime of year, monk seals haul out on Hawai'i beaches and Po'ipū is a favored spot. Volunteers are frequently on hand to help protect the seals from curious onlookers. Protection may take the form of erecting an occasional fence but, more often, it is just friendly conversation to educate people about the seals' endangered status and their special needs.

WILDLIFE TO WATCH

The two big attractions at this site are **monk seals** and reef fish. This is perhaps the best place in Hawai'i to reliably see the rare monk seals, which have a total population of 1,200 to 1,300 animals. These puppy-faced marine mammals are endangered because of disturbance at their breeding grounds in the remote Hawaiian Islands. They are somewhat tame by nature and lack a natural instinct to flee when approached. However, if they are with their young, mothers may charge intruders and, in the process, abandon their young. Many young monk seals die from malnourishment or being abandoned, helping to lead to their decline.

Hawaiian monk seal

Po'ipū Beach is an excellent place to learn how to snorkel. While the water clarity along the sandy shore isn't the best, expect to see schools of **goatfish** (weke) feeding on the sandy bottom. The rocky breakwater will provide the best water clarity and diversity of colorful reef fish, including the **Hawaiian triggerfish** (humuhumunukunukuapua'a). If you didn't come to get wet, keep your binoculars handy because you can often see the 400- to 600-pound monk seals and 200-pound **green sea turtles** from shore. You may also spot **wedge-tailed shearwaters**.

VIEWING TIPS

Snorkeling is good year-round. There is also excellent snorkeling for more advanced swimmers at the adjacent beaches. Near the rocky breakwater, water clarity and fish diversity are best. Try floating awhile to watch for shy fish to appear. Notice the markings on the different species of fish: some markings help related species of fish to find each other while others are intended to fool predators. Monk seals are present all year and there are good chances of seeing them in the surf or hauled out on the beach. Between April and September is the best time of year to see nursing pups. The green sea turtle is the most common sea turtle in Hawai'i. They feed on kelp growing on the rocky promontories surrounding Po'ipū Beach. If you are interested in Kaua'i's rich botanical life, call ahead to see if you can visit the Allerton Garden located on Lāwa'i Road.

Site Notes The beach park offers extremely easy access to the shoreline and water. Parking is usually available. It is about a 50-foot walk to the beach from the parking area. The Park can provide an all-terrain wheelchair for those with limited mobility. If possible, contact the County of Kaua'i, Office of Community Assistance, Recreation Agency, at (808) 241-4467. A restaurant/deli across the street makes impromptu picnics possible. If you want a more secluded experience, ask locals for directions to the nearby beaches and coves. Some also offer opportunities to spot seabirds and other marine life. Also in the area is the 10-mile Kōloa Heritage Trail, where you can walk, bike or drive amid beautiful scenery and learn about the area's historical, cultural and environmental features from 14 marked sites. For more information, go to www.koloaheritagetrail.info.

Hours 7:30 AM–4:30 PM

Nearby Services Gas and food are available in Po'ipū and Kōloa. Lodging is available in Po'ipū. For more information, contact the Kaua'i Visitors Bureau, (808) 245-3971, www.kauaidiscovery.com.

Special Tips Monk seals occur throughout the 1,500-mile Hawaiian Island chain and are endangered. Volunteers monitor the seals during the birthing and nursing season between April and September to help visitors avoid disturbing seals resting on the beaches. Please remain at least 50 yards from the seals at all times while you are enjoying the water or viewing.

Contact Information Kaua'i County Office of Community Assistance, Recreation Agency Permits Section, 4444 Rice Street, Suite 150, Pi'ikoi Building, Līhu'e, Kaua'i, 96766, (808) 241-4467

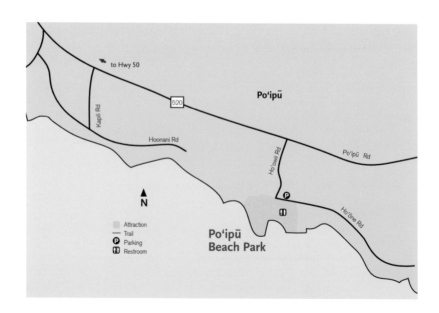

Hawaiian Monk Seal

Its Hawaiian name is "ʻĪlio holo i ka uaua," sometimes translated to "dog running in the sea or surf." With its puppy-like face, whiskered snout and playful antics in the water, the monk seal resembles a big dog playing in the surf. The collar of fat arrayed like a monk's cowl around its neck and its solitary nature may be responsible for its English name. The entire species numbers only around 1,300 animals, making it one of the rarest marine mammals on earth.

It is a rare treat to see monk seals in the main Hawaiian Islands, as most of the animals live at a half-dozen pupping islands in the remote Northwestern Hawaiian Islands. Their numbers have so declined that they were declared endangered in 1976 and their pupping sites on these remote islands were protected to help them recover.

As the monk seal population has expanded in the main Hawaiian Islands, the animals are making more frequent appearances. Your best chance of seeing them is on Kauaʻi, especially around Poʻipū Beach Park. You may see these 4- to 7-foot-long, brownish gray mammals swimming near shore or hauled out on the beach. You can also visit the Waikiki Aquarium in Honolulu to view monk seals that cannot be released into the wild.

Monk seals are especially sensitive to disturbance by humans and dogs (and they are vulnerable to human and canine diseases), so they tend to seek out quiet beaches to rest and give birth away from areas of high human use. Monk seals are sound sleepers when on the beach, which puts them in danger of being approached too closely by misguided humans. Too much activity on the beach can discourage them from coming ashore or staying there. In rare instances when pups are born in highly public areas, misguided beachcombers and swimmers who get too close can inadvertently disrupt nursing and displace mother and pup from their favored habitat. Don't be misled by their puppy-like faces; monk seals can and do bite. Federal and state laws require that you avoid disturbing monk seals and common sense dictates that you resist the urge to get close to these imperiled animals.

See pages 21–25 for ethical viewing tips.

Cloud-topped views, rare forest birds and secluded rain forests

BACKGROUND

When you hear the word "swamp," you may envision a dark, closed-in place with slithering creatures and eerie sounds. A visit to Alaka'i Swamp adjacent to Kōke'e State Park, one of the most pristine native forests in Hawai'i, will transform your preconceptions. Hawaiian lore recounts how the swamp was formed when the goddess Pele stomped her foot in anger while standing on top of Mount Wai'ale'ale. The area is volcanic in origin and today is topped with an impenetrable bog marked by stunted vegetation.

A multilayered canopy of lush green vegetation blankets cliffs reaching toward a sometimes cerulean sky. There is a feeling of spaciousness in this misty realm of clouds and rainbows, with views encompassing the pictur-esque Kalalau Valley and extending to Hanalei Bay. The sweet songs of forest birds punctuate the soulful silence. And forest birds that are rare else-where are plentiful here; many are visible year-round.

DESCRIPTION

The drive to Kōke'e State Park is an experience in itself. Beginning at sea level, the winding highway climbs through a dry and sparse landscape, past the gateway to Waimea Canyon, and continues ascending into the rain forests of Kōke'e State Park. Plan on spending time at Waimea Canyon to view the red, water-carved gorges sometimes described as the "Grand Canyon of the Pacific." (See Waimea Canyon sidebar on page 56). This hot, arid landscape provides a sharp contrast to the verdant rain forest that grad-ually appears as the highway ascends. Make time to enjoy the scenic views.

The 4,345-acre Kōke'e State Park has been a recreational area since the early 1900s. There are numerous cabins, orchards and facilities from the 1930s and 1940s throughout the Park.

Stretch your legs at the Kōke'e Natural History Museum set amid forest-fringed meadows. You may see junglefowl (moa) as you approach the

Museum. Nēnē can also be spotted. Enjoy numerous interpretive displays at the Museum that focus on the flora and fauna of the rain forest or ask for helpful trail maps. Take the .1-mile hike on the nature trail behind the museum to see many native mesic forest plants; being able to recognize the two dominant trees, koa and 'ōhi'a, will help you locate many forest birds.

Leave Kōke'e Museum and drive to the Kalalau Lookout. From here you can walk to the Pu'u o Kila Lookout, where you'll find the Pihea Trailhead. This is the gateway to the Alaka'i Wilderness Area. Take some time to look for birds in the parking area and enjoy the views of the Pacific Ocean thousands of feet below, if the weather cooperates. Hike some or all of the 3.7-mile Pihea Trail into the swamp to see a bonanza of forest birds. This 30-square-mile network of 20 bogs is recharged by runoff from Mt. Wai'ale'ale, which receives 450 inches of annual rain. Fog and mist are common in this primeval setting, where trees and ferns grow densely in the murky waters.

Wooden boardwalks thread through much of the swamp, but be prepared for muddy trails before you reach the boardwalk. Hiking is slow and slippery in this sodden and rugged landscape; whether you like birding or incredible scenery, the effort is worth every step.

WILDLIFE TO WATCH

As the swamp evolved, the birds came: vibrantly-hued native birds, such as the **'apapane**, **'ākepa** and **'anianiau**; less colorful native birds, such as the **puaiohi** and **nēnē**; and non-native species, such as the **cardinal**, **dove**, **thrush** and **myna**. You may even see introduced **black-tailed deer** along the hiking trails. As you approach the Museum, watch for **junglefowl**.

This is one of the best places in Hawai'i to easily see numerous forest birds year-round. At least nine species reside here. Begin watching for forest birds as soon as you see your first koa or 'ōhi'a trees! There are excellent chances of seeing the **Kaua'i 'elepaio**, **'amakihi** and 'apapane almost anywhere in the Park. The 'apapane is the same color as the red flowers of the 'ōhi'a from which it feeds, nature's way of providing camouflage. The yellowish green 'amakihi may often be spotted creeping on branches or hanging upside down from them, mining the bark for a meal. There are very good chances of seeing the 'i'iwi and 'ākepa in the swamp. Deer and goats occur throughout the Park. Look for non-native birds around the Visitor Center and along the overlooks at lower elevations in Waimea Canyon. And scan the cliffs from April to November for nesting **Newell's shearwaters** ('a'o).

VIEWING TIPS

View from the hiking trails, but also watch for birds at parking areas and lookouts, especially when native 'ōhi'a trees are in bloom. The 'apapane, 'amakihi and Kaua'i 'elepaio reliably occur in trees near the restroom area at the Kalalau Lookout. Any area above tree top level may provide good views into the canopy, where the birds often feed and rest. The unusual koli'i plant

(*Trematolobelia spp.*), which blooms in late summer, has long stems with clusters of bright pink blossoms that attract many honeycreepers. Bring binoculars to improve the chances of seeing and identifying birds. You might even see the rare puaiohi, a thrush-like bird that has been reintroduced to the area.

'I'iwi

Look in the canopy of the 'ōhi'a tree and you may see a bright vermillion bird with black wings, using its curved orange beak to feed on nectar. If you are close enough, you may also notice that its dark eye is encircled in yellow.

This distinctive bird is the 'i'iwi, one of Hawai'i's colorful and rare forest birds. It is common on Hawai'i, Maui and Kaua'i, where it makes a home in koa and 'ōhi'a forests located above 2,000 feet. 'I'iwi also reside on O'ahu and Moloka'i, though sightings are infrequent. Like many Hawaiian species, forest bird numbers have declined as forests were cleared for cultivation or for their wood.

Several excellent native forests remain on Hawai'i, Maui and Kaua'i, each offering good forest bird viewing. Begin your search for the 'i'iwi by scanning high in the tree canopy. Then look in the understory, where you may see it sipping nectar from tubular flowers or foraging for insects. Other nectar-feeding birds may compete with each other to feed; however, other birds retreat wherever the 'i'iwi is drinking because this crimson bird with the call like a squeaky hinge is at the top of the pecking order.

In Hawaiian lore, red birds like the 'i'iwi were symbols of royalty. The Hawaiians made capes and helmets from the feathers of the 'i'iwi and other red birds. Its feathers were also a symbol of the highest chief, and where they appeared, others showed deference. Early Hawaiians composed many songs or chants in which the monarchy and the 'i'iwi were linked.

See pages 21–25 for ethical viewing tips.

KAUA'I • *Kōke'e State Park*

Waimea Canyon

Water is the engineer of what many have called the Grand Canyon of the Pacific. Waimea Canyon was formerly an ancient volcano that partially collapsed. The Waimea River then sliced through this opening, cutting and scouring the canyon for five million years and exposing rich color and texture in the lava walls. This exceptional geologic attraction is adjacent to Kōke'e State Park and is similarly protected. As you ascend the highway toward the canyon, you'll pass through non-native dryland trees, such as eucalyptus. With elevation, 'ōhi'a and koa appear, along with the opportunity to see forest birds.

If you're interested in learning more about the native vegetation, including unusual plants such as iliau, a cousin of silversword found on Haleakalā, stop at the Iliau Nature Trail. You can also take the Kukui Trail, which makes a steep descent to the Waimea River. You may see introduced goats and some of the erosion they have created in the valley.

One of the most popular stops is the Waimea Canyon Lookout. The wind can howl and mist can obscure the view, but when it is clear the deeply cut ridges, spires and other-worldly formations are stunning. Look for white-tailed tropicbirds (koa'e kea) riding wind currents in the canyon. You may occasionally spot an Erckel's francolin at the parking lot. Francolin are chukar-like birds that feed on the ground and run to escape.

Farther up the road is Waipo'o Falls, which plunges some 800 feet during the wet season. Beyond the falls, Pu'u Hinahina Lookout provides contrasting views of Ni'ihau Island and the rugged Waimea Canyon. You may see the 'amakihi and 'elepaio in trees near the parking lots. Feral goats are commonly seen balancing on lookout precipices, and at night during spring and summer, you may hear calling seabirds which come up the canyon to nest. Nighttime listeners may also hear the short-eared owl (pueo) and barn owl. Look for owls especially at dawn or dusk, when they are most active.

If you have only a short time to visit and your interest is forest birds, visit Kōke'e State Park first and experience Waimea Canyon on your return.

Site Notes The trip to the Park is a 45-minute drive from Waimea or Kekaha and includes a long, winding road. Plan to spend an entire day so you can also enjoy a visit to Waimea Canyon. The Park has 12 rustic cabins that you can rent; plan this in advance as they are popular. Make reservations through Kōke'e Lodge, (808) 335-6061.

Hours Open during daylight hours. Museum open daily, 10 AM–4 PM

Nearby Services Gas, food and lodging are available at Waimea and Kekaha. Food is available at Kōke'e Lodge. For more information, contact the Kaua'i Visitors Bureau, (808) 245-3971, www.kauaidiscovery.com.

Special Tips Check at the museum for road and trail conditions. High elevation trails may be steep and slippery. Good hiking boots are a must; plan on getting wet and muddy. A walking stick is helpful. Some dirt roads can become slippery and impassable with abundant rain, which is why 4WD vehicles are required for dirt roads in the Park. The weather can be cold due to the higher elevation. Pig hunting occurs in the Park.

Contact Information Department of Land and Natural Resources, Division of State Parks, 3060 'Eiwa Street, Rm. 306, Līhu'e, HI 96766, (808) 274-3444, www.hawaii.gov/dlnr/dsp

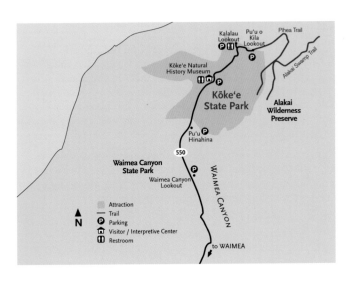

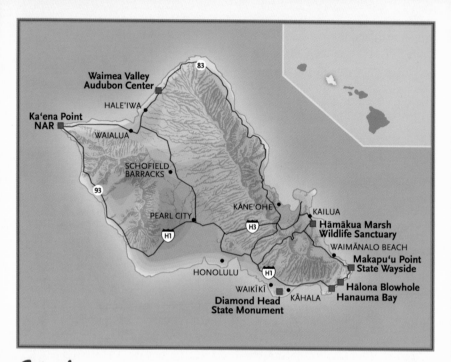

O'ahu - The Gathering Place

ISLAND FLOWER
Pua 'ilima

Say "O'ahu" and most visitors immediately envision Waikīkī with its perfect turquoise water, a sweeping crescent of sandy beach and arched palms backed by towering high-rise buildings. Undoubtedly, Honolulu and its famous beach are big draws for many O'ahu visitors, offering signature tropical beauty that is uniquely Hawaiian in a setting that is also a hub for the state's political, cultural and commercial activities.

Honolulu means "protected bay" in Hawaiian and this sheltered embayment, so friendly to ships, was one of the first areas to develop in the islands. The city brims with history, from the 'Iolani Palace built during King Kalakaua's reign to Mission Houses that are among the oldest western style buildings in the state.

You don't need to stray far from the city to enjoy nature and wildlife, even on the state's most populated island. O'ahu is known for its picture postcard beaches backed by steep rugged mountains and its many opportunities to experience the island's rich cultural history.

A few minutes' drive from Waikīkī, you can climb through a tunnel and up stairs to the top of Diamond Head, savoring the scenic views while doing some birding as you climb. Hanauma Bay is also close, offering the chance to experience several hours of world-class snorkeling among colorful reef fish. Another popular site close to Honolulu is the Hālona Blowhole, where you can see waves explode through a hole in the coastal lava while watching for humpback whales (koholā) as they pass by during winter.

A trip to Makapu'u Point offers a chance to stretch your legs with a vigorous walk to this picturesque lighthouse. The hike provides many opportunities to see seabirds and passing whales during winter. Still within a half hour's drive from Honolulu, you can visit Kailua. While most people visit Kailua to relax on the exquisite beach, birders should also fit in a stop at Hāmākua Marsh for up close views of endangered Hawaiian stilts (ae'o) and other waterbirds.

If you're willing to spend a day and drive a distance to the north shore of the island, you can visit Waimea Valley Audubon Center, where the high priests of O'ahu lived for more than 1,000 years. The site combines birding with cultural and botanical experiences in a terraced setting that includes ponds and a waterfall. To really experience wild O'ahu, add a trip to isolated Ka'ena Point to your travel list. This stretch of dunes is an excellent site to view seabirds that build their nests adjacent to the trails. A bonus for making the trek to Ka'ena Point will be the chance to see an occasional monk seal ('īlio holo i ka uaua) or green sea turtle (honu), and to experience an untamed and less visited side of this popular tourist destination.

brown booby

BACKGROUND

The unique profile of Diamond Head (Lēʻahi) sits prominently near the eastern edge of Waikīkī's coastline. Hawaiʻi's most recognized landmark is known for its stunning coastal views, military history—and as a prime area to view many non-native birds. Even novice birders should be able to spot and identify several familiar and distinctive species.

This broad, saucer-shaped crater was formed about 300,000 years ago during a single eruption that sent ash and fine particles into the air. As these materials settled, they cemented together into a rock called tuff, creating the crater and appearing on trails throughout the park. Most of the vegetation and local birds were introduced from the late 1800s to the early 1900s. Eight acres of the 350-acre Park are developed for public access.

DESCRIPTION

You will see birds as you climb to the summit, but your attention will shift to the site's military and geological history. The trail to the summit of Lēʻahi was built in 1908 as part of Oʻahu's coastal defense system. The .8-mile hike from the trailhead to the summit is steep and strenuous, gaining 560 feet as it ascends from the crater floor. A concrete walkway built to reduce erosion shifts to a natural tuff surface about .2 mile up the trail; many switchbacks traverse the steep slope of the interior crater. The ascent continues up steep stairs and through a lighted 225-foot tunnel to the Fire Control Station, completed in 1911. Built on the summit, the station directed artillery fire from batteries in Waikīkī and Fort Ruger, outside of Diamond Head crater. At the summit, you'll see bunkers and a huge navigational light built in 1917. The postcard view of the shoreline from Koko Head to Waiʻanae is stunning, and during winter the scene may include passing humpback whales (koholā), visible when they breach or spout.

WILDLIFE TO WATCH

Diamond Head offers good to excellent opportunities to see more than a dozen non-native birds year-round, concentrated in a single location. Many non-native species have readily adapted to island conditions and are frequently more visible than native Hawaiian birds, which they sometimes displace. You will see drab-colored **doves, house finches** and **sparrows** mixed with richly marked **red-crested cardinals** and **red-vented bulbuls**. The red-crested cardinals may be seen in pairs or larger groups. In winter you should also see the area's only native species, the **Pacific golden-plover** (kōlea), in the grassy areas of the park. This plover is so common that it is often one of the first birds that Hawaiian children learn to identify. Along the trail, you may hear the distinctive piercing call of

the **francolin** and you may see a **mongoose** moving through the brush. **Zebra doves** are common and easy to recognize by the distinctive barring on their chest. Another bird covered with a barred pattern is the **common waxbill**. This 4-inch bird also has a red bill and red stripe across each eye. You may also spot **humpback whales** from the summit.

VIEWING TIPS

From the moment you step out of your vehicle in the parking area, you can usually enjoy excellent birdwatching. You don't need to walk far from the parking lot or trailhead to see birds. Watch for zebra doves and common waxbills in algaroba (kiawe), a tropical, non-native tree related to mesquite, and candlenut trees (kukui), or locate them by their melodious songs. For help identifying the local birds, stop at the visitor booth interpretive sign to see photos and learn about their habits. From the summit, humpback whales can be seen spouting and breaching from January to March.

Site Notes There is an entrance fee to the park. Allow 1.5 to 2 hours for your hike. The site is accessible to those with disabilities from the parking lot to the trailhead kiosk.

Hours Daily 6 AM–6 PM; gates are locked at 6 PM

Nearby Services Gas and food are available at Kapāhulu, Kahala and Waikīkī. There is lodging in Waikīkī. For more information, contact the O'ahu Visitors Bureau at (808) 524-0722, www.gohawaii.com/oahu.

Special Tips The park is crowded between 9 AM and 2 PM. Come early in the morning or late afternoon for a better hiking and viewing experience. The hike to the summit is very steep and uneven in some areas. The last .1 mile is all stairs and especially steep. Wear good walking shoes, bring water, wear a hat and apply sunscreen. Although the existing trail can, at times, be crowded, do not leave the trail to hike along the crater rim. The rim soils are highly erodable. Some areas are also very steep and several hikers must be rescued each year. The entire crater area is extremely dry, so smokers should appropriately dispose of their cigarettes before starting the trail.

Contact Information Department of Land and Natural Resources, Division of State Parks, 1151 Punchbowl Street, Room 310, Honolulu, HI, 96813, (808) 587-0300, www.hawaii.gov/dlnr/dsp/oahu.html

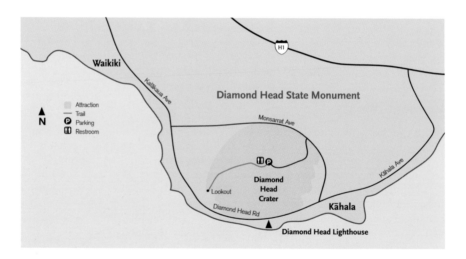

Pacific golden-plover

African silverbill

BACKGROUND

As a common translation of its Hawaiian name suggests, Hanauma (hana: bay; uma: curved) is a crescent-shaped bay flanked by steep volcanic cliffs. The rugged dome of Koko Head sits above the turquoise waters of this famous embayment. A series of volcanic events formed Hanauma's underlying landscape. Over time, the land eroded and encircled a network of reefs that are home to some of the most colorful and unique marine life in the Hawaiian Islands.

This once isolated stretch of coast, located a short distance from urban Waikīkī, was King Kamehameha V's favorite fishing grounds and served as a sheltered place for canoes to await favorable winds before crossing to Moloka'i. Today, several overlooks offer dramatic views of this 301-acre site (includes both land and water), counted among Hawai'i's most photographed beaches.

DESCRIPTION

Hanauma Bay is not only beautiful, it is also one of Hawai'i's most popular snorkeling spots. Despite the crowds, its reefs continue to support abundant fish populations. In 1990 the City and County of Honolulu began controlling visitor numbers and emphasizing education to stem environmental damage (the bay was being "loved to death") and improve the quality of the visitor experience. As soon as the preserve's parking lot is full, vehicle access to public parking from the highway is temporarily closed. As parking becomes available, vehicles are able to enter the preserve. An award-winning Visitor Center is the gateway to the site and features informative exhibits and displays. All visitors are required to watch a short video that provides an orientation to Hanauma and encourages stewardship of the bay and other living reef environments. The entry procedure at the Visitor Center also helps control over-crowding by regulating the rate of flow of visitors to the beach. If you need to wait to enter the preserve, you won't be disappointed: the views and snorkeling are superb.

WILDLIFE TO WATCH

Nearly 100 species of fish inhabit the nearshore reefs. Schools of fish sometimes form a shimmering rainbow of color and may include many large fish, such as **parrotfish** (uhu) and **jacks**. Symmetrical rows of black dots on the sides of the bright yellow **milletseed butterflyfish** (lauwiliwili) make this favorite easy to spot. The **sergeant major** (maomao) with its five bold stripes is a regular reef inhabitant and can often be seen swimming in groups. Other abundant signature reef fishes include the **surgeonfish** (kole), **convict tang** (manini) and **saddleback wrasse** (hīnālea). You may occasionally spot **green sea turtles** (honu). While you are on the beach, notice the fragments of white coral limestone and dark basalt rock embedded in the cliff walls. They are remnants of the violent volcanic explosions that created the crater. When you're in the parking lot, look for non-native birds.

VIEWING TIPS

Snorkeling is excellent much of the year, especially within the line of exposed boulders that provide protection from heavy surf. Visibility is usually best at low tide and early in the day, before sediment is kicked up by other snorkelers. Look in the crevasses on the surface of nearshore reefs for fish hiding from predators. Abundant reef life can be viewed within the reef flat. Ask volunteers at the beach kiosk for information about the bay and animals observed while snorkeling. The lifeguards and posted signage provide information about hazardous marine life and dangerous areas to avoid.

green sea turtle

Parrotfish

A bright turquoise fish swims lazily beneath the water's surface, nibbling on the living coral. Suddenly, a wispy cloud of matter is emitted from under its tail. This colorful reef inhabitant is the parrotfish, or uhu, whose eating habits are helping to form many Hawaiian beaches. The cloudy emission is fine particles of crunched coral. Parrotfish are among the biggest producers of coral sand in the tropical world. A large parrotfish can produce hundreds of pounds of sand each year!

This blunt-headed fish is named for its teeth, which are fused into a beak-like mouth. The Hawaiian name for one of the seven species found in the state translates to "loose bowels," probably in reference to the plumes of sand it excretes while eating.

Parrotfish are often brilliant turquoise and green, but may also be tinged with red or other rainbow coloring. They are big fish, ranging from one to three feet in length. They use their teeth to scrape seaweed or algae from coral, sometimes biting off chunks of coral in the process. It is not unusual for snorkelers or scuba divers to hear them crunching underwater.

At night, these wily fish hide among the rocks, where they may swath themselves in a cocoon of mucous to ward off night predators. They are also hermaphrodites. The largest, dominant fish transforms into a male and turns blue; the remaining fish are often red females and juveniles. If the male dies, the most dominant female transforms into a male, even changing its color to blue.

Hawaiian folklore includes many references to the uhu. This was a favorite eating fish among ancient Hawaiians and when a fisherman saw two parrotfish rub noses, he believed it meant that flirting may be going on at home. Many Hawaiian sayings about uhu relate to longing or admiration. The uhu is a tasty, attractive fish so comparing a person to the uhu is complimentary, suggesting the person will be satisfying. However, the uhu excretes a mucous secretion making them difficult to catch, so comparing a person to the uhu can also suggest the person is wily and difficult to catch off-guard or trip up.

See pages 21–25 for ethical viewing tips.

O'AHU • *Hanauma Bay Nature Preserve*

Premier
– SITE –

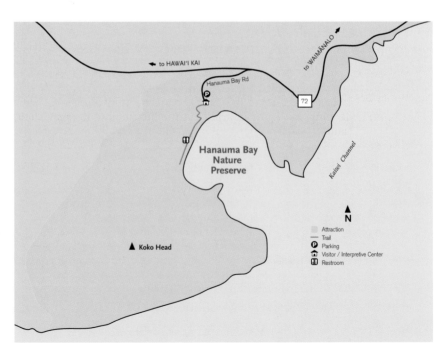

to HAWAI'I KAI →

Hanauma Bay Rd

to WAIMĀNALO

72

Hanauma Bay
Nature
Preserve

Kaiwi Channel

▲ Koko Head

N

Attraction
Trail
P Parking
Visitor / Interpretive Center
Restroom

Site Notes There are entrance and parking fees. Entrance fees are waived for residents of Hawai'i with valid proof of residency and for children under the age of 13 years. You can enjoy the scenery and Visitor Center at cliff level. Walk down the steep hill to the beach or pay for a shuttle ride. Many overlooks and facilities are accessible to those with disabilities.

Hours Preserve is always closed all day on Tuesdays. Otherwise, open daily 6 AM–6 PM from October through March. Open second Saturday of the month until 10 PM. Open 6 AM–7 PM from April through September. Open second and fourth Saturdays of the month until 10 PM. Hours may vary. Please check before visiting by calling the park's information line at (808) 396-4229, or check online at www2.hawaii.edu/~hanauma or www.co.honolulu.hi.us/parks/facility/hanaumabay/index1.htm.

Nearby Services Gift shop, snack bar, snorkel rental on premises. Gas and food are available about a mile away in Hawai'i Kai. Lodging is available in Waikīkī. For more information, contact the O'ahu Visitor Bureau at (808) 524-0722, www.gohawaii.com/oahu.

Special Tips This area is exceedingly popular and crowded. During the summer and winter tourist seasons, try to avoid the midday crowds. When in the water, remember that the rocks are an important part of the living reef and are very vulnerable to damage; swim or snorkel over them and avoid standing on them. They can also be slippery, sharp or abrasive. The inner reef surface has many crevices to explore that are deeper than standing depth. The ocean is unpredictable and can be dangerous, especially at high tide or periods of high surf (See pages 19–20 for safety tips). The preserve prohibits fishing; feeding, taking or injuring marine life (including eggs), shells, sand, coral or other geological features; walking on the reef; or carrying equipment used for those purposes. Smoking is also prohibited in the preserve. Please, do not feed the fish.

Contact Information Hanauma Bay Nature Preserve, 100 Hanauma Bay Road, Honolulu, HI 96825, (808) 396-4229, www.hanaumabayhawaii.org. For more information, contact the O'ahu Visitors Bureau at (808) 524-0722, www.gohawaii.com/oahu

O'AHU • Hanauma Bay Nature Preserve

Premier
– SITE –

Hālona Blowhole

Spouting whales and gushing surf get top billing

DESCRIPTION

When waves reach just the right angle and height, they shoot like a geyser through a large lava tube located just east of Hanauma Bay. Hālona means "a lookout or peering place," an apt description of this scenic vantage point for watching the surf boil through the offshore rock formations. In perfect form, this popular blowhole also mimics the sound of spouting humpback whales (koholā).

Near the blowhole, a small rock shrine bears the image of O-Jizosan, the Japanese guardian spirit of protection. Movie buffs may recognize the beach cove below as the site of many scenes from the film *From Here to Eternity*.

WILDLIFE TO WATCH

This is one of the best sites on O'ahu for watching **humpback whales**. These waters are so important to these winter visitors that they are part of the Hawaiian Islands Humpback Whale National Marine Sanctuary.

Hālona blowhole is also an excellent place to look for **green sea turtles** (honu) and an occasional **Hawaiian monk seal** ('īlio holo i ka uaua). **Wandering tattlers** ('ūlili) and **ruddy turnstones** ('akekeke) prowl the shore during winter. Throughout the year the open water includes views of **sooty terns** ('ewa 'ewa), **great frigatebirds** ('iwa) and other seabirds. **Mynas** and **doves** are year-round regulars around the lookout.

VIEWING TIPS

You can see the Hālona blowhole and the humpback whales from a large paved parking lot overlooking the beach.

SITE NOTES

The paved parking area adjacent to highway can hold 20 vehicles. The lookout offers access to those with disabilities. The head cove is attractive for sunbathing and picnicking, but it is not advisable to swim there.

Hours Open 24 hours a day

Nearby Services Gas and food are available in Waimānalo and Hawai'i Kai. Lodging is available in Waikīkī. For more information, contact the O'ahu Visitors Bureau at (808) 524-0722, www.gohawaii.com/oahu.

Special Tips The area is subject to occasional high winds. Heed the warning signs and do not stand near or on top of the blowhole. Do not leave valuables in your car.

Contact Information National Oceanic and Atmospheric Administration/ Hawaiian Islands Humpback Whale National Marine Sanctuary, 6600 Kalani'ana'ole Highway, Suite 301, Honolulu, HI, 96825, (808) 397-2651, 1 (800) SS-WHALE, http://www.hawaiihumpbackwhale.noaa.gov

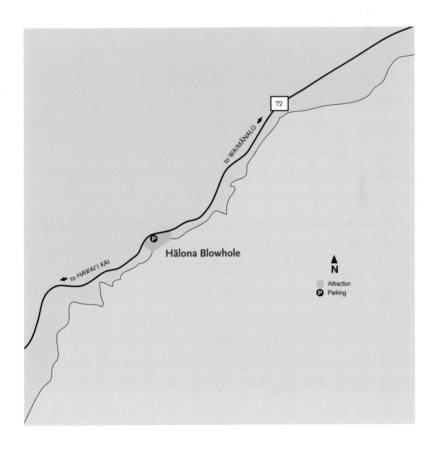

BACKGROUND

If you want an invigorating hike, spectacular coastal scenery and the chance to enjoy whale and seabird viewing from one of the best sites on O'ahu, a trip to the historic Makapu'u Lighthouse is a must. The white-sided, red-roofed lighthouse built in 1909 is perched on rugged lava cliffs on the easternmost point of O'ahu. This functioning lighthouse was automated in 1946. Its original lens, the largest of its type in the world, is still in use.

DESCRIPTION

A mile-long trail along a paved service road to this historic beacon passes through dryland habitat to an elevated viewing platform. The trail initially climbs past algaroba trees (kiawe), cactus (pānini) and other non-native dry-land plants. As it ascends toward Makapu'u Head, you are treated to views of grassy meadows and coastal wetlands in the Kealakīpapa Valley extending toward the ocean in the distance. Most of these coastal wetlands have been filled and developed over the last century throughout O'ahu. As you pass through the arid landscape, watch for doves, mynas and red-vented bulbuls.

As the trail hairpins to the north, the point extends into the windy Ka Iwi Channel. This offers hikers welcome ocean breezes and incredible views of the Pacific and surf pounding hundreds of feet below. The vistas are breath-taking, so stop often to savor the views of Koko Head and Diamond Head and also keep an eye out for leaping spinner dolphins (nai'a).

The ocean below is part of the Hawaiian Islands Humpback Whale National Marine Sanctuary. Each winter, humpback whales (koholā) often come remarkably close to shore. To spot them, look for their blows, which can rise over 20 feet. If you're lucky, you may even see a mother and calf breaching, slapping or just resting offshore. Other wildlife, such as green sea turtles (honu) and Hawaiian monk seals ('īlio holo i ka uaua), also inhabit this beautiful area.

The trail eventually leads past the weathered cement foundations of a for-mer lightstation and positions you above the red-roofed lighthouse. There is an elevated viewing platform 647 feet above the sea that overlooks the

rugged coastline and two offshore islands (Kāohikaipu and Mānana islands) that are sanctuaries for Hawai'i's seabirds, such as the great frigatebird ('iwa) and tropicbirds (koa'e). One of the sanctuaries is known as Rabbit Island. On a clear day, you may see colorful hang gliders on thermal updrafts near the cliffs, or views of Moloka'i and Lana'i in the distance. If the hike back heats you up, stop off at nearby Makapu'u Beach Park to cool off or watch bodysurfers catch the big waves.

WILDLIFE TO WATCH

It's possible to spot an occasional **dove**, **myna**, **red-vented bulbul** or **mongoose** near the trail, but for many, the real attraction is the seabirds, **humpback whales** and **spinner dolphins**. The offshore island sanctuaries attract **red-tailed tropicbirds** (koa'e 'ula), **great frigatebirds** and other seabirds, such as **red-footed boobies** ('ā), **brown noddies** (noio kōhā) and **sooty terns** ('ewa 'ewa) throughout the year. Thousands of sooty terns seek the islands to breed from March to August. Whales are present during winter and you can spot spinner dolphins throughout the year. You may also spot **green sea turtles** and **monk seals**.

VIEWING TIPS

Your chances of seeing seabirds and whales are excellent during winter from December through April, with the very best viewing from January to March. Watch for mongooses scurrying between bushes and exotic birds perched on the brush. Views of seabirds, whales and dolphins can be distant, so bring binoculars or a spotting scope. You should see seabirds on the islands, on offshore waters or in flight. To see whales or dolphins, stop for a while and scan the horizon for spouts or movement. Remember, whales often breach more than once in the same general area. The Hawaiian Islands Humpback Whale National Marine Sanctuary occasionally offers hikes and can provide information about marine mammals.

You can also see an array of captive marine species at Sea Life Park, north on Highway 72. The park displays everything from small whales to penguins and rehabilitates marine mammals that are injured.

Site Notes Two trails lead to the top of Makapu'u Point. The safest and best trail is the old access road to the light station, which begins at a pipe gate about one-third mile south of the Rabbit Island Lookout. A second unimproved trail leads from the Rabbit Island Lookout above Makapu'u Beach. This rugged climb up the ridge is not recommended.

It takes about 30 to 45 minutes to reach the lighthouse and overlook on the access road trail. There are no restroom facilities, though there is an interpretive panel about humpback whales and a spotting scope. Hike in the morning to avoid midday heat. The lower portions of the trails to the lighthouse can be exceedingly hot from late morning to afternoon. Be sure to bring a hat, sunscreen and plenty of water.

Hours Sunrise to sunset daily

Nearby Services Gas and food are available at Hawai'i Kai and Waimānalo. There is lodging in Waikīkī. For more information, contact the O'ahu Visitors Bureau at (808) 524-0722, www.gohawaii.com/oahu.

Special Tips The Division of State Parks will complete two new parking lots south of the Rabbit Island Lookout above Makapu'u Beach in 2006. Until then, you may use the small parking area at the Rabbit Island Lookout; avoid parking along the highway shoulder because of the heavy traffic.

Contact Information Department of Land and Natural Resources, Division of State Parks, 1151 Punchbowl Street, Room 310, Honolulu, HI 96813; phone (808) 587-0300; www.hawaii.gov/dlnr/dsp. Hawaiian Islands Humpback Whale National Marine Sanctuary, 6600 Kalani'ana'ole Highway, Suite 301, Honolulu, HI, 96825, (808) 397-2651, 1 (888) 55-WHALE, http://www.hawaiihumpbackwhale.noaa.gov

O'AHU • Makapu'u Point State Wayside

red-footed booby

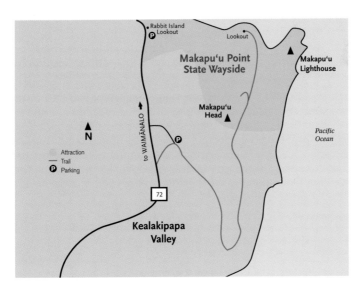

black-crowned night-heron

BACKGROUND

Hāmākua Marsh is a remnant of once extensive wetlands, fishponds and agricultural terraces that have been replaced by urban Kailua. The 22-acre site lies downstream from Kawainui Marsh, the largest remaining freshwater wetland in the state. Hāmākua Marsh is now bordered on one side by a busy suburban street. It is flanked by the lush green of the Hill of Spray. The Hawaiian name, Pu'u o 'Ehu, reflects an earlier age when ocean waves crashed against the base of this promontory. Today, the marsh is largely dependent on the adjacent Hāmākua Canal and surrounding watershed for water.

DESCRIPTION

Amid the buzz of city traffic, Hawaiian stilts (ae'o) balance on long pink legs as they probe the shallows of Hāmākua Marsh for worms, fish and other submerged delectables. This distinctive black-and-white waterbird is one of three endangered waterbirds that is common at this urban wetland located on O'ahu's windward side.

Even though bird populations fluctuate due to seasonal changes in the water supply, this marsh supports impressive wildlife diversity, including numerous fish and rich aquatic life. Native avian survivors have prompted a restoration program that is now improving water quality and marsh conditions. A canal between the street and the marsh provides an added buffer for the birds, allowing them to adjust to the ebb and flow of people and traffic. There is excellent viewing from a grassy berm between the road and the wetland– and from the adjacent coffee shop.

WILDLIFE TO WATCH

This is the best place on O'ahu for year-round, reliable, close-up views of the **Hawaiian stilt**, **Hawaiian coot** ('alae ke'oke'o) and **Hawaiian moorhen** ('alae 'ula). Look for the tallest shorebird and it will be the Hawaiian stilt, which stands 16 inches tall. It has a glossy black back that contrasts sharply with its white breast. Birds that appear slightly tinged with brown are female. According to Hawaiian lore, the stilts originally came to the area to feed on the small fish that flourished in the area's taro patches. The moorhen, with its bright red forehead and bill, was also important in Hawaiian mythology for bringing fire to the early Hawaiians. The **Pacific golden-plover** (kōlea) can be spotted in the winter along with other shorebirds, including the **ruddy turnstone** ('akekeke), **wandering tattler** ('ūlili) and **sanderling** (hunakai). At dawn and dusk, you may see a **black-crowned night-heron** ('auku'u) hunkered down on an elevated mound waiting to feed or flying to its nighttime roost. It is also possible to spot non-native **mynas** and **zebra doves**.

Hawaiian moorhen

VIEWING TIPS

Birds are present throughout the day, though the best viewing occurs in the morning. Interpretive panels along the grassy shoulder will help you identify the common birds. Park near the sign and enjoy strolling along the berm as you view. You may even see birds while driving by the site.

You can also enjoy similar species at the privately-owned Ka'elepulu Wetland located nearby. To reach this nearly 6-acre marsh, travel south on Hāmākua Drive, then turn right on Keolu Drive. Proceed about .8 mile and turn left on Kiuke'e Place. The Wetland is in a small residential neighborhood, so please respect the privacy of the residents.

Site Notes	This very accessible site offers exceptional, year-round views of many waterbirds. The marsh has no facilities, but nearby restaurants and markets offer food and provide restrooms for their patrons. Arrive in the morning for the best viewing and on-street parking.
Hours	Dawn to dusk
Nearby Services	Gas, food and lodging are available in Kailua. For more information, contact the O'ahu Visitor Bureau at (808) 524-0722, www.gohawaii.com/oahu.
Special Tips	Parking along Hāmākua Drive is restricted in the afternoon during the rush hours of 4 PM–6 PM. Be cautious when parking and viewing from the grassy shoulder of this busy street. People sometimes feed wildlife at this location, but please don't be tempted to join them.
Contact Information	Department of Land and Natural Resources/ Hāmākua Marsh Wildlife Sanctuary, 1151 Punchbowl St., Honolulu, HI, 96813, (808) 587-0166, www.hamakuamarsh.com

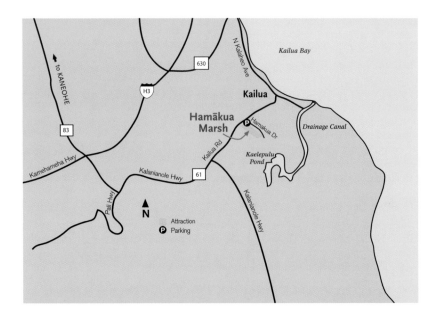

Hawaiian stilt

O'AHU • *Hāmākua Marsh Wildlife Sanctuary*

O'ahu Offshore Island Seabird Sanctuaries

Many people visit Hamakua Marsh because it offers such good opportunities to see the Hawaiian stilt (ae'o), Hawaiian coot ('alae ke'oke'o) and Hawaiian moorhen ('alae 'ula). This urban wetland is also a magnet for Pacific golden-plovers, wandering tattlers, ruddy turnstones and other shorebirds that travel between offshore islands dotting O'ahu's windward coast.

These islands, islets and rocks are so important to nesting seabirds that they have been protected as the O'ahu Offshore Island Seabird Sanctuaries. Some of the islands were once connected to the mainland while others are former reefs, dunes or volcanic cones. They were severed over time from mainland O'ahu by erosion and changes in the sea level.

These unpopulated landscapes have become a haven for seabirds, shorebirds and other avian travelers within the Hawaiian Islands chain. As the main islands have become more populated and altered to meet human needs, these offshore outposts have taken on great importance as one of the last nesting areas for noddies, shearwaters, petrels and other seabird species. For this reason, access to most of the islands is highly restricted. For information, call the Division of Forestry and Wildlife office at (808) 973-9778.

Even though the islands are located from a few hundred yards to a half mile from the mainland, some of these sanctuaries are vulnerable to visitors, non-native plants and predators. Mongooses, rats, cats and dogs all pose a threat to ground-nesting seabirds. So do non-native plants, which have spread to such an extent that they are now present in some nesting areas.

The Offshore Islet Restoration Committee was formed from several concerned agencies and organizations to promote restoration and public education. Communities along the coast have been active in helping to eradicate or remove non-native plants and animals. Even school children in Lanikai have studied the Mokulua islets and made and posted signs to show visitors how to avoid harming the island landscape or its species.

The Sanctuary stretches from Kahuku to Makapu'u Point on O'ahu's windward side. As you drive between these areas, make time to stop and scan the shore for seabirds traveling to and from these critical island sanctuaries. Binoculars will help extend your view and enable you to identify some of the more common species.

Hawaiian moorhen

BACKGROUND

Wind and rain carved this lush valley nestled against the Ko'olau Mountain range beginning over two million years ago. Rain funnels off the forested mountains and gathers into Kamananui Stream as it zigzags through Waimea Valley. The stream cascades over 45-foot Waihī Falls, meanders past world-class botanical gardens and empties into Waimea Bay. No wonder the high priests of O'ahu lived in this beautiful setting for more than 1,000 years.

Much of the valley floor was originally cleared for the cultivation of taro. You can visit the Hale 'O Lono Heiau, a shrine dedicated to the god of agriculture, located at the end of the Visitor Center parking lot. There are two additional heiau sites on cliffs above the valley, fishing shrines honoring Kū'ula, the god of fishermen and remnants of agriculture structures associated with cultivation of taro, sweet potatoes and other crops.

DESCRIPTION

While many visitors consider the valley's scenery, gardens and waterfall the main attractions, wildlife lovers will be rewarded with views of several native and non-native species, including breeding populations of the endangered Hawaiian moorhen ('alae 'ula), four species of Hawaiian freshwater gobies ('o'opu) and beautiful Hawaiian dragonflies and damselflies (pinao). The Audubon Society has recently assumed management of the 1,875-acre park to "protect and enhance Waimea Valley's cultural, botanical and ecological resources and interpret those resources through quality educational programs." About 200 acres are open to the public.

Park at the Visitor Center and then walk on paved pathways past some of the 35 botanical collections from around the world. The gardens feature plants native to Hawai'i and from distant locations, such as Sri Lanka and South America. Be sure to allow a few extra minutes to tour the Makai Hawaiian garden, which showcases many native and rare species found only in Hawai'i and provides a glimpse of some very rare hibiscus that no longer exist in the wild.

Each of the four ponds next to the walkway offers very reliable views of the endangered Hawaiian moorhen. Stream shallows in the estuary attract wintering shorebirds. Colorful peacocks abound.

WILDLIFE TO WATCH

Waimea Falls

The endangered **Hawaiian moorhen** is common at ponds within the valley. There are fewer than 500 moorhens on Oʻahu and Kauaʻi and about 20 individuals reside in this valley. You can watch them walk on pond lilies, spreading their long, unwebbed toes to maintain balance on the floating vegetation. Native **black-crowned night-herons** (ʻaukuʻu) are often visible hunting along the stream or within the ponds. **Pacific golden-plovers** (kōlea) and **wandering tattlers** (ʻūlili) appear during winter. From spring through fall, you may catch a glimpse of the **white-tailed tropicbird** (koaʻe kea) gliding along the valley walls. When you see their long, elegant tails, you'll understand why ancient Hawaiians coveted them for their feather decorations. **Common peafowl** (pīkake) abound; these natives of India were reputed to be a favorite of Princess Kaʻiulani. You may see an occasional **mongoose** scurrying past the ground level plants. You may also spot **Hawaiian hoary bats** (ʻōpeʻapeʻa).

VIEWING TIPS

Most of the wildlife can be seen during the first 20 minutes of walking along the trail to the waterfall. Educational tours focus on many aspects of the valley's natural and cultural history. These tours are your best chance to learn about the less visible residents, such as the diverse populations of Hawaiʻi's only native freshwater fish, the goby (ʻoʻopu), and Hawaiʻi's only native land mammal, the Hawaiian hoary bat.

Site Notes The Center charges an admission fee. Wildlife programs are currently offered several times a month. Botanical tours are offered on Mondays, Thursdays and Sundays. Historical Tours are offered on Fridays and Saturdays. Call to confirm tour availability and to learn about new educational opportunities or events.

Hours 9:30 AM–5 PM daily, except Christmas and New Year's Day

Nearby Services Waimea Falls Grill, located on site, serves a variety of sandwiches and plate lunches featuring locally grown produce and fresh seafood. Gas, food and lodging are available in Haleʻiwa. For more information, contact the Oʻahu Visitors Bureau at (808) 524-0722, www.gohawaii.com/oahu.

Special Tips Audubon asks visitors not to feed the birds because it leads to a host of problems, from dependency on handouts and the spread of diseases to reduced caution around humans. The round-trip to the falls is 1.5 miles and includes a short section with an 11 percent grade. Bring your bathing suit for a swim at the falls when conditions permit. The decision to allow swimming or not is made daily by 10 AM. Please do not jump or dive into the water or drink from the stream. Lifeguards and changing rooms are provided.

Contact Information Waimea Valley Audubon Center, 59-864 Kamehameha Highway, Hale'iwa, HI, 96712, (808) 638-9199, www.audubon.org/local/sanctuary/hi.html

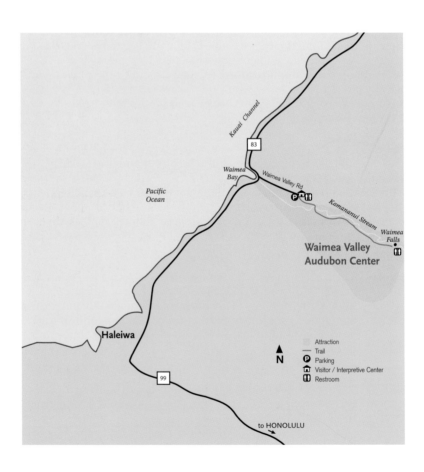

Hawaiian Moorhen

The Hawaiian moorhen ('alae 'ula) was a supernatural being that possessed the secret for making fire. According to Hawaiian lore, the demigod Māui decided to get the secret of fire from the moorhen. The moorhen, however, is very secretive. It has long, unwebbed toes, allowing it to walk upon and hide within heavy marsh vegetation; it can also remain underwater by holding onto marsh plants.

Despite these traits, Māui finally caught the moorhen. Unbeknownst to the demigod, the moorhen lied about how to make fire, so Māui's efforts failed. Finally, Māui coerced the secret from the moorhen: rub hard wood upon soft wood until it bursts into flame. And then the angry demigod punished the moorhen by rubbing its head against wood, making it so hot that it glowed red ('ula'ula). Even today the moorhen wears a distinct red shield between its eyes that extends to the top of its bill, a reminder of its lie to Māui.

Māui's effort to find the moorhen may parallel your own efforts to see these endangered birds. They are very shy and secretive, hiding when threatened instead of flying away. Try to remain in one place for a while and watch for motion and that flash of red on its head.

These endangered marsh birds are found only on O'ahu and Kaua'i. If you see them feeding in water from a distance, the white feathers under their tails may appear as they tip up to search for submerged mollusks and insects. The moorhen's voice is a distinctive high pitched crackle or croak. Early Hawaiians sometimes reserved the name 'alae 'ula for a person at an important meeting whose voice was persuasive or whose reasoning influenced the group.

See pages 21–25 for ethical viewing tips.

O'AHU • Waimea Valley Audubon Center

Ka'ena Point Natural Area Reserve

Spectacular scenery, rare native plants and seabirds galore

Laysan albatross

BACKGROUND

This impressive coastal Reserve is located on the opposite end of O'ahu from Waikīkī; it is as wild as Waikīkī is developed. It offers rugged beauty, isolation and terrific seasonal opportunities to see nesting seabirds and passing humpback whales (koholā). Together, Ka'ena State Park and Natural Area Reserve (NAR) wrap around the westernmost point of O'ahu, an expanse of volcanic rock sustaining the most intact coastal dune ecosystem remaining on O'ahu. The sand includes fragments of coral that have washed ashore to form this coastal formation of dunes. The 50-acre NAR was created within the Park in 1983 to help heal the fragile dune ecosystem and numerous native plants from years of disturbance by dirt bikes, all-terrain vehicles and 4WD vehicles.

DESCRIPTION

This is O'ahu at its wildest. You can enjoy unmarred views of both the north and south coasts. Today, the scars from tire tracks have somewhat disappeared beneath carpets of colorful wildflowers and the anchoring tentacles of native plants, such as the vine called the sarong of Hi'iaka (pā'ū-o-Hi'iaka). According to Hawaiian mythology, this vine protected Hi'iaka, Pele's baby sister, as she napped in the scorching sun. Other unusual species inhabit this windswept, arid and salty environment, such as the Ka'ena spurge (ka'ena 'akoko), a plant found only at Ka'ena Point, and the endangered 'ohai, a shrub with salmon-colored flowers that is a member of the pea family. The Point is also home to the Laysan albatross (mōlī) and wedge-tailed shearwater ('ua'u kani), which returned once the area was closed to motorized vehicles. With peace reigning, the albatrosses and shearwaters have resumed nesting. Hiking to the Point can be rigorous but rewarding: during the nesting season, the trail passes so close to the shearwaters' nesting burrows that the odor of the fish consumed by the youngsters is evident.

A cadre of volunteers is actively removing generations of non-native plants, fencing off areas and trapping mongooses and feral cats to restore the dune ecosystem. These efforts are allowing the return of such plants as 'ilima papa, whose golden flowers are a common symbol for O'ahu. Along the trail to the Point, a sacred rock called Leina a ka 'uhane is revered by Native Hawaiians as a "souls' leap," which is a place where spirits depart from earth to enter the ancestral realm. This is considered a sacred site, so please respect the site and remain on the trail.

WILDLIFE TO WATCH

If you make this rigorous trip to see wildlife, you shouldn't be disappointed. **Wedge-tailed shearwaters**, **noddies** (noio) and **Laysan albatrosses** wheel through the air offshore. The shearwater has a gray back and moves through the air with a graceful, soaring flight. The large, white albatrosses are especially easy to spot. **Humpback whales** pass by during winter. Look for **green sea turtles** (honu) in the water and watch for **Hawaiian monk seals** ('īlio holo i ka uaua) that sometimes haul out on the beach or rocks. Ka'ena Point is one of the few places on O'ahu to see these playful seals. The albatross and shearwater are the only species that nest near the point, but you may see other seabirds, including **black-footed albatrosses**, **glaucous gulls** and **glaucous-winged gulls**.

VIEWING TIPS

Most of the seabirds are present year-round. Albatrosses nest and raise their young from November through April; some fledglings stay until July. Some albatrosses nest in shallow depressions in the dunes right next to the trail, providing you with frame-filling views. Shearwaters nest and tend their young from April through November. The shearwaters dig nesting burrows under vegetation. You can see many burrows along the Wai'anae side of the reserve. While you may not see young in the nest, you should see parents bringing fish to the nest or burrow. If you're there in December, you have a chance of seeing the youngsters' first flights. Contact the Division of Forestry and Wildlife for a brochure about wildlife and plants.

wedge-tailed shearwater

Laysan Albatross

They soar effortlessly, looping from high elevation air currents down to breezes near the ocean's surface, but they are so awkward on land they are often called "gooney birds." Albatrosses are the largest of the Hawaiian seabirds and the mostly white Laysan albatross (mōlī) with its dark back is easy to differentiate from other seabirds. These unusual birds have salt glands in their nostrils that allow them to drink saltwater, concentrate the salt and then discharge it in droplets from the end of their bill—almost like a runny nose.

Most Laysan albatrosses breed in the remote northwest Hawaiian Islands, where nesting sites are so dense they appear to be flocked with white. Some albatrosses in the remote Hawaiian Islands with young in the nest have been tracked making flights to the Aleutian Islands to fish, then returning to feed their young on Laysan Island—a distance of several thousand miles. Their nest is little more than a scrape in the sand and the cacophony of their whistles, whinnies and moans can be deafening. In recent years, Laysan albatrosses have also found safe nesting sites at Ka'ena Point, O'ahu, and Kīlauea Point, Kaua'i, where efforts to remove predators have been successful.

To Native Hawaiians, any soaring bird is admired, so references to the albatross symbolize admiration. Hawaiians were also keenly aware that the albatross and other species generally appeared during a specific season. Winter, for example, is viewed as the season of the albatross or the humpback whale because both are present. The albatross also symbolized a time of year when no warfare was allowed. It came to Hawai'i to breed, so the season was also a time of fertility and celebration. During winter, Hawaiians led great processions along the shores of islands carrying white banners adorned with white albatross feathers and leis. These so-called "makahiki" activities are enjoying a comeback among Hawaiians today.

See pages 21–25 for ethical viewing tips.

O'AHU • Ka'ena Point Natural Area Reserve

Premier
– SITE –

Site Notes Ka'ena Point is about a 1-hour drive from the Honolulu area, so plan on spending a full day.

Hours Sunrise to sunset daily

Nearby Services Gas, food and lodging are available at Wai'anae and Mākaha on the west side; on the east side, Waialua (gas and food only). Contact the Hawai'i Visitors & Convention Bureau, 1 (800) GoHawaii, www.hvcb.org/, or the O'ahu Visitors Bureau, (808) 524-0722, www.gohawaii.com/oahu.

Special Tips Due to fragile vegetation and the shearwaters' underground burrows, it is important to stay on the trails. The hike can be hot and dry, so bring sunscreen, a hat and drinking water, and wear sturdy shoes. Time your visit for morning to avoid the midday heat. The 2.5-mile hike or trail bike ride from the parking area follows an unpaved dirt road through the State Park; off-road recreational vehicles still use this area. A 4WD vehicle can be used to reach the reserve, but the road is still sometimes impassable. This site is very remote and unstaffed. Be sure to leave your valuables where you are staying and lock your vehicle. Pets are not allowed in the reserve. Commercial operators are not allowed to operate in the NAR without a Special Use Permit. This permit is also required for research, collection, large groups or other large-scale disturbance. For information, contact (808) 587-0063.

Contact Information Department of Land and Natural Resources, Division of State Parks and Division of Forestry and Wildlife, 1151 Punchbowl Street, Honolulu, HI, 96813, (808) 587-0300 (State Parks) www.hawaii.gov/dlnr/dsp, and (808) 587-0166 (Division of Forestry and Wildlife/NAR), www.dofaw.net/

Ka'ena Point
Natural Area
Reserve

Ka'ena Point State Park

930

to WAIALUA

Ka'ena Point State Park

Pacific
Ocean

930

Mākua

Attraction
Trail
Parking

N

to MĀKAHA

Hawaiian monk seal

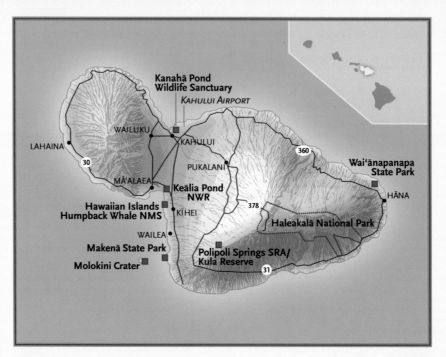

Maui - The Valley Island

One might expect that an island named for a Hawaiian demigod known to have lassoed the sun would be a magical place—and Maui does not disappoint. From sweeping beaches ringed by submerged coral gardens to the massive, dark crater of Haleakalā perched at 10,023 feet, Maui is an island known for its diversity of landscapes, wildlife viewing experiences and rich Hawaiian history and culture.

A predawn drive up the winding road to the windswept crater of eastern Maui provides the chance to witness sunrise at what Hawaiians called Haleakalā, the house of the sun. Here, morning light reveals a rugged landscape dotted with the unusual silver spiked plant, silversword, and occasional views of the endangered nēnē, a small relative of the Canada goose surprisingly at home in this arid, high elevation environment.

The upcountry towns on Haleakalā's flanks cultivate many types of produce and flowers, while nature supplies most of the greenery growing luxuriantly in rain forests hugging the Hāna Coast. Seabirds abound offshore and forest birds appear in gem colors among the dense vegetation.

Moisture subsides on the drier southern side of Haleakalā, producing an arid, brown landscape that supports the Tedeschi Winery and cattle, sheep and elk at the 18,000-acre 'Ulupalakua Ranch. Here, Maui's native scrub forest, dominated by the yellow-flowering māmane, is home to a host of colorful forest birds.

Commercial Kahului includes a surprisingly rich wetland at Kanahā Pond, where many birds thrive just a stone's throw from the island's busy airport. Silence and tranquility reign, by contrast, at Keālia Pond National Wildlife Refuge across the island, near Māʻalaea. A new boardwalk skirts the edge of this large wetland, which is vital to many resident and migratory waterbirds. The adjacent sandy beach and surf often yield views of sea turtles (honu) and during winter, humpback whales (koholā).

Maui's beaches are world famous and those in West Maui provide vistas of Lanaʻi and Molokaʻi. These three islands were once joined as one island in the geological past and now encircle a sanctuary for humpback whales. Catamarans and wide-beamed tour boats ply the waters here, giving visitors front row seats as dolphins (naiʻa) swim and leap alongside the boats and whales blow, breach and crest through the waves.

Farther east, snorkelers paddle and float in wonder as they watch fish in rainbow colors glide in and out of coral reefs within Molokini Crater's protected cove. Coral reefs border many Maui beaches, offering warm water, beautiful scenery and a chance to explore the underwater coral gardens and see many colorful reef fish.

iʻiwi

BACKGROUND

The West Maui Mountains form a backdrop for this 234-acre wetland gem set a stone's throw from industrial buildings, commercial centers and the airport in Kahului. Despite this strong urban influence, Kanahā Pond remains a large and productive wetland that sustains three endangered Hawaiian birds and over 80 species of migratory shorebirds, ducks and waterbirds.

DESCRIPTION

This protected freshwater marsh is an example of the wetlands once common on Maui's coastal plain. A short trail from the small parking lot off of Airport Road leads to a roofed observation area offering views of the wetland. Benches allow you to remain awhile to enjoy the tranquil setting. There are excellent chances of seeing Hawaiian stilts (ae'o) feeding in the shallows and Hawaiian coots ('alae ke'oke'o) in the open water. A black-crowned night-heron ('auku'u) may stalk fish near the muddy shoreline, sometimes among a scattering of shorebirds pecking for insects and invertebrates. You will also see 2-foot-tall stands of smooth flatsedge (makaloa) and bulrush (kaluhā), native plants prized by Hawaiians for matmaking. If you fly to Maui, you don't need to make an effort to visit the site. It is right next to the airport and makes a perfect stop upon arrival or before you depart.

WILDLIFE TO WATCH

Hawaiian ducks (koloa) are regulars at Kanahā pond. Since many hybridize with look-alike mallards, it is often hard to distinguish them. If you dabble in Hawaiian lore, you can "safely" observe **Hawaiian coots** as they cruise the pond during a daytime visit; however, if you hear the chirp of the coot at night, it may be an omen of bad luck or death. During fall and winter, many shorebirds will be present, including the **Pacific golden-plover** (kōlea), **ruddy turnstone** ('akekeke) and **wandering tattler** ('ūlili). Migratory ducks also abound, including **lesser scaup**, **northern pintail** (koloa māpu), **Eurasian wigeon**, **American wigeon**, **blue-winged teal**, **green-winged teal** and **northern shoveler** (koloa mohā). You may also spot **Hawaiian stilts** and **black-crowned night-herons**.

VIEWING TIPS

The endangered Hawaiian stilt, Hawaiian coot and Hawaiian duck are year-round residents. By Hawaiian standards, birding in the back areas can be spectacular. You will see a greater diversity and higher number of birds if you get a permit to visit these quieter areas of the marsh.

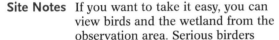

Hawaiian coot

Site Notes If you want to take it easy, you can view birds and the wetland from the observation area. Serious birders who want to spend more time enjoying the wetland from September through March can gain access to the back areas of the marsh by getting a free back area permit in Wailuku at the Division of Forestry and Wildlife/Maui District Office. The dirt roads in the back area allow hiking only.

Hours 8 AM–3 PM Mon–Fri for permitted areas, from September through March. Observation area is always open.

Nearby Services Gas, food and lodging are available in Kahului and Wailuku. For more information, contact the Maui Chamber of Commerce, (808) 871-7711, www.mauichamber.com, or the Maui Visitors Bureau, (808) 244-3530, www.visitmaui.com.

Special Tips If you want to get a back area permit from the Forestry and Wildlife office, call first to be sure the office is open. Office hours are Mon–Fri, 8 AM–4 PM.

Contact Information Department of Land and Natural Resources/Division of Forestry and Wildlife, 54 S. High Street, Room 101, Wailuku, HI 96793, (808) 984-8100, www.state.hi.us/dlnr/dofaw

MAUI • *Kanahā Pond Wildlife Sanctuary*

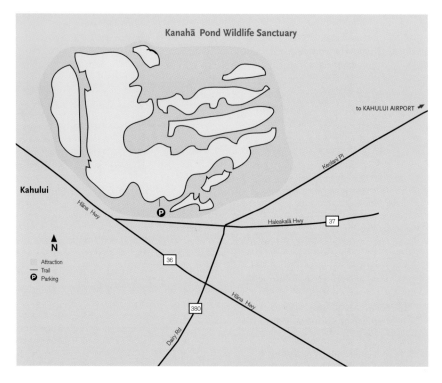

Kanahā Pond Wildlife Sanctuary

Hawaiian duck

From Wetlands to a Volcanic Monolith — the Ī'ao Valley

Maui is known for its sharply contrasting scenery, from rugged lava fields to azure beaches. If you have time and would like to juxtapose the flat, tranquil vistas of Kanahā Pond with a near-vertical setting steeped in Hawaiian history, drive west of the town of Wailuku to the Ī'ao Valley.

A sheer-walled rock pinnacle called the Ī'ao Needle presides over the rugged chasm that defines this lush valley. The 2,250-foot vertical monolith has been used as a natural altar over the eons. Ī'ao Stream gently cuts through this verdant gorge, past rock walls almost a mile high. It is hard to imagine that this serene waterway was once blocked by the bodies of so many dead warriors that it was called Kepaniwai, or "damming of the waters."

Their slaughter occurred in 1790, when Hawai'i's famous king, Kamehameha I (or Kamehameha the Great), vanquished the Maui army in order to unite all of the Hawaiian Islands. He was reportedly aided by western advisors and a ship's cannon. The success on Maui was a springboard to other victories and by 1795, unification of the islands was realized. A bronze tablet at the base of the Ī'ao Needle commemorates Maui's history-making battle.

You can enjoy the 6.2-acre park via two paved walkways that offer beautiful views of the Ī'ao Needle and picturesque valley. If you're still interested in picturesque scenery, stop at Kepaniwai Park and Heritage Gardens, located near the valley entrance, to walk through landscaped gardens that showcase Hawai'i's various cultures. To reach the Park, from Wailuku take Highway 32 (Kaahumanu Road) west. This road becomes Highway 320, which leads to Ī'ao Valley State Monument. Stop at the Hawai'i Nature Center before you reach the Ī'ao Needle.

BACKGROUND

Volcanic eruptions, the arrival of many plant and wildlife species over the millennia and the effects of extreme isolation have combined to form what is now Haleakalā National Park, a remote area that still retains many of Hawai'i's original natural ecosystems. Topped by a vast basin marked by cinder cones, Haleakalā (house of the sun) rises from the sea to its 10,000-foot summit. It is so tall that it is exposed to both the moist windward tradewinds and dry leeward air, conditions that help to create an amazing variety of natural ecosystems. The 30,200-acre Park's central offering is geologic—the massive volcano, cinder cones and unusual lava flows—but there is also wildlife to enjoy. It offers many viewing options, depending on the length of your visit. If you enjoy Hawaiian history, you will see stone cairns and other evidence of early Hawaiian use throughout the Park.

DESCRIPTION

Haleakalā is divided into two sections with different access routes: the summit area, where you may see forest birds, nēnē and a wealth of insects, and the Kīpahulu area on the coast (see page 108), perfect for viewing seabirds and marine mammals.

The summit area includes several major habitat types roughly associated with elevation, each supporting its own plants and wildlife. Begin your trip at Park headquarters to orient yourself. Take a break at Hosmer Grove, located below the headquarters. This collection of trees from around the world was planted to determine which varieties might be best suited for timber harvest and reforesting Hawai'i. Although much of the grove is non-native pine, eucalyptus and cedar, you can often see native honeycreepers and other forest birds here.

As you continue to gain elevation, you'll pass through sparsely vegetated subalpine shrublands. The native Hawaiian short-eared owl (pueo) often hunts over the shrubland during the day. You may see ring-necked pheasants and house finches or an occasional 'amakihi and 'apapane fluttering through the shrubs. You can sometimes spot the nēnē, an endangered Hawaiian goose.

Vegetation thins out considerably as you gain the summit. Be prepared for a long drive through alpine aeolian habitat that is rocky, harsh and dry, where few insect and plant species survive. Day and nighttime temperatures here can be extreme. The dominant endangered plant, Haleakalā silversword (hinahina), has a shallow root system and silvery hairs that gather or hold moisture. It is one of about 250 flowering plants at the Park. In addition to the spectacular views, you may hear Hawaiian petrels ('uaʻu) calling if you're outside of the House of the Sun Visitor Center after dark, from March to September. Nighttime visitors may also catch a glimpse of the Hawaiian hoary bat ('ōpeʻapeʻa).

short-eared owl

On your return trip, stop to enjoy the panoramic vistas at Kalahaku lookout, about halfway down the summit road on a sharp curve. The overlook has an interpretive display about the silversword plant. This is a good place to look for chukars and Hawaiian short-eared owls hunting for food.

WILDLIFE TO WATCH

The **nēnē** that are now visible near the Park Headquarters, in the subalpine shrublands and along the road were reintroduced here from captive bred populations in 1962. Please resist feeding them, even if they beg! This goose has reduced webbing on its leathery feet and can travel across the rugged lava with ease.

At Hosmer Grove, hike the .5-mile self-guided loop trail and look for forest birds, including the 'apapane, 'iʻiwi and **Maui 'alauahio**, in 'ōhiʻa trees. Brushy areas may produce views of the yellowish green **Maui 'amakihi**.

As you drive, look for **short-eared owls** and **ring-necked pheasants** in the shrublands, **sky larks** along the road, and **red-billed leiothrix, house finches, house sparrows, northern cardinals** and **melodious laughing-thrush** in the brushy areas. **Pacific golden-plover** (kōlea) can be seen throughout the Park during winter. The endangered **Hawaiian petrel** ('uaʻu) is present from mid-February through October. This is the world's largest protected nesting population of these birds, which use their wings and feet to excavate nesting burrows high on the crater. You may also spot **Hawaiian hoary bats, chukar** and **white-tailed tropicbirds**.

VIEWING TIPS

Hosmer Grove's hiking trail provides excellent opportunities for viewing native honeycreepers. There is a "bird overlook" where you may spot honeycreepers feeding on the nectar of the lehua flower at the tops of 'ōhiʻa trees.

You can improve your chances of seeing some of Maui's native forest birds by learning their feeding habits. It may be easy to spot the crimson colored 'iʻiwi and 'apapane in the spring feeding on nectar from the yellow blossoms of the māmane. Those hiking in Kaupō Gap have excellent chances of seeing white-tailed tropicbirds (koa'e kea) soaring around the cliffs, as well as native honeycreepers.

Take a guided tour of the Waikamo'i Preserve, a 5,200-acre natural area next to Hosmer Grove Campground. The diverse range of habitats here support some of the rarest species in Hawai'i and some of the state's best remaining forests. Make reservations in advance with the Park or The Nature Conservancy.

Numerous books and publications have been written about Haleakalā's natural history; consider investing in some to help plan your visit. Also, take time to appreciate the miles of fencing the Park has erected around the crater to exclude non-native pigs and goats, which nearly eliminated many native plant species.

Site Notes The Park is vast and there are numerous ways to experience it. Become familiar with what the Park offers so you can plan a satisfying visit based on the time you can spend. Many excellent publications are available, from those on rare wildlife to mile-by-mile hiking guides. Bicyclists can rent bikes and be transported to the summit for a spectacular 36-mile downhill ride. You can spend the night at drive-in or hike-in campgrounds and primitive cabins.

Hours The Park is open 24 hours a day. Park Headquarters, Haleakalā Visitor Center and Kīpahulu Visitor Center are open daily year-round, subject to staff availability. Hours are: Park Headquarters 8 AM–4 PM; Haleakalā Visitor Center 7:30 AM–3:30 PM; Kīpahulu Visitor Center 9 AM–5 PM.

Nearby Services Limited gas, food and lodging are available in Kula; more services are available in Pukalani. For more information, contact the Maui Chamber of Commerce, (808) 871-7711, www.mauichamber.com, or the Maui Visitors Bureau, (808) 244-3530, www.visitmaui.com.

Special Tips You will see lots of people in the developed areas of the Park. To escape the crowds, consider hiking a few miles on the Halemau'u Trail. Be prepared for extremes and rapid changes in temperatures, from rain or icy wind and frigid temperatures on the summit to heat in the lower elevations. Bring warm clothing, rain gear, sturdy shoes, sunscreen and hat, drinking water, snacks and a flashlight for night walks. Nēnē are often near roads, so drive carefully.

Contact Information Haleakalā National Park, P.O. Box 369, Makawao, HI, 96768, (808) 572-4400 (recording) or (808) 572-4459, www.nps.gov/hale.

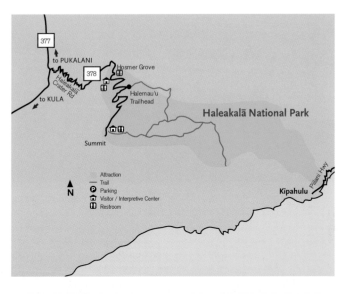

nēnē

Polipoli Springs State Recreation Area and Kula Forest Reserve

Forest birds and hiking on the flanks of Haleakalā

BACKGROUND

Most avid birders know that you sometimes have to work a little to see unusual species and this is the case with forest birds in Hawai'i. Maui visitors are fortunate because some of the islands' best forest birding occurs in the high elevation native scrub forests that grow within the Kula Forest Reserve amid the exotic pines, cypress and redwoods on the west flank of the volcanic crater, Haleakalā.

DESCRIPTION

While it may take some effort to reach Polipoli Springs State Recreation Area and the excellent viewing sites within the forest reserve, you should quickly be rewarded with views of colorful forest birds that are rare elsewhere but common here, such as the 'apapane, 'amakihi, 'alauahio and 'i'iwi.

Polipoli Springs is surrounded by dense pine forests dotted with native scrub forest. The most common tree is māmane, noted for its bright yellow, pea-like flowers that are a magnet for nectar-feeding birds. Once you find these distinctive native scrub trees, viewing is easy because the birds will find you! Even the native shrubs around the parking area offer excellent views of Maui creepers and 'amakihi. It's possible to see several different species in just a few minutes. In addition to a bonanza of native birds, you should also see introduced species, such as the red-billed leiothrix and house finches.

When the weather is clear, there are spectacular views from the road into the area between the flanks of Haleakalā and Pu'u Kukui, stretching into the distance from Kahului to Keālia Pond.

WILDLIFE TO WATCH

The two most common native forest birds are the **'amakihi** and the **'apapane**. On Maui, the 'amakihi is predominantly bright yellow and is often seen in small flocks. Look for it among the leaves on branches, searching for nectar, fruit and insects. The 'apapane is largely crimson, with some gray and black feathers on the wings and tail. This songster has numerous calls and its wings make a distinctive whirring sound in flight. It moves quickly and frequently lights on flowering māmane and koa. The ʻiʻiwi is similar in size to the ʻapapane. It is also red and black, but has a very long, curved salmon-colored bill that should make it easy to identify. The ʻiʻiwi is the subject of many Hawaiian folktales and its feathers, and those of the ʻapapane, were often used in Hawaiian featherwork. The small bright yellow warbler-type bird you may see is the **Maui ʻalauahio**. It gleans nectar and insects from branches and trees and frequently moves through the forest in small groups. You may also spot **Maui creepers**, **red-billed leiothrix** and **house finches**.

ʻapapane

VIEWING TIPS

There are excellent viewing opportunities for forest birds year-round. You don't need to hike inland as you can see many birds while walking on road. If you do hike, become familiar with the appearance of native scrub vegetation because this is where you will find many native forest birds. Enjoy this unique opportunity to easily see many species of forest birds that are becoming more and more difficult to find due to habitat destruction and loss.

Bring binoculars and bird and plant guides to make the trip meaningful. Plant lovers may want to visit the nearby Kula Botanical Gardens.

Site Notes	This site is remote and takes time to reach. Bring a picnic and enjoy the views from the grassy hillsides. If you plan in advance and want an overnight stay, the recreation area offers a cabin for overnight rental.
Hours	No posted hours (and no gates)
Nearby Services	Gas and food are available in Kula. Lodging is available at Kahului and Polipoli Spring State Recreation Area. Those wishing to stay in a Park cabin must obtain a cabin permit from State Parks. For more information, contact the Maui Chamber of Commerce, (808) 871-7711, www.mauichamber.com, or the Maui Visitors Bureau, (808) 244-3530, www.visitmaui.com.
Special Tips	The road is winding and one lane. The pavement snakes up to 7,000 feet and turns to dirt for the final 3.5 miles to the springs, which are fairly flat. A high clearance vehicle or 4WD vehicle is recommended for the last 3.5 miles during rainy weather. If you're in doubt about road conditions, park the car where the pavement ends and walk along the road. You'll pass several trailheads along the dirt road. Select a trail

or just walk along the lightly-traveled road. The area is very primitive with few facilities and no interpretation. It can be foggy, so be prepared for limited visibility and chilly weather. This is also a popular hunting area. Hikers should stay on the trails or roads and wear bright colors.

Contact Information Department of Land and Natural Resources, Division of State Parks, 54 S. High Street, #101, Wailuku, HI 96793, (808) 984-8109, www.hawaii.gov/dlnr/dsp

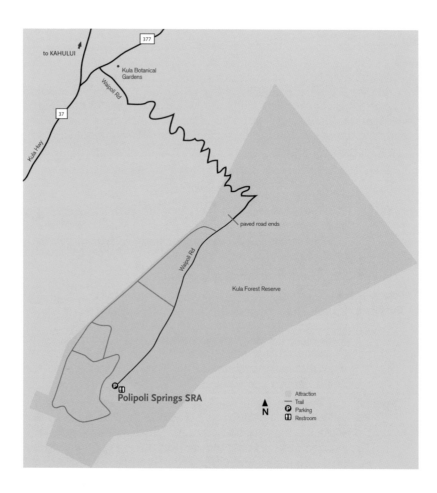

Maui creeper

red-billed leiothrix

Wai'ānapanapa State Park

Seabirds, turtles, lava formations and black sand beach

green sea turtle

BACKGROUND

The black sand beach at Pailoa Bay in Wai'ānapanapa State Park is probably one of Maui's most photographed sites. It also provides a welcome
respite after a long, winding drive on the Hāna Highway. Here, black lava
cliffs and promontories carpeted with the bright green plant, naupaka
kahakai, meet the turquoise waters of the Pacific Ocean. Wind and water
have eroded the lava to form an array of spires, arches and blowholes along
the picturesque Hāna coast. They have beaten the lava into black pebbles
and sand on Pailoa Bay, forming a beautiful swimming beach and a perfect
location for watching seabirds, spinner dolphins (nai'a) and green sea turtles
(honu) all year long. When the ocean is calm, the bay offers great snorkeling
at this 110-acre Park.

DESCRIPTION

A coastal trail provides access to excellent ocean views and cultural sites.
The Wai'ānapanapa Cave supports native shrimp ('ōpae 'ula) and is a
favorite swimming spot. According to Hawaiian lore, the shrimp sometimes
turn red in memory of a princess who was slain there by her jealous husband. In addition to views and water sports, the secluded area is a seasonal
home to many species of seabirds. A coastal trail heading north of the beach
provides great views of seabirds and lush hala forests. Hala, also called
screwpine or pandanus, grows on the steep cliffs and throughout the park. It
bears a conspicuous fruit that resembles a pineapple. Early Hawaiians used
the leaves of this native plant to weave mats or as thatch for their houses.
Scan the coastal waters often. You may see great frigatebirds ('iwa) soaring
on thermal currents or black noddies (noio) leaving in groups from their
roosting areas on offshore rocks.

WILDLIFE TO WATCH

The **great frigatebird** is unmistakable. With a wingspan of 90 inches this
largely black bird with a long split tail is the largest native bird you will see.
In flight, his wings are not flat but each is bent in an A shape. You may also

identify it by antics responsible for its Hawaiian name, which means thief. The great frigatebird often harasses smaller seabirds that have a mouthful of fish, forcing them to drop their catch and then scooping up the lost meal in midair. You will enjoy excellent views of **black noddies**, which gather in a nesting colony during late spring that can be viewed from the coastal trail on the small islet just below the caretaker's residence. They nest in small caves or on rocky ledges, often flying out to sea to feed at dawn and dusk. **White-tailed tropicbirds** (koa'e kea) with their elegant, 16-inch tails are common, gliding effortlessly in graceful flight. The tail can account for half the length of the body. You will need to be lucky to see **spinner dolphins** arching through the air as they crest through the waves, but **green sea turtles** are quite common.

great frigatebird

VIEWING TIPS

Seabird viewing is excellent year-round. You will see birds roosting or nesting on offshore rocks or in flight. Views are distant, so bring binoculars. Green sea turtles can often be seen in the surge zones of the bays.

Site Notes The park offers several amenities, including a scenic trail that follows the coast into historic Hāna. Ohala Heiau, an important temple site, is located along the trail and about a .5-mile walk from the Park entry. The Park offers camping, and the cabin rentals are among the best deals for lodging in Hawai'i.

Hours No posted hours

Nearby Services Gas and food are available in Hāna. Lodging is available in Hana and Wai'ānapanapa. For more information, contact the Maui Chamber of Commerce, (808) 871-7711, www.mauichamber.com, or the Maui Visitors Bureau, (808) 244-3530, www.visitmaui.com

Special Tips This is a popular site, so be prepared to share the experience with other visitors. Good footwear to protect your feet from the sharp lava, hat, sunscreen and water are musts. Bring binoculars to enjoy the distant views. The road to Hāna is extremely winding; those with tendencies toward motion sickness may want to consider over-the-counter medication. There are no lifeguards at the beach, so exercise caution as there can be big surf. Permits from State Parks are required for camping and cabins. You can get them from the Maui or Honolulu offices. The phone number is (808) 587-0300 on O'ahu and (808) 984-8109 on Maui. Check the website for permit details and rates.

MAUI • Wai'ānapanapa State Park

Contact Information Department of Land and Natural Resources, Division of State Parks, 54 S. High Street, Room 101, Wailuku, HI 96795, (808) 984-8109, www.hawaii.gov/dlnr/dsp/maui.html

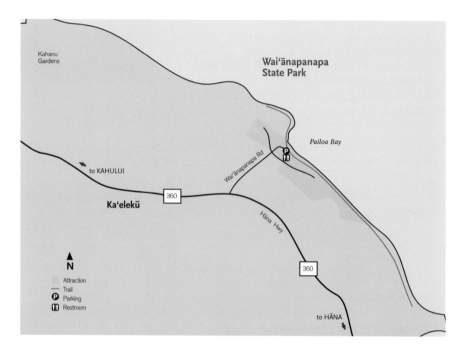

black noddy

The Road to Hāna

If you've contemplated a trip to the Hāna coast and shared the notion with an islander, the first question you may be asked is whether you know about the "highway" to Hāna. Travel along this narrow, two-lane road with its numerous single lane bridges is as much a part of the Hāna coast experience as the sights themselves. The road climbs in switchback turns through lush rain forests and along coastal precipices. Unforgettable scenery and physical isolation from population centers, create a feeling reminiscent of Maui before it was developed into a vacation mecca.

To complement this feeling of falling back in time, you will have numerous opportunities to see cultural sites that were once important to early Hawaiians. Make time to see the Kaulanapueo Church in Huelo. This community once supported more than 75,000 Hawaiians and the church has been serving their religious needs since 1853. Likewise, the old facade of the 'Ihi'ihi o lehowa o na Kaua Church in Ke'anae hints of its 1860s roots.

After you leave Nāhiku, a short, unmarked road leads to the Pi'ilanihale Heiau, perhaps the largest of Hawai'i's ancient places of worship. The beautifully landscaped shrine within Kahanu Gardens has been included in the National Register of Historic Sites.

At Waiānapanapa State Park, you can visit a cave where, according to legends, an Hawaiian princess was slain by her husband. At certain times of year, tiny red shrimp turn the water red, a visible reminder of the slain princess' blood.

Depending on weather, the trip from Kahului to Hāna can take at least three hours one way, and probably more, depending on how many times you stop. Here are a few tips to make this an enjoyable trip:

- Drive as early in the day as possible. The road gets busier with each passing hour.

- Check the weather in advance. Wet weather limits your visibility and ability to get outside of the car and enjoy the scenery; it also makes you more vulnerable to landslides, slippery turns and other driving hazards.

- Top off your fuel tank in Pa'ia or before. There is no gas along this route until you reach Hāna. Also use this opportunity to pick up water, food for a picnic or other supplies.

- Don't be discouraged if there is heavy traffic. Many travelers do not stop, so some roadside areas may be uncrowded.

- Try to visit popular destinations before 11 AM to avoid crowds.

- Stay alert on the road and be safe. If you are tired, pull over in a safe area. If traffic piles up behind you because you are traveling slow enough to enjoy the scenery, pull over and let the traffic pass.

BACKGROUND

About 900,000 years ago, an undersea volcano emerged from the Pacific Ocean, forming East Maui. Known today as Haleakalā (house of the sun), eruptions continued for another 400,000 years, building a towering mountain much taller than the present-day volcano. Time, combined with water, wind and perhaps even glaciers, carved deep valleys along the volcano's flanks. Kīpahulu Valley lies on Haleakalā's eastern shoulder. Today, streams and waterfalls continue to slice through the valley's lush rain forest and the drier shrublands below it, finally flowing into the sea at the wave lashed foot of the volcano. The Kīpahulu Valley Biological Reserve protects the rare plants and forest birds found in one of the last intact native rain forest ecosystems on the islands. While this important reserve is closed to the public to protect many fragile species, the dry forest and coastal lowlands below it are open and should be added to any trip made to the distant Hāna Coast. The coastal scenery is superb and there are good opportunities to see wildlife.

DESCRIPTION

Haleakalā is divided into two sections with different access routes: the Kīpahulu area on the coast, perfect for viewing seabirds and marine mammals, and the summit area (see page 96), where you may see forest birds, nēnē and a wealth of insects.

After leaving the town of Hāna, near the ʻOheʻo bridge you will enter the National Park—and a stream habitat zone much different than the upper reaches of the Park's famous volcano. The Kīpahulu Valley section covers about 5,000 acres. Well-maintained gravel trails offer access points below the bridge to view several tiered pools, then lead to the mouth of ʻOheʻo Gulch. ʻOheʻo Stream originates high in the Kīpahulu Valley and is one of Hawaiʻi's finest unimpaired natural streams. At its lower reaches, you will see many non-native plants, such as bamboo (ʻohe), Christmas berry, guava (kuawa) and java plum. Native naupaka kahakai grows closer to the ocean.

Be sure to stop at the Visitor Center at Kukui Bay to become oriented with this 5,000-acre section of the Park and see interpretive panels that focus on cultural relationship between Hawaiians, the land, wildlife and the ocean. If you have just a short time, take one of the trails along the coast. If you have more time, walk upland from the Visitor Center on the Pīpīwai Trail. You'll wind through a non-native forest so dense that the sun is heavily filtered. In just under 2 miles you'll pass the falls at Makahiku and reach Waimoku Falls, where water cascades 400 feet down a vertical slab of rock. When you reach overlooks of the Pacific, watch for seabirds and shorebirds. Black noddies (noio) nest along the cliffs and many seabirds often fish just off the shoreline.

black noddy

WILDLIFE TO WATCH

Mongooses and **feral cats** sometimes roam the parking lot. If you park close to the bridge near the park entrance, you can wander along the 'Ohe'o Stream. As you enjoy this stunning setting, look for resident **black-crowned night-herons** (auku'u) hunkered down in the shallows as they watch for prey. The stream shore and rocky coastline areas may attract the **wandering tattler** ('ulili), a small shorebird that arrives in August and normally remains through April.

Stop frequently to peer through openings in the vegetation toward the sea. There is an excellent chance that you'll see **black noddies** fluttering near the cliffs. These small tern-like birds often seem tame and tend to approach people more closely than other seabirds. Near the coast you may also see the **great frigatebird** ('iwa) and **wedge-tailed shearwater** ('ua'u kani). Wherever you are, watch for **Pacific golden-plovers** (kōlea), which are regular winter visitors to the Park, mostly in open fields. You may also glimpse them along trails leading toward the ocean.

Waimoku Falls, located on the Pīpīwai Trail, is a good place to look for birds, such as the **myna**, **northern cardinal**, **Japanese white-eye**, **red-billed leiothrix** and the **melodious laughing-thrush**. Enjoy the dramatic coastal views, making time to scan the water for **green sea turtles** (honu) near the surf line. Look for the shiny head and back of an occasional **monk seal** ('īlio holo i ka uaua). Watch for **spinner dolphins** (nai'a), and in winter, **humpback whales** (koholā).

VIEWING TIPS

You should see some birds and marine species. Some forest birds repeatedly return to feeding sites; if you have seen birds, try stopping and standing quietly for five to ten minutes and they may return. Other than humpback whales, which pass by during winter, you may see spinner dolphins and monk seals throughout the year. Views of sea turtles and other marine mammals are usually distant, so bring binoculars.

Site Notes If you make time to drive to this remote site, become familiar with what the Park offers so you can plan a satisfying visit based on the time you can spend.

Hours The Park is open 24 hours a day. The Kīpahulu Visitor Center is open daily year-round, subject to staff availability. Kīpahulu Visitor Center hours are 9 AM–5 PM.

Nearby Services Gas, food and limited lodging are available in Hāna. For more information contact, the Maui Chamber of Commerce, (808) 871-7711, www.mauichamber.com, or the Maui Visitors Bureau, (808) 244-3530, www.visitmaui.com.

Special Tips The road to this section of the Park is narrow, winding, heavily-traveled and subject to rock falls. Flash flooding can occur during the winter months. Even though this section of the Park is isolated, it can be crowded at midday, especially when the weather is good. Bring binoculars; many views are distant. Swimming in pools or streams is dangerous and may be prohibited.

Contact Information Haleakalā National Park, P.O. Box 369, Makawao, HI, 96768, (808) 572-4400, www.nps.gov/hale

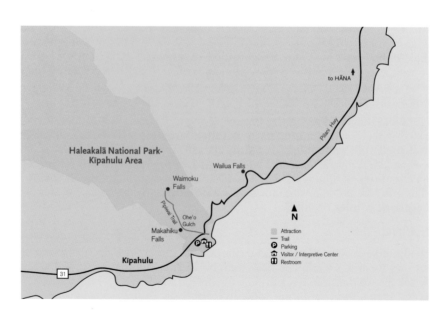

Dragonflies

Dragonflies have large compound eyes with thousands of lenses, four long, lacy wings—and they mate in the air. They do not fold their wings back, but rest them by holding them horizontally. With these long, rapidly beating wings, dragonflies look like the helicopters of the insect world. They can hover, but also fly at speeds of 35 mph and faster, if they can surf on favorable wind currents. They have huge biting mouthparts, the perfect tool for catching a meal.

Hawaiians call them pinao and there are almost three dozen different species of dragonflies and damselflies that are native to the islands. Among them is one whose six-inch wingspan makes it the largest insect in the United States. This species lives on the wet montane flanks of Haleakalā.

Dragonflies often reside near fresh water because it is a vital part of their life cycle. After mating in the air, dragonflies lay their eggs on submerged plant stems. The tiny eggs may take two or three years to hatch. The nymph, or young dragonfly, lives part of its life underwater. The large adult insects are active and easy to see, especially around taro fields where they breed.

In ancient times, Hawaiians named a temple (heiau) on Kaua'i after the dragonfly. The nymph, which Hawaiians call lohelohe, is sacred for those who practice hula, Hawai'i's native dance. A young hula dancer must be very attentive to memorize the meaning of the songs and learn the dance steps. In Hawaiian, lohe means "to listen attentively." Masters of hula often presented a dragonfly nymph, or lohelohe, to the deity of dance so that their students would be attentive learners.

See pages 21–25 for ethical viewing tips.

MAUI • *Haleakalā National Park: Kīpahulu Area*

Keālia Pond National Wildlife Refuge

Scenic pond bordered by beach attracts waterbirds

Hawaiian stilt

BACKGROUND

The West Maui Mountains and Haleakalā provide a dramatic backdrop for this expansive National Wildlife Refuge pond bordered by coastal dunes and beach. The pond and wetlands originally formed as rainwater collected behind a series of sand dunes along the shore. The outlet is normally plugged with sand, cutting off the pond from the ocean; however, high tides or winter rains can clear the outlet, allowing saltwater and fish into the pond and making the water brackish. The pond can swell to over 400 acres with heavy winter rains, creating one of the largest remaining wetlands in the state. Ancient Hawaiians collected salt here, naming the pond keālia, which means "the salt-encrusted place." Other salt gathering places in Hawai'i bear the same name. A rock platform near the refuge is probably a heiau or possibly a fishing shrine, hinting at the importance of the pond to early inhabitants.

DESCRIPTION

Though the marsh appears natural, it is actually a great example of intensive management. The refuge staff aggressively fights introduced plant species that threaten the wetland and also controls water flow to maintain adequate levels to support foraging and nesting birds.

You can now enjoy intimate views of the marsh and shore from a new elevated boardwalk that meanders for 2,200 feet and includes interpretive signs and shaded viewing kiosks overlooking the wetland. The new structure offers expansive vistas of a variety of birds drawn to this 700-acre site. The adjacent beach access may yield seasonal views of passing whales (koholā) and endangered hawksbill turtles (honu).

The water in the pond recedes during the summer months, creating shallow water mudflats rich in invertebrates and small fish—just in time to provide a meal for fall migrants and nesting birds. Fish concentrate in the shallows, offering an easy meal for black-crowned night-herons ('auku'u) and cattle egrets. When the water recedes, you may see the crater-like nests of tilapia in the sand, a fish introduced in the 1950s.

The beach is one of Maui's nesting sites for endangered hawksbill turtles, so scan the sand during summer for the tracks of nesting females. They arrive in the evening, crawling ashore to dig nests to incubate their eggs. Two to three months later, tiny hatchlings emerge from the nest all at once and make their way to sea under the relative safety of darkness. Early morning walkers should report any turtle tracks on the beach to the refuge staff so the potential nest can be surveyed and monitored. Every day during summer, Turtle Watch volunteers patrol this and other nesting beaches, looking for signs of activity. Please avoid disturbing the nest sites.

sanderling

WILDLIFE TO WATCH

You will have good to excellent chances of seeing three of five native Hawaiian waterbirds here year-round: the **black-crowned night-heron**, endangered **Hawaiian stilt** (ae'o) and **Hawaiian coot** ('alae ke'oke'o). **Hawaiian ducks** (koloa) are present but due to interbreeding, they are difficult to differentiate from mallards. The introduced **cattle egret** is common year-round.

Eighteen species of ducks and geese visit during fall and winter, among them the **northern pintail** (koloa māpu) and **northern shoveler** (koloa mohā). When the early Hawaiians named the northern pintail koloa māpu, or wind-blown duck, they were recognizing its long migration across the seas. The refuge attracts some rarities that ride the wind from North America and Asia, including the **garganey** and **Eurasion wigeon**. Of the more than 20 species visiting during fall and winter, common shorebirds include the **Pacific golden-plover** (kōlea), **ruddy turnstone** ('akekeke) and **wandering tattler** ('ūlili). You will recognize the turnstone as it flips pebbles and flotsam to search for food, a habit resulting in its name. Other predictable winter visitors include **terns** ('eki'eki) and **osprey**. You will undoubtedly see some of Hawai'i's non-native birds, such as **doves**, **finches** and **cardinals**.

In the pond, you may spot **tilapia**. At the beach, watch for **humpback whales** in winter, **green sea turtles** (honu) and **hawksbill turtles**.

VIEWING TIPS

To enjoy the site's diversity, consider beginning your visit on the boardwalk to view birds and walk back along the beach. There are wildlife species to see year-round. During fall and winter look for shorebirds foraging on mud-

Hawaiian Stilt

Standing 16 inches tall, the Hawaiian stilt (ae'o) is one of the largest Hawaiian waterbirds and also the easiest to identify. It is black above and white below, with long pink legs and a long, straight black bill. Its Hawaiian name means "one standing tall," but also translates to "stilt," its exact English name. The Hawaiian stilt is a distinct species. Its North American relative is known as the black-necked stilt. In Hawaiian lore, ae'o refers to a dance by people using wooden stilts to mimic the movements of this distinct black-and-white waterbird.

You can readily see this endangered bird on all of the Hawaiian Islands, most often in shallow, open water and on mud or salt flats. In the water, they use their long legs to wade into the deeper areas to probe for larvae, insects and fish. Their coloration makes them easy to spot and you can enjoy watching them use several hunting styles.

Stilts move rapidly through the water, sometimes up to their bellies, as they actively search for worms, small fish or other edibles. Their long bills are perfectly suited for jabbing prey below the surface, though stilts also may raise their heads to snag insects in flight. If you don't see these conspicuous waterbirds, you can often locate them by their insistent "kek kek kek" or "yip yip yip" calls.

Stilts nest in several protected natural areas, including Kanahā and Keālia ponds on Maui. You may see one of the pair vigorously defending its nest and chicks. Some stilts splash water on their breasts to distract predators, others feign a broken leg; occasionally, a few birds even join forces to attack and drive off intruders.

See pages 21–25 for ethical viewing tips.

flats, near the outlet and on beaches that border the refuge. When the mud-flats are more extensive as the water evaporates, a spotting scope will help bring distant birds into view. Doves, finches and cardinals often perch in the scrubby algarroba trees (kiawe) located along the boardwalk and near kiosks. Viewing is best in the morning. Also, keep your eyes open for green sea turtles swimming offshore. While 90 percent of these turtles nest in the remote Hawaiian Islands, they can regularly be seen at many main Hawaiian Island locations, such as this one. Scan the horizon for spouting or breaching humpback whales in the winter months.

wandering tattler

Site Notes There are interpretive panels and shade structures along the boardwalk to enrich your visit and provide relief from the sun. The boardwalk is accessible to those with disabilities.

Hours Boardwalk viewing during daylight hours. Office hours are Mon–Fri, 8 AM–4 PM (excluding federal holidays).

Nearby Services Gas, food and lodging are available in Kīhei. For more information, contact the Maui Chamber of Commerce, (808) 871-7711, www.mauichamber.com/ or the Maui Visitors Bureau, (808) 244-3530, www.visitmaui.com.

Special Tips Parking is very limited and you can only turn right into the parking lot from the south bound lane of Highway 310 heading toward Kīhei. This is a narrow, two-lane undivided highway and there is no left turn allowed across traffic coming from the north. Arrive early in the morning or late in the afternoon for the best chance of finding a parking spot, and for the best and coolest viewing. Bring drinking water.

Contact Information Keālia Pond National Wildlife Refuge/Administrative Office, Milepost 6 on Mokulele Highway (Hwy. 311), P.O. Box 1042, Kīhei, Hawai'i 96753, (808) 875-1582, www.fws.gov/pacific/pacificislands/wnwr/mkealianwr.html

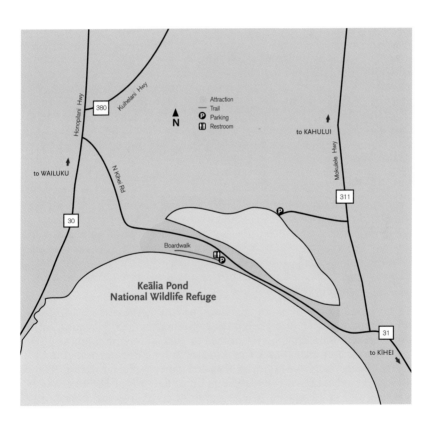

BACKGROUND

Perhaps the most spectacular snorkeling in Hawai'i involves a fun, 3-mile boat trip from Maui to a tiny islet off the southwestern coast. Molokini is the crescent-shaped rim of an extinct volcanic crater located in the crystal clear waters of 'Alalākeiki Channel. According to Hawaiian lore, Molokini was once a beautiful woman. She and Pele, the fire goddess, fell in love with the same man. Pele grew jealous and cut Molokini in two, then turned her into stone. The woman's head is supposedly Pu'u ōla'i, the cinder cone by Mākena Beach.

DESCRIPTION

Dozens of species of colorful reef fish live amid the coral heads and basaltic boulders forming this sheltered 77-acre cove. Whether you're a beginner or avid snorkeler or scuba diver, this can be a half or full day adventure that becomes the experience of a lifetime. Non-swimmers can enjoy the riches of Molokini, too, as many tour boats have underwater windows for viewing the reef and fishes. There are no beaches, sitting areas or facilities on Molokini; it is strictly for snorkeling or scuba.

The cove area slopes off from the shoreline to a depth of about 100 feet before dropping off. The sheltered inner circle provides protection from heavy surf and incredible opportunities to view a moving rainbow of fish and delicate coral formations. Coral grows in long fingers, branching rounded heads, huge mounds or lobes and other fantastic shapes. The back side of the cove wall is steep, dropping off to a depth of 200 feet, and is more exposed to the ocean. Patches of black coral are now reappearing on the back wall, following years of over-harvesting.

While on the boat, watch for seabirds, sea turtles (honu), spinner dolphins (nai'a) or humpback whales (koholā) during winter.

WILDLIFE TO WATCH

This is fish watching in full technicolor! More than 100 species of interesting fish inhabit this coral reef. **Parrotfish** (uhu) come in bright colors, from turquoise to brilliant red. If a male dies, the most dominant female can transform into a male and change color from red to vibrant blue or turquoise green. You will see many **butterflyfish**; many have vivid yellow coloring overlaid with stripes, spots and other markings. The raccoon butterflyfish, with the conspicuous black mask and white stripe behind the eye, may be spotted swimming in large schools. Where there is prey, there are predators, so watch for **reef whitetip sharks** (manō lālākea), **gray reef sharks** and several species of **jacks**. The sandy channels on the crater's northwest slope often yield views of **garden eels** that are two feet

pyramid butterflyfish

long. These greenish gray animals dangle out of the sand, waving back and forth, with most of their bodies hidden from view. The same deep sand channels are also home to **manta rays** (hāhālua), which slowly swim in circles as they feed on plankton carried by the strong ocean currents. You may also spot **sea turtles**, **spinner dolphins** and **humpback whales**.

VIEWING TIPS

Fish are so abundant you only need to look through your tour boat's observation window or put your face in the water and remember to paddle around for more variety. Check weather conditions before your trip. Bring fish identification cards or guidebooks so you can identify the fish while they are fresh in your mind.

Try to visit the Maui Ocean Center in Māʻalaea before your Molokini trip. This thoughtfully designed aquarium displays many of the fish you will see at Molokini and offers excellent information about marine life in Hawaiʻi.

Site Notes	Access to Molokini Crater is by boat only, and charter boats operate out of Lahaina, Māʻalaea Harbor and Kīhei. Tour boats are highly regulated and mooring buoys are provided to protect the fragile reef from anchors. The crater basin, just 35 feet deep, is perfect for beginning snorkelers and scuba divers. The underwater wall is 70 feet deep, a good setting for intermediate divers. The back wall, more than 200 feet deep, is suitable for very experienced divers only.
Hours	Open 24 hours a day
Nearby Services	Gas, food and lodging in Kīhei. For more information, contact the Maui Chamber of Commerce, (808) 871-7711, www.mauichamber.com, or the Maui Visitors Bureau, (808) 244-3530, www.visitmaui.com.
Special Tips	The crater is protected, but heavy swells and storms can make the trip unpleasant. Before choosing a tour boat operator, find out if there is a naturalist on board. Naturalists can

enrich your experience by helping you spot whales, dolphins and sea turtles and identify the fish that you've just seen. The boat should provide snorkel equipment, float vests for beginners, beverages and food. Be sure to bring waterproof sun screen, a change of clothes, a hat, an inexpensive underwater camera and a towel.

Contact Information Department of Land and Natural Resources/Division of Aquatic Resources, 130 Mahalani Street, Wailuku, HI 96793, (808) 243-5294, (808) 243-5294, www.hawaii.gov/dlnr/dar/mlcd/molokini.htm

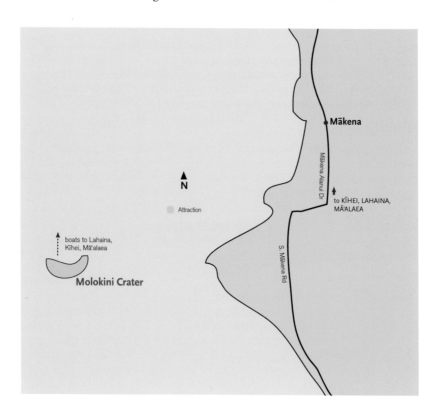

milletseed butterflyfish

Hawaiian Islands Humpback Whale National Marine Sanctuary

humpback whales

BACKGROUND

You've arrived on Maui and heard about the superb whale watching from tour boats and at coastal locations throughout the island. As you scan the water, you hope you'll be treated to the sight of spouts, tails slapping the surf or entire bodies suspended in air as these 45-ton giants breach. If you'd like to know more about the habits of humpback whales (koholā) and have an excellent chance of seeing them, be sure to plan a visit to the Hawaiian Islands Humpback Whale National Marine Sanctuary headquarters in Kīhei. The building that houses the sanctuary office was formerly used by the Navy during wartime. The Sanctuary took over the dilapidated building with peeling paint in 1994 and renovated it to better achieve its important mission of marine conservation and education. The site now offers an educational center and programs, interpretive displays about whales and a beachside platform with perfect views of these giants as they pass by Māʻalaea Bay. The Sanctuary Headquarters presides over the waters between Maui, Molokaʻi and Lanaʻi that form the core of the sanctuary. Almost every island has ocean waters preserved as part of the Whale Sanctuary and field offices located on Oʻahu, Kauaʻi and the Big Island of Hawaiʻi offer information and other resources. The Sanctuary is managed by the National Oceanic and Atmospheric Administration (NOAA) in partnership with the Hawaiʻi Department of Land and Natural Resources.

DESCRIPTION

It's easy to feel the draw of the ocean as soon as you arrive at the site. A grassy viewing area with spotting scopes lies just behind the blue-walled Sanctuary office, a quiet, relaxing area that invites you to spend time looking seaward. Volunteer interpreters are usually on site and can provide interesting anecdotes about marine mammals and tips for spotting whales and understanding their behavior.

Premier
- SITE -

The whale viewing platform is next to an ancient Hawaiian fishpond, one of many once found along coasts throughout the Hawaiian Islands. These rock-walled fishponds provide a tangible link to an era when early Hawaiians used aquaculture to raise fish that entered the ponds through a special sluice gate built to trap the fish. The Sanctuary is working with a local fishpond association to restore the pond to use for educational programs about Native Hawaiian culture and the traditions of ocean stewardship.

Most visitors are so anxious to watch for whales they pass by the Sanctuary's education center in favor of reaching the platform. If classes aren't in session, make time to explore this treasure trove of hands-on experiences, where you'll find everything from specimens and models to interactive displays. The center routinely gives talks for visitors that are publicized in many local tourist publications. They are interesting and informative, with ample opportunities to ask questions.

The Sanctuary is also trying to reestablish native plants at the Kīhei headquarters. Today, more than 30 varieties have been planted on site, a project that is helping to restore native vegetation, reestablish plants that could become extinct and control coastal erosion. The effort also honors Hawaiian culture and the plants' use for food, thatching, boats, cloth, medicines and more. You can learn about the plants and this restoration effort on a self-guided tour of the grounds.

WILDLIFE TO WATCH

Humpbacks are in Hawai'i from November through May, with the peak season occurring from the beginning of January through the end of March. Because the whales are so numerous in Sanctuary waters during whale season, there is an excellent chance of seeing some activity during your visit. In addition, you may see **pilot whales** and **spinner** and **bottlenose dolphins** (nai'a). As a bonus, the beaches on either side of the sanctuary have coral reefs that offer good snorkeling.

VIEWING TIPS

Take advantage of the spotting scopes and binoculars on the viewing platform to close the gap on distant views. As you scan the horizon, look for whales spouting as they exhale and inhale on the surface. If you're lucky, you'll see them slap their tails, spy hop (stick their heads up in the air) or breach (jump partially or completely out of the water). If you see a whale breach, keep watching the same spot as whales often appear several times in the same area. Beginning in January, calves may breach near their mothers.

One of the most exciting ways to view whales is by boat. While the trips often focus on humpbacks, you may also see bottlenose and spinner dolphins and pilot whales. Look for boat operators who have naturalists on board to guide and enrich the experience. Some even have hydrophones that will allow you to hear the underwater songs of passing whales.

Humpback Whale

Humpback whales (koholā) are huge when mature, sometimes reaching 45 feet in length with a weight of 45 tons. They are also known for their incredible leaps, spins and breaches. Sometimes they slap the water with their pectoral flippers or tail flukes. The males sing precise and eerie songs of groans, crackles and whistles that can last several minutes and are repeated throughout an entire day.

Humpbacks sing while they are in Hawaiian waters, ceasing as soon as they migrate back to Alaska, where they spend spring and summer feeding on incredibly rich concentrations of krill, herring and other small fish. They then migrate south for the winter by themselves or in small groups to the warm Hawaiian waters, where they will mate and females will calve after a gestation of one year. The calf may weigh two tons at birth. Many humpback whales nurse and have their young in Hawaiian waters that have been designated a National Marine Sanctuary in order to further protect these endangered marine mammals. The humpbacks have made a remarkable comeback, thanks to federal and state protection.

Like other creatures of the sea, the whale figures prominently in Native Hawaiian legends and chants. Pu'ukoholā Heiau, one of Hawai'i's largest temples, was so named because it was built upon "whale hill." Whales were considered sacred and revered as an 'aumakua, the spirit of a family ancestor that has assumed the shape of an animal or object that protects the family. In return for this protection, the family cared for these animals or objects and passed on lore about them to the younger generations. This respectful ethic continues today through laws and regulations aimed at giving whales the undisturbed space they need to prosper.

See pages 21–25 for ethical viewing tips.

If you time it right and are keen to do something to help managers help the whales, you can volunteer to participate in the annual Sanctuary ocean count and learn about humpback whales in the process. The counts occur at 65 different shore sites around Maui, O'ahu, Kaua'i, Kaho'olawe and Hawai'i on the last Saturday in January, February and March each year. Call 1 (888) 55WHALE for information.

More Whale Watching Sites

Papawai Point, Maui
Directions: Near mile marker 8 on the Hono-a-Piʻilani Highway, between the town of Māʻalaea and Lahaina. Look for the paved pull off area on the ocean side of the highway. There are several marked parking places. You can view from your vehicle. Avoid standing too close to the edge of this steep overlook.

Makapuʻu Point Lighthouse, Oʻahu
Directions: From the Koko Marina Shopping Center on the Kalaniʻanaʻole Highway, travel approximately 4.5 miles toward Makapuʻu Point. The trail leading to the lighthouse is on the right hand side of the road, before the scenic lookouts. A black gate marks the start of the trail. Be cautious when selecting a place to park or when walking to the trailhead. See page 72 for Makapuʻu Lighthouse description.

Hālona Blowhole, Oʻahu
Directions from Honolulu: Travel east on the Kalaniʻanaʻole Highway toward Hanauma Bay. Hālona Blowhole is the second lookout area past Hanauma Bay. Park in a large paved parking lot and enjoy views from the lookout.

From Kailua: Travel south on the Kalaniʻanaʻole Highway, through Waimānalo, past Sea Life Park and Makapuʻu Point. The parking area is adjacent to the large lookout just past Sandy Beach. See page 70 for Hālona Blowhole description.

Puʻukoholā Heiau National Historic Site, Hawaiʻi
Directions from Kona: Take Highway 19 north past Waikōloa/Hāpuna and Spencer Park. Turn left at Highway 270; proceed .5 mile and turn left at the National Park sign.

Directions from Waimea: Take Highway 19 south to Highway 270, then turn right or north on 270. Proceed .5 mile north and turn left into park. You'll see the National Park sign on the highway—easy to find. Turn right into paved parking area.

Kīlauea Point National Wildlife Refuge, Kauaʻi
Directions: Take the Kūhiō Highway to the town of Kīlauea. Turn right on Kolo Road, then left on Kīlauea Road. Proceed to refuge entrance. You will take a short walk from the parking lot to the lighthouse. See page 43 for Kīlauea Point description.

Site Notes This New-England style structure is located between two picturesque beaches. Bring a snack and use Sanctuary picnic tables to enjoy the scenery after you've taken in the interpretive displays and whale watching. The site is very accessible to those with disabilities. Sanctuary staff and volunteers are on duty weekdays, 8 AM–5 PM, to provide information and answer questions.

Hours Education Center open Mon–Fri, 10 AM–3 PM. Sanctuary office and viewing platform open 8 AM–5 PM.

Nearby Services Gas, food and lodging are available in Kīhei. For more information, contact the Maui Chamber of Commerce, (808) 871-7711, www.mauichamber.com, or the Maui Visitors Bureau, (808) 244-3530, www.visitmaui.com.

Special Tips If you plan to take a whale watching tour, select an operator who puts the needs of marine mammals first.

Contact Information NOAA's Hawaiian Islands Humpback Whale National Marine Sanctuary, Maui Headquarters: 726 S. Kīhei Road, Kīhei, HI, 96753, (808) 879-2818 or 800/831-4888 (off Maui). Oʻahu office: 6600 Kalaniʻanaʻole Hwy, Suite 301, Honolulu, HI, 96825, (808) 397-2651. Kauaʻi Office: 4370 Kukui Grove St., Suite 206, Līhuʻe, HI, 96766, (808) 246-2860. Kona (Big Island) Office: 73-4460 Queen Kaʻahumanu Hwy, #112, Kailua-Kona, HI, 96740, (808) 327-3697, http://hawaiihumpbackwhale.noaa.gov

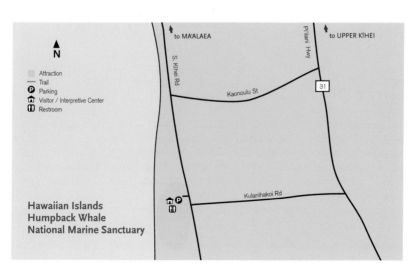

Hawaiian Islands Humpback Whale National Marine Sanctuary

- Attraction
- Trail
- **P** Parking
- Visitor / Interpretive Center
- Restroom

N

to MAʻALAEA

S. Kīhei Rd

Piʻilani Hwy

to UPPER KĪHEI

Kaonoulu St

31

Kulanihakoi Rd

Mākena State Park

Snorkeling, water sports and wetland viewing at unspoiled beach

BACKGROUND

Where can you find something for everyone? Excellent snorkeling, great water sports, wetland ponds and wildlife, perfect beaches and memorable views combine to set Mākena State Park apart from many other sites. Pu'u Ola'i is a cinder cone on the southwestern slope of Haleakalā crater. This starkly beautiful landmark straddling the shoreline separates Naupaka, a black sand beach to the north, from Oneloa, a white sand beach to the south. Crowded parking areas are testimony to the popularity of these two beaches.

DESCRIPTION

If you want to do some birding and then cool off with some snorkeling or water sports and finish up with more birding, plan a visit to these two beautiful beaches. Begin your visit at Naupaka Beach. Behind the sand dunes lies Maluaka, a wetland that teems with bird life. Waterbirds here are benefiting from efforts to restore this wetland pond. You should also see many non-native birds, such as finches and cardinals, flitting in and out of the underbrush surrounding the ponds.

If you want to do some snorkeling, remain at Naupaka Beach. If beach and water play are your preferences, return to your vehicle and continue driving south to the parking lot on the opposite side of the cinder cone. Oneloa, or "long sands," also known as Big Beach, is an expanse of glimmering white sand that stretches 3,300 feet. One of Maui's most scenic beaches also offers excellent swimming and boogie boarding. If you walk inland from the beach, you'll see a barrier of algarroba trees (kiawe), a relative of mesquite, that screens a large wetland from view. To reach the pond, turn into the trees and cross low sand dunes carpeted with morning glories and naupaka kahakai, a conspicuous beach shrub covered with green succulent leaves. There are fewer birds at the pond to the south, which does not always contain water, but you may see Hawaiian stilts (ae'o) and a variety of shorebirds during winter.

From either beach throughout the year, enjoy the views of Molokini Crater and the neighboring island, Kaho'olawe. Sit awhile and scan the water for green sea turtles (honu), particularly near the cinder cone. Scientists are now buzzing because endangered hawksbill turtles (honu'ea) have recently begun to nest on Oneloa Beach.

WILDLIFE TO WATCH

The water is clear and you can see **green sea turtles** and many colorful fish while snorkeling at Naupaka Beach, including **saddleback wrasse** (hīnālea) and **parrotfish** (uhu). Scan the shoreline occasionally during winter and there's a chance you'll also spot passing **humpback whales** (koholā). At Maluaka Pond, the sharp "kek kek kek"

ruddy turnstone

of the **Hawaiian stilt** (ae'o) reverberates across the wetland. **Ruddy turnstones** ('ūlili) and **Pacific golden-plovers** (kōlea) fan out on the mudflats and **black-crowned night-herons** ('auku'u) roost in the surrounding trees. The **Hawaiian coot** ('alae ke'oke'o) is also a visitor. Black-crowned night-herons are present year-round, but are often very secretive. By contrast, stilts are conspicuous throughout the year. The wetland ponds should offer excellent chances of seeing other shorebirds in winter. You may also spot **hawksbill turtles**.

VIEWING TIPS

Snorkeling is best at Naupaka Beach. You'll find good snorkeling below the cliffs and along the rocky shore where green sea turtles are common. Walk along the shoreline towards the Maui Prince Hotel and watch for the turtles directly offshore as they surface for air. The turtles feed on sea lettuce growing on the nearshore rocks. There are no formal trails to the wetland ponds, so do your best to avoid trampling sensitive dune plants. Approach the ponds quietly; birds will be less likely to flush. Shorebirds are present from fall through spring, but viewing will be sporadic if the wetlands dry out early.

Site Notes	To reach Naupaka Beach on the Wailea, or north side, of the Park, take the unimproved dirt road next to the cinder cone. The small dirt parking lot can only hold about six vehicles. It is a short walk from the parking lot at Naupaka Beach to reach Maluaka Pond, the best place for viewing the waterbirds. There is parking for about 25 cars at either end of Oneloa Beach.
Hours	5 AM–9 PM
Nearby Services	Gas, food and lodging are available at Wailea and Kīhei. For more information, contact the Maui Visitors Bureau, (808) 244-3530, www.visitmaui.com.
Special Tips	Be cautious at Oneloa. Locals call it "Break Neck Beach" because of the steep beach entry and occasional heavy surf.

Contact Information Department of Land and Natural Resources, Division of State Parks, 54 S. High Street, Room 101, Wailuku, HI 96793, (808) 984-8109, www.hawaii.gov/dlnr/dsp/maui.html

male spectacled parrotfish

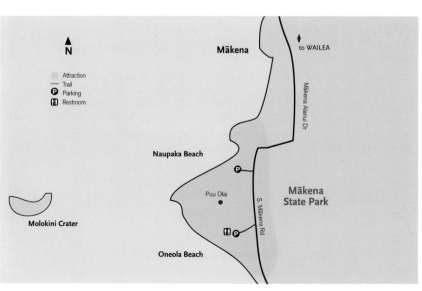

N

Attraction
Trail
P Parking
ℍ Restroom

Mākena

to WAILEA

Mākena Alanui Dr

Naupaka Beach

P

Puu Olai

**Mākena
State Park**

S. Mākena Rd

ℍ P

Molokini Crater

Oneola Beach

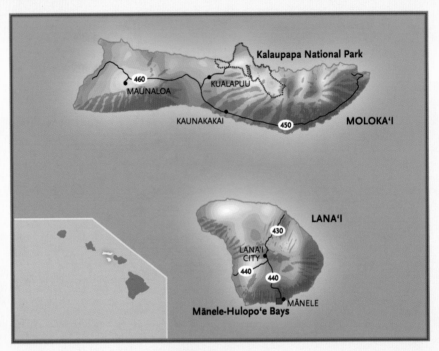

Lana'i & Moloka'i -
The Pineapple & The Friendly Islands *ISLAND FLOWER*
Native Dodder (Kauna'oa)

As you relax on a West Maui beach, four islands are visible across the channel: Molokini and Kaho'olawe are the closest, while Lana'i and Moloka'i are more distant. Lana'i and Moloka'i each have a unique history and both offer unspoiled ruggedness and some limited wildlife viewing opportunities.

If you need to get away from it all while in Hawai'i, the retreat you seek might be on the island of Lana'i. With the exception of three hotels and Lana'i City, where almost all of the island's 2,800 residents live, the entire island is largely undeveloped. There are probably less than 25 miles of paved roads on Lana'i and the island's dirt roads are only accessible with 4WD vehicles.

In ancient times, early Hawaiians shunned the island, believing it was inhabited by spirits. After the son of a Lahaina chief rid the island of the spirits and its bad reputation, early Hawaiians came and so did westerners, who ran sheep and cattle and planted sugarcane. In 1922, James Dole purchased 98 percent of the island and founded the famous Dole Hawaiian Pineapple Company. Dole planted 13,000 acres of pineapples, developed a deep water harbor and other facilities and eventually sold his company to the Castle and Cooke Corporation. Castle and Cooke has since built two luxury hotels, golf courses and other amenities on the island.

Four-wheel drive tracks and rugged trails lead to volcanic, boulder-strewn landscapes, lush rain forests and high elevation peaks with breathtaking views. Tour boats transport beachcombers and snorkelers to beautiful Mānele and Hulopoʻe bays, where unspoiled beaches, outstanding snorkeling opportunities and the appearance of spinner dolphins (naiʻa) and sea turtles (honu) are reason enough to visit these bays. This is the only site on Lanaʻi that is featured in the guide, but it is a highly popular destination for visitors who can combine marine mammal viewing with a superb snorkeling experience on an island that feels like it has been forgotten by time.

Across the channel, two volcanoes created Molokaʻi, an island known for dramatic coastal cliffs considered to be among the tallest in the world. Most people remember Molokaʻi as a place of exile for thousands of people suffering from leprosy, a then incurable, contagious disease, now referred to as Hansen's Disease. Some 8,000 people afflicted with the disease were forced to live in the colony at Kalaupapa during the 1870s and 1880s with Father Damien. Some individuals still live in the colony by choice and the Kalaupapa Peninsula is now protected as a National Historic Park. You can see this historic site from Pālāʻau State Park, located more than 1,500 feet above the peninsula.

Compared to other Hawaiian Islands, Molokaʻi remains fairly undeveloped and much of its land is devoted to agriculture. Its forested peaks, wetlands, dunes and superb beaches are home to a variety of birds, from cattle egrets to Pacific golden-plovers (kōlea). Migratory birds, such as the wandering tattler (ʻūlili) and ruddy turnstone (ʻakekeke), also make seasonal visits to Molokaʻi beaches and wetlands. Many of the sites used by these birds are small or remote, or lack the infrastructure needed to accommodate visitors and protect the habitat and wildlife. For this reason, no wildlife viewing destinations are currently featured for Molokaʻi, although visitors staying at its many bed and breakfasts or luxury resorts will undoubtedly have opportunities to see a variety of birds and passing humpback whales during winter. Numerous Hawaiian fishponds are situated along the coast as you drive out of Kaunakakai.

BACKGROUND

If you want to know what it feels like to be in an aquarium, a snorkeling trip to Mānele and Hulopo'e bays will provide it. These two bays are separated by a volcanic cone that includes its own inlet called Pu'u Pehe cove. Sea stacks and other rocky sentinels add character to these stunning turquoise bays where fishing has been restricted, resulting in a great diversity of coral reefs and the colorful fish that inhabit them. There are also stone ruins from an ancient fishing village in Mānele, underscoring the importance of this marine resource to early Hawaiians. Today the park at Hulopo'e Bay is owned by the Castle and Cooke Corporation, which also operates a luxury hotel sitting on the rocky promontory overlooking the bay. Just below the hotel, there are rock foundations that have interpretive signs.

DESCRIPTION

The most common way to reach these beautiful embayments is on a commercial tour boat or ferry from Lahaina on Maui, which takes about 45 minutes. Many offer partial or full day trips, complete with meals, beverages and natural history talks. The boat trip provides great opportunities to spot humpback whales (koholā) during winter and spinner dolphins (nai'a) as you travel to and from the island. If you like snorkeling or scuba, the unspoiled bay waters will offer great viewing. The clear water at Pu'u Pehe Cove is rich in marine life. Corals lie next to large patches of sand in 10 to 15 feet of water and are distant from the beach, where the water is often clear. This is a favorite spot for scuba divers, who use a guided dive boat to reach an area not accessible from the shoreline.

Snorkelers are drawn to Hulopo'e Bay. The bay has large tidepools on the eastern side of the baypoint and a shallow offshore reef. The variety of beautiful coral formations include cauliflower, finger, lobed and other shapes. Fish in many hues swim in and out of underwater arches and openings. The diversity is outstanding, from parrotfish and butterfly fish to tangs. The fish are also exceptionally large because of the protection afforded by the bay's designation as a Marine Life Conservation District.

While Mānele Bay corals are abundant along the bay close to the cliffs, snorkeling is generally not recommended here because of the boat traffic. However, the area outside of the western edge of the bay near Pu'u Pehe rock is a popular destination, particularly for those who like scuba.

WILDLIFE TO WATCH

Whether you're sitting on deck or at an inside window seat on your boat ride across the channel, keep a sharp eye out for spouting and breaching **humpback whales** in the winter. **Spinner dolphins** may ride the bow wake and swim alongside the boat for a while. When you reach the bay, prepare yourself for an uncrowded beach and prime snorkeling. Experienced snorkelers and divers have identified as many as 20 fish during one swim. One conspicuous family of fishes is the **tang**, which includes 23 species. Tang are thin, flat, oval fish that may have two sets of scalpel-like spines at the base of its tail fin that can slice and cut, hence the nickname "surgeonfish." You will see them graze along the surface of coral for algae. They often move in groups, which affords protection. **Wrasse** (hīnālea) are known for their speed, using their pectoral fins to fly through the water. This is the principal way they avoid predatory fish. They are extremely colorful in their youth, but fade with age. Most wrasse eat other fish or plankton. However, one species, the cleaner wrasse, waits in one location for fish to drop by for a cleaning. The small blue and yellow wrasse will swim in and out of the mouths and gills of much larger fish, removing and eating parasites from their host.

VIEWING TIPS

Invest in a fish identification book or chart to enrich your experience, because some of the fun is identifying the creatures you've just seen. Snorkeling is generally best in the morning, before it becomes windy. It is best along the north and western shores from May through September. Diving is best on southern and southeastern shores from October to April. Although tides vary, they usually don't affect snorkeling or diving. If you take a commercial boat trip, choose a boat operator who has a naturalist on board and advertises that he or she abides by marine regulations.

Site Notes The ferry and most tour boats dock at Mānele Harbor. Hulopo'e Bay is about a 10- to 15-minute walk, so wear suitable walking shoes. If you're interested in identifying the local birds, stop at the visitor booth interpretive sign to see photos and learn about their habits. There are no food services on the beach or at the harbor, although you can eat at the upscale restaurant at the Mānele Bay Resort.

Hours Open 24 hours a day

Nearby Services None

Special Tips Stairways are steep. If you're not getting a meal on your tour boat, bring a lunch and drinking water. Come prepared for a long day with such necessities as hat, sunblock, sunglasses, shoes, bathing suit and towel. Heavy wave surges can make snorkeling more difficult and dangerous. There is no lifeguard on duty. Be aware that local surfers use the same beaches, so pay attention to "traffic."

Contact Information Division of Aquatic Resources, Maui Office, 130 Mahalani Street, HI, 96793, (808) 243-5294, www.hawaii.gov/dlnr/dar/

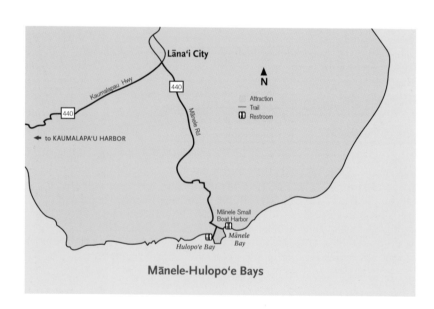

Mānele-Hulopo'e Bays

humpback whale

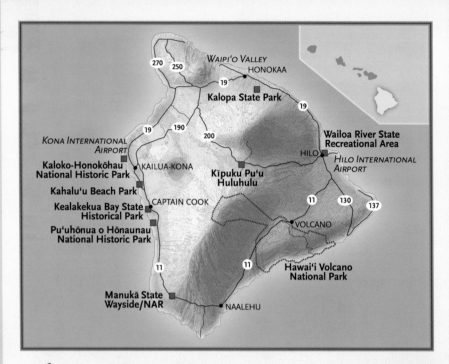

Hawai'i - The Big Island

ISLAND FLOWER
'ohia lehua

All of the Hawaiian Islands are volcanic in origin and nowhere is volcanism more evident than on the Big Island. Hawai'i was born when a hot spot deep within the earth erupted. The youngest of the Hawaiian Islands continues to grow today, fueled by blasts from Kīlauea volcano in Hawai'i Volcanoes National Park, where lava flows build in layers to form new land along the wave-beaten shore.

It is an island rich in Hawaiian cultural history and legends. The first Polynesians reportedly landed at what is now Ka Lae, the southernmost piece of land in the United States. The godess Pele once resided at the Halema'uma'u Crater, located within the caldera of Kīlauea volcano. And Kamehameha I was born on the west side of the island, a place rich in petroglyphs, temples (heiau), royal fishponds and other sacred sites.

The evidence of volcanism is everywhere: Wander carefully past hissing cinder cones and belching steam vents, where the acrid odor of sulfur dioxide lingers. Visit a sacred site that inspires the story of Pele, the volcano goddess. Hike across vast fields of crumbling lava to reach a secluded oasis. Or dig your feet into a black sand beach, the remains of lava pulverized by the surf.

As the earth spat fire and snaking rivers of lava parted and coalesced, they cooled in many forms, from softly rounded mounds and thick ribbons twisted like whipped taffy (pāhoehoe) to endless fields of brutal, jagged-edged rock ('a'ā). On this harsh substrate, ferns, 'ōhi'a and other pioneering plants took hold, gradually forming specialized environments that supported many native wildlife species.

On the windward side of the island, heavy rainfall produces a carpet of tropical vegetation. The swollen Wailoa River flows through ponds in urban Hilo, creating wetlands and deep water habitat that attract a rich variety of waterbirds.

The tradewinds drop most of their load of moisture as they encounter Mauna Kea and Mauna Loa, resulting in drier conditions on much of the western side of the island. At Kaloko-Honokōhau National Historic Park, ancient fishponds set amid a field of lava are a magnet for endangered resident waterbirds and many migratory species. Forest birds, dainty butterflies and Hawai'i's only native land mammal, the Hawaiian hoary bat, thrive at Manukā State Wayside and Natural Area Reserve. Dolphins come to rest each day at Kealakekua Bay, and the coral reefs along the Kona Coast provide some of the best snorkeling in Hawai'i. Wherever you visit on the Big Island, you will find a rich assortment of wildlife viewing experiences.

Hawaiian squirrelfish

BACKGROUND

Pick up any book about the Big Island and chances are there will be photos of Kahalu'u Bay, one of the island's most beautiful embayments and perhaps its best snorkeling spot. Traditionally, Hawaiians also sought these waters, where cool, fresh water flows from nearshore springs and mixes with warmer ocean water, creating an ideal environment for fish. A breakwater that shelters the calm inner bay may have been built by Hawaiians in days of old. An outer reef protects the bay from waves and choppy water and the water entry at the shore is gradual, making it an ideal place for beginning snorkelers. Some of the locals call it "baby beach" because it is popular among families with youngsters who want to enjoy the warm water and easy snorkeling. It is also an ideal environment for large heads of lobed coral and a thriving population of green sea turtles (honu).

DESCRIPTION

The site is a snorkeler's dream because schools of colorful fish congregate around submerged rocky reefs and coral heads in water less than ten feet deep. These are the tropical fish that make Hawai'i famous: the multihued puffers, tang, parrotfish, butterflyfish and scores of others that delight snorkelers and divers. Green sea turtles are drawn to the algae carpeting the rocky shoals. Turtles sometimes feed amid snorkelers, who can enjoy watching the show if they keep their distance and refrain from disturbing the turtles. Interpretive signage on shore provides information about reef fish and reminders about snorkeling etiquette. As you watch the reef fishes feeding in the nearshore coral, take advantage of this opportunity to swim among some of the most impressive coral gardens on the island without needing to use scuba gear to enjoy them.

Those who want to avoid getting wet can enjoy an elegant, out-of-water viewing experience by visiting the bar at the adjacent Keauhou Beach Resort, where you can have a drink or snack while overlooking reef fish and sea turtles in the shallow tidepool located below the bar.

WILDLIFE TO WATCH

The two big attractions are **reef fish** and **green sea turtles**. All can be readily enjoyed year-round. Get out your fish identification book or card and tally your observations because you may see many species, from **white goatfish**, **bluefin travally** and **flying gurnards** to at least a half-dozen species of conspicuous **butterflyfish**. The butterflyfish have flattened, disk-like bodies with patterns of stripes and speckles in blue, yellow and white. Many have distinctive snout-like noses. They often travel in pairs and use their streamlined bodies to thread their way through narrow spaces.

green sea turtle

VIEWING TIPS

Because the site is popular with inexperienced snorkelers, the entry area and shallows are often crowded. You will find more space and lots of fish if you swim beyond these areas. Years of snorkeling and swimming popularity have caused major damage to the fragile coral, a continuing concern for resource managers. Eels (puhi) are sometimes visible in the shallows near the Keauhou Resort, drawn to the area because misguided people feed them. On calm days, very experienced snorkelers can venture outside of the reef, where huge schools of fish often congregate in the boulder environment. There are frequently reports of turtles feeding on sea lettuce or grasses at the south end of the bay.

Site Notes You can usually rent snorkeling gear on site. Lifeguards are on duty 9 AM–4 PM daily. The most convenient place to enter and leave the water is a small sandy area in front of the lifeguard stand. To avoid damaging the coral, inexperienced snorkelers should wear a flotation device, but no fins.

Hours 7 AM–11 PM

Nearby Services Gas, food and lodging are available in Kailua-Kona. For more information, contact the Big Island Visitors Bureau, (808) 961-5797 (Hilo Office), (808) 886-1655 (West Hawaiʻi Office), www.bigisland.org.

Special Tips This site is popular and can be very crowded. There is limited parking in a paved lot next to the beach. Come early in the morning to enjoy the best snorkeling and avoid the crowds. Stay within the reef where the water is usually calmer; a strong current often exists throughout the bay. Please keep your distance from sea turtles.

Contact Information Hawai'i County Parks and Recreation, (808) 961-8311, www.hawaii-county.com

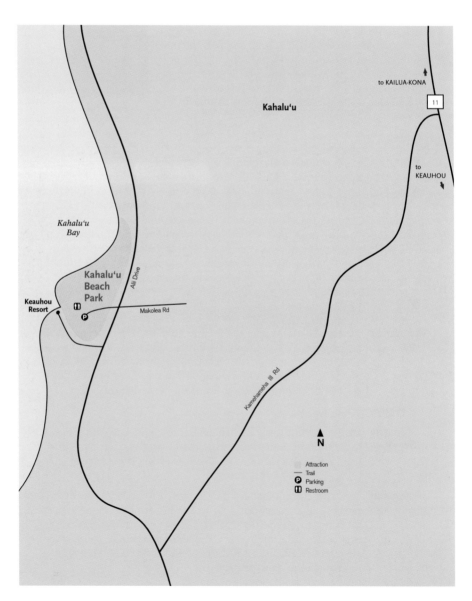

to KAILUA-KONA

Kahalu'u

11

to
KEAUHOU

*Kahalu'u
Bay*

**Kahalu'u
Beach
Park**

Alii Drive

**Keauhou
Resort**

Makolea Rd

Kamehameha III Rd

N

Attraction
Trail
Parking
Restroom

yellowfin goatfish

BACKGROUND

This stunning bay with clear, turquoise water is known for its extraordinary coral reefs and snorkeling and the regular appearance of spinner dolphins. The popular bay has also played an important role in Hawaiian history. Captain James Cook unexpectedly discovered the Hawaiian Islands in 1778. His explorations took him to Kealakekua Bay during the time of the annual festival (makahiki) when Lono, the god of land fertility, was dominant. Because of this timing, Hawaiians may have believed that Captain Cook was Lono. Cook was treated very well by the Hawaiians during his stay and departed, only to quickly return because a mast broke. Tensions increased when a British rowboat was stolen and a fracas ensued that resulted in Cook's death. To commemorate his discovery of the Hawaiian Islands, the British erected a monument to Cook at Ka'awaloa. The monument and the land upon which it is located are still maintained by the British Government. The Hikiau Heiau at Nāpō'opo'o at the south end of the bay remains an important shrine in Hawaiian cultural history. The Park has recently rebuilt restrooms and a picnic area at this fully accessible site so visitors can linger and enjoy one of Hawai'i's most significant historic sites.

DESCRIPTION

In addition to its rich history, Kealakekua Bay is one of several embayments along the Kona Coast where spinner dolphins (nai'a) rest during the day. They are drawn to the clear, shallow, sandy bottom of the bay, which provides a safe place for them to rest after a night of hunting in deeper offshore waters. If you've come for the snorkeling, you won't be disappointed. Kealakekua Bay is also a state designated Marine Life Conservation District, so posted fishing rules must be followed in the bay. These regulations ensure that a rich diversity of mature reef fish can be found among the healthy coral heads. The best snorkeling is at Ka'awaloa Cove, near the Captain Cook monument at the north end of the bay. If surf conditions aren't too heavy, you will have excellent views of many colorful fish. This is a great place for beginners to enjoy some successful snorkeling. You will feel far away from the urban scene here as there is little modern development on the bay and much of the viewscape is very natural.

WILDLIFE TO WATCH

Researchers, dolphin lovers and wildlife viewers have been coming to Kealakekua Bay for decades because the **dolphins** regularly appear. Do your part to protect the dolphins by viewing from a distance. Please do not swim with them. If you want to view the bay from a boat, select a tour operator who puts the needs of the dolphins first and abides by marine regulations.

spinner dolphins

VIEWING TIPS

Come early in the morning for an excellent chance to see dolphins in the bay throughout the year. Locate them by their exuberant spinning jumps or look for groups of them arching through the waves. Keep your distance and refrain from approaching them. The best ways to see the dolphins are with binoculars from the sea wall at the end of the road next to Hikiau Heiau, by sea kayak or on a tour boat excursion. However you see the dolphins, wear polarizing sunglasses to cut down the glare from the water. If you want to snorkel, get there early to avoid the crowds. Invest in a fish identification book to help you attach names to the colorful fish that you will see. If you'd like to see the Cook Monument and do some snorkeling, you can hike down a steep, 2-mile trail on old Ka'awaloa Road, but the best way to view the monument is by boat.

Site Notes Parking can be limited so arrive early, particularly if you plan to rent a sea kayak in Captain Cook and drive it down to Nāpō'opo'o Landing to launch (note there are no kayak rental operations at the bay). Commercial tour operators offer snorkel and spinner dolphin combo trips out of Kailua Pier, Keauhou Bay and Honokōhau Harbor.

Hours No posted hours

Nearby Services Gas and food are available in Kealakekua and Captain Cook. Lodging is available in Kealakekua and Kailua-Kona. Big Island Visitors Bureau, (808) 961-5797 (Hilo Office), (808) 886-1655 (West Hawai'i Office), www.bigisland.org.

Special Tips Remember, the spinner dolphins are in the bay to rest. You must remain at least 150 feet away from them. Exercise caution when using sea kayaks as large swells can make boating hazardous. If you're in a kayak, please refrain from landing on the coral reefs or walking on them as this damages the

HAWAI'I • Kealakekua Bay State Historical Park

fragile coral. The road to the beach is narrow and winding and passes through a residential area.

Contact Information   Department of Land and Natural Resources, Division of State Parks, 75 Aupuni St., Hilo, HI, 96720, (808) 974-6200; www.hawaii.gov/dlnr/dsp

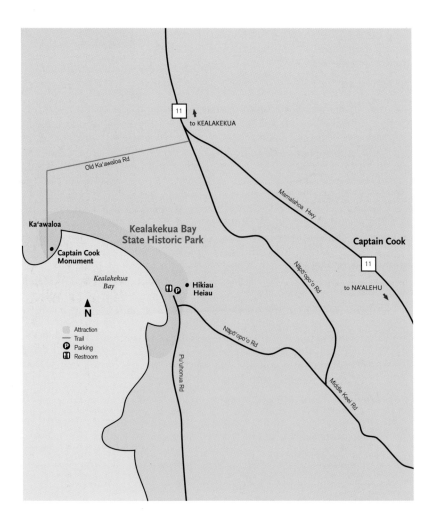

Spinner Dolphins

After a night of hunting in large groups in the deep waters off the Hawaiian coasts, spinner dolphins (naiʻa) often return to shallow, sandy-bottomed bays throughout the Hawaiian Islands during the day to rest, care for their young and avoid predators. There is safety in numbers so the dolphins frequently travel in groups, ranging from a few to several dozen individuals.

The aptly named spinners are among the most spectacular acrobats of the cetaceans (dolphins and whales). Their leaps and spins out of the water may include up to seven complete turns as they ascend and descend. Some scientists believe they leap to help synchronize movements within a group. Others think that they may be removing small living organisms that are clinging to their skin.

You can identify spinner dolphins by their distinctive coloring and appearance. They have a prominent, long, thin beak and are three-toned: dark on the top, gray on the sides and light on the belly. They have a prominent triangular dorsal fin situated midway along their back. If you are fortunate to see them riding the bow of your vessel, try to look for the dark stripe extending from the eye to the flipper to distinguish them from bottlenose dolphins and spotted dolphins.

For many Hawaiians, spinner dolphins are an important ʻaumakua, a physical manifestation of an ancestral spirit. Many of the sites associated with these animals are also sacred to people of that area, so respect and sensitivity are both required when viewing dolphins.

There are several types of spinner dolphins in the world's oceans, and the ones that inhabit the waters around the Hawaiian Islands are unique to the area.

Hawaiʻi's population of spinner dolphins has not been impacted by the tuna fishery, but there is increasing concern about the welfare of this population due to human encroachment in the dolphins' resting areas. Please remember that anytime you see dolphins while enjoying Hawaiʻi's coastal waters, you should remain at least 50 yards away to avoid disturbing their resting and social behaviors.

See pages 21–25 for ethical viewing tips.

HAWAIʻI • Kealakekua Bay State Historical Park

Pu'uhonua o Hōnaunau National Historic Park

Unique cultural site, beautiful scenery and best snorkeling on the Big Island

BACKGROUND

For centuries, the black lava flats bordering Hōnaunau Bay became one of the most important residences of early Hawaiian chiefs. A beautiful sheltered cove provided an ideal spot for canoe landings. There was no palace in this tranquil coconut grove; instead, a dozen thatched buildings served the family's needs. One of the most prominent structures is a massive stone wall that separated the royal grounds from a sanctuary created to give defeated warriors and others unfortunate people a second chance. No bloodshed was allowed at this pu'uhōnua, or Place of Refuge, as it is called. In Hawaiian lore, anyone who broke one of the many taboos (kapu) would be punished by death. If the law breaker escaped, however, and made it to the sanctuary, he or she could be absolved and return home safely. This important cultural site was occupied until 1819, when King Kamehameha abolished some of these old traditions. Today, you can visit and see a model of the site, re-created structures, bowls carved into rock and even papamū, a stone slab "board" used for playing kōnane, a form of Hawaiian checkers.

DESCRIPTION

You can stand next to the Great Wall at Pu'uhonua o Hōnaunau and feel a sense of awe and wonder. The 1,000-foot-long wall made of native rock is ten feet high and 17 feet thick. It separates this grass and white sand compound from the rugged lava surrounding it. You can easily stroll on the .5-mile self-guided walking tour and possibly hear one of the many cultural or historical stories from volunteers that are present on the grounds. Throughout the year there are good chances of seeing many non-native birds while you are in the compound. Some of the best wildlife viewing will not be on the site, but next to it, at the network of coral reefs just offshore. Hōnaunau Bay is one of the premier snorkeling and diving spots in the

LEFT: green sea turtle

HAWAI'I • Pu'uhonua o Hōnaunau National Historic Park

Premier
— SITE —
149

state. The coral gardens are spectacular and are honeycombed with areas to see colorful fish.

WILDLIFE TO WATCH

Green sea turtles (honu) are common in the protected cove. Some come ashore and bask on the sandy beach. Shrubs and trees within the compound may produce year-round views of many non-native birds, including the **yellow-billed cardinal**, **lavender waxbill** and **java sparrow**. The snorkeling experience outside the Park is superb. The coral formations are magnets for many colorful fish, including several types of **butterflyfish**, **wrasse** (hīnālea), **surgeonfish**, **parrotfish** and the **Hawaiian triggerfish** (humuhumunuku-nukuapua'a). Watch for **moray eels** in the crevices and **barracuda** (kākū) in the open water. If you visit at dusk, you may catch a glimpse of **Hawaiian hoary bats** ('ōpe'ape'a) as they leave their daytime roosts to hunt. **Spinner dolphins** (nai'a) are frequently seen within the bay where they rest during the day.

VIEWING TIPS

Advanced snorkelers can enter the adjacent bay at a shelf of lava called "two step." Beginning snorkelers may feel more comfortable at the boat launch where there is calm water, a sandy bottom and a gradual entry into the surf. After you're done snorkeling, watch for spinner dolphins that frequent the bay. You may see their shiny backs as they surface to breathe or spot them leaping and spinning midair.

stout moray

Raccoon, or Masked, Butterflyfish

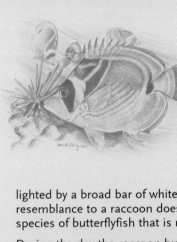

There are more than a two dozen species of butterflyfish in the Hawaiian Islands; this fellow is one that may be a bit harder to spot during daylight hours. The raccoon butterflyfish (kīkākapu) gets its name from the distinct black mask over its eyes, high-lighted by a broad bar of white above the mask and eyes. The resemblance to a raccoon doesn't stop there, for this is the only species of butterflyfish that is nocturnal.

During the day the raccoon butterflyfish is bright yellow and rests in the water by hiding among schools of other colorful fish. At night, the bright yellow appears drab brown, making it less noticeable while hunting. The black bar over its eyes may confuse other fish by effectively hiding its eyes.

Like its cousins, the raccoon butterflyfish is disk-shaped and narrow. It is good at evading predators by fitting through small openings. It uses its long snout to probe into crevices for algae, invertebrates, coral and other food.

Butterflyfish are among the most colorful of Hawaiian reef fishes. They are also very spiny, so the bright coloration could be a warning to other fish that they would not be tasty mouthfuls. They were nevertheless important to early Hawaiians, who considered some of the fish "kīkākapu." This meant that taking these specific fish was "strongly prohibited," as they were considered sacred. The "kapu" part of their Hawaiian name accentuates their restricted status.

See pages 21–25 for ethical viewing tips.

Site Notes Snorkeling and swimming are not allowed within the National Park, but the adjoining Hōnaunau Bay is accessible to snorkelers from a road next to the Park entrance. There is limited parking along the bay, so park in the National Park lot and walk to the bay. The entry point called "two step" is a shelf of lava that drops off into deep water. It can be a rough entry when the ocean is choppy. Picnic tables and BBQs at the southern end of the Park provide a nice place for a mid-day picnic or sunset meal.

Hours Visitor Center is open 8 AM–5:30 PM daily

Nearby Services Gas, food and lodging available in Captain Cook. For more information, contact the Big Island Visitors Bureau, (808) 961-5797 (Hilo Office), (808) 886-1655 (West Hawai'i Office), www.bigisland.org.

Special Tips This Park is popular and the parking lots can become full. Please respect local residents and their property, especially along Hōnaunau Bay outside of the Park.

Contact Information Pu'uhonua o Hōnaunau National Historic Park, P.O. Box 129, Hōnaunau, HI, 96726, Headquarters (808) 328-3236, Visitor Information (808) 328-2288, www.nps.gov/poho

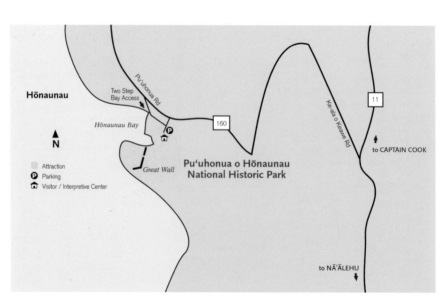

Hawaiian hoary bat

Kamehameha butterfly

BACKGROUND

Mauna Loa volcano has been growing for almost one million years, adding to its mass and height with accumulations of its own molten lava. As the lava streamed down the flanks of Mauna Loa, strips of native trees and plants survived between the dense and chunky lava. Following years of eruptions, layers of lava have accumulated, and upon this rugged base a wealth of vegetation has taken hold. These islands of vegetation on the older lava flows are called kīpuka. Younger vegetation occurs on the more recent lava flows. At the 5,000-foot elevation of this site, the dominant forest trees are 'ōhi'a—unusually tall, shaggy-barked trees that have become a haven for native forest birds. Rock mounds set in terraces on the lava are evidence of early Hawaiians, who farmed the area, probably growing sweet potatoes, taro and other crops. The 13.4-acre Wayside Park is located within the Manukā State Natural Area Reserve. It includes a small arboretum that features many native plant specimens.

DESCRIPTION

If you enjoy lush plants and vegetation along with wildlife viewing, this compact reserve should be on your "must see" list. You can experience the mature forest that has sprung from this 2,300- to 4,000-year-old lava flow on a self-guided nature trail. The 2-mile loop leads you through 20 stations that include native plants, rock walls and planting mounds, and even a stop devoted to Hawai'i's only native land mammal, the Hawaiian hoary bat ('ōpe'ape'a). The trail begins at the parking area with samples of native plants scattered across the manicured grounds. At the first stop, for example, native 'ōhi'a are interspersed with introduced plants such as strawberry guava (waiawī). The second stop describes the older lava flows and the much newer lava near the trail. The sixth station teaches you about the mesic forest community, which contains vegetation from both rain forest and dry lowland habitats. The eleventh station points out the māmaki plant. This relative of nettle is the host plant for the caterpillar that transforms into the reddish orange Kamehameha butterfly (pulelehua), one of Hawai'i's two native butterflies. At station 18, late afternoon or evening visitors are urged to watch for the Hawaiian hoary bat. Throughout the forest you should look for native and non-native forest birds.

WILDLIFE TO WATCH

The primary focus of the Reserve is clearly plants, but you can use your knowledge of plants to help locate wildlife. The well-developed understory attracts many insect eating birds, such as the 'elepaio. This active little bird plucks insects from vegetation and catches them on the wing. It often perches with its tail held high or cocked and seems

Japanese white-eye

very used to humans. Hawaiian canoe makers consider this bird their guardian spirit. The 'apapane haunts the forest canopy, a red bird searching for nectar among the red blossoms of 'ōhi'a and other flowering trees. This is one of the most visible birds in the Reserve and among honeycreepers, the most vocal. Their repertoire includes many songs, whistles, buzzes, trills and clucks. The 'amakihi is also present. The bright yellow bird with black curved bill is sometimes visible in the white-flowered wiliwili trees near the picnic area, creeping along the branches in search of nectar or insects. Non-native birds are numerous, from the **Japanese white-eye** to the **cardinal**. The **Hawaiian hoary bat** sometimes makes afternoon appearances throughout the Reserve. You may also spot **Kamehameha butterflies**.

VIEWING TIPS

There are few places you can see the Hawaiian hoary bat and this is one of them. You can distinguish them from birds by the darting and fluttering flight. Time your visit for late afternoon or evening for the best chances of seeing one. The Kamehameha butterfly is a winged beauty that is seasonally present at the Reserve. The tree canopy is quite dense; bring binoculars and use them to scan the canopy, especially where you see flowering blossoms.

Site Notes	Allow 2 to 3 hours to make the loop hike. There is an elevation gain of 400 feet. Picnic tables and restrooms make this a nice stop between Mauna Loa Volcano and Kona.
Hours	No posted hours
Nearby Services	Gas, food and lodging are available at Nā'ālehu. Camping is allowed at the wayside with a permit from State Parks. For more information, contact the Big Island Visitors Bureau, (808) 961-5797 (Hilo Office), (808) 886-1655 (West Hawai'i Office), www.bigisland.org.
Special	The trail is well maintained but is rocky and may be muddy

Tips and slippery when wet. Wear sturdy, protective shoes. Because of the tall, closed canopy, it gets dark early here. Mosquitoes are fierce; long pants, long sleeves and insect repellent are highly recommended. (One of the stops along the trail discusses the accidental introduction of mosquitoes from seafaring westerners.) Be sure to bring your own water as none is available on site. A brochure is now available. Call (808) 974-4221.

Contact Information Department of Land and Natural Resources, Division of State Parks, 75 Aupuni Street, Room 204, Hilo, HI 96720; (808) 974-6200, www.hawaii.gov/dlnr/dsp

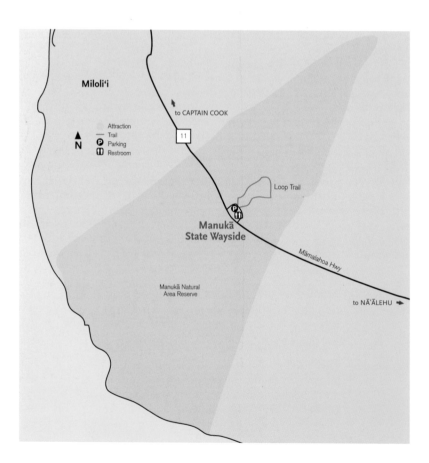

'elepaio

Hawaiian hawk

BACKGROUND

When you visit the Hawaiian islands, remember that the ground beneath your feet was entirely created by volcanoes. Cataclysmic eruptions and rivers of molten lava have accumulated layer upon layer, forming a wild and rugged landscape on which life has taken hold and evolved. The island of Hawai'i is topped by two of the world's most active volcanoes, Kīlauea and Mauna Loa, fueled by subterranean magma that periodically gushes forth in flaming streams and blazing fountains. They are among the best understood volcanoes on earth, providing invaluable insights into the processes of volcanism. Here, at Hawai'i Volcanoes National Park, you can safely see a live volcano in action, both on site and by live remote camera. You can also enjoy excellent wildlife viewing, thanks to active programs to eliminate feral pigs, non-native plants and other unwanted pests that compete with native species. The Park supports a wide range of native and non-native species, from the nēnē and Hawaiian hawk ('io) to several species of honeycreepers and butterflies. The Park has been recognized as an International Biosphere Reserve and a World Heritage site.

DESCRIPTION

Visitors to this 300,000-acre park are often amazed by the contrasting landscapes. Fields and gullies of lava still smoke and fume adjacent to lush strips of native forest. You absolutely must begin your visit with a stop at the Kīlauea Visitor Center. There is an excellent Park orientation film to prepare you for your visit and help you select areas to see. Numerous displays help you understand 70 to 80 million years of volcanism that created the Hawaiian Islands and the changes occurring in the Park today. The center provides trail maps, brochures, an outstanding bookstore, daily activities and safety precautions. You can take a one-mile hike from the Visitor Center, passing 'ōhi'a trees where 'apapane and other nectar-feeding birds often feed. The route skirts steam vents that will remind you that the volcano is active beneath your feet. Many people simply drive the 11-mile Crater Rim Drive, stopping at the overlooks and Hawaiian Volcano Observatory. If you have only a short time for a hike, descend through the 'ōhi'a and fern forest leading to the Thurston Lava Tube. A lava tube forms when lava starts to cool around the edges but flows continue, eventually forming a round tunnel. This popular site can be crowded, but the overlook to the lava tube entrance offers outstanding views into the 'ōhi'a tree canopy, where you might see 'apapane, 'amakihi and other forest birds. For those with more time, take the Chain of Craters Road, a 40-mile trip that ascends 3,700 feet to ocean. Numerous overlooks provide views of pit craters and lava flows and, at the lower reaches, seabirds, wintering whales (koholā) and dolphins (nai'a). You can hike onto the lava flows at the end of the road. When lava reaches the ocean, huge steam plumes are visible.

WILDLIFE TO WATCH

On the Chain of Craters Road, watch for the endangered **nēnē**. In the winter, you may spot adults and goslings feeding on grasses and tender leaves growing along the roadside. **Hawaiian hawks** may be seen soaring overhead or perched in trees, particularly off of Crater Rim Drive, Chain of Craters Road and Mauna Loa Road. **White-tailed tropicbirds** (koa'e kea) frequent Halemaumau Crater at the summit of Kīlauea and also nest in the pit craters in the Ka'ū Desert. Listen for their harsh, staccato calls as they circle Halema'uma'u. **Kalij pheasants** in family groups are common in Kīpuka Puaulu, along Mauna Loa Road and on other Park roadsides early in the morning. You may hear the loud, cackling laugh of introduced **Erckel's francolins** in dry shrubland areas, especially in the morning. **Black noddies** (noio) are quite common along the ocean cliffs, where they nest on ledges or in caves during spring. These tern-like birds have a black body with a distinctive white cap and forehead. Seaward, look for spouting and breaching **humpback whales** during winter, and **spinner dolphins** throughout the year. In areas with a good forest canopy, watch for forest birds such as the 'apapane, a red honeycreeper that spends much of its time high in the trees. You may also spot the 'amakihi.

VIEWING TIPS

This is a huge landscape. Bring binoculars to bring distant views closer. Forest birds are most active in the mornings and late afternoons. Stop anytime you see blossoms and you may spot some of the nectar-feeding honeycreepers. Try standing in one spot for a while and listen for their calls. Sometimes it's hard to look straight up into the canopy and see these tiny birds. Try looking from gaps in the forest, such as parking lots, which offer a better viewing angle. In good weather, the patio (lanai) behind Volcano House also offers views of the tree tops below.

White-tailed Tropicbird

White-tailed tropicbirds (koa'e kea) are among a handful of seabirds that are so distinctive they are almost signatures of Hawai'i. The strikingly white bird has black eye stripes and bold black bars on the wings, but it's the tail that attracts notice. These elegant streamers may be as long as 16 inches, formed of narrow, glossy feathers.

White-tailed tropicbirds occur on all of the main Hawaiian Islands, some even nesting far inland in volcanic calderas. Even those that nest inland fly daily to the ocean to feed, often hovering above the water then plunging 50 to 100 feet in a steep dive to pick up fish, squid or other edibles near the surface. Their flight is one of easy grace and has linked them to poetic descriptions of cliffs and other places where they nest. Such steep locations are called "pali lele koa'e," which translates to "cliff where the tropicbirds soar."

You can be sure that these conspicuous white birds caught the attention of ancient Hawaiians. Only chiefs and other high ranking individuals possessed the rare and beautiful feathers. They were a symbol of rank and were principally used to make the kāhili, a large staff or standard, with a crown of long, beautiful feathers. Many of the very narrow tropicbird's tail feathers were required to make a kāhili, which was placed inside a chief's home or carried before the individual, announcing his or her presence, as in a procession.

See pages 21–25 for ethical viewing tips.

HAWAI'I • Hawai'i Volcanoes National Park: Chain of Craters Road

Premier
– SITE –

Mauna Loa Road

The Mauna Loa Road exposes you to a different view of this vast park on the world's most massive mountain, Mauna Loa. The road winds through kīpuka, or islands of native forest and other vegetation, that are surrounded by more recent lava flows. These areas afford panoramic views of the summit of Kīlauea. Here the landscape is transitioning from native koa-'ōhi'a forest to open shrublands dominated by 'a'ali'i, Hawaiian heath (pūkiawe) and tufted hairgrass. This is forest bird country and you have excellent chances of seeing many resident forest birds.

Access Mauna Loa Road on Highway 11 south from the Visitor Center. One mile in, pause at Kīpuka Puaulu (sometimes called Bird Park) and take the short loop trail, which offers close-up views of a rich mesic forest, an increasingly rare ecosystem in Hawai'i. Local birds include the native Hawaiian thrush ('ōma'o), which is more often heard than seen. If you notice a plump, drab bird that quivers its wings while perched, it is probably the Hawaiian thrush. This also is a good place to spot the perky native 'elepaio and the colorful introduced red-billed leiothrix.

The remainder of Mauna Loa Road traverses rugged lava flows, koa forests and mixed forests of 'ōhi'a and māmane as it winds up to Mauna Loa lookout. Part of the way up, the narrow, two-lane road turns into a single lane. Once at the top of the road, take the trail at the lookout, leaving the forested kīpuka and entering more open countryside. Look for 'apapane, 'amakihi and 'i'iwi in the scattered 'ōhi'a and māmane trees.

On the way back down the road stop at one of several small pull-offs and scan the trees and shrubs for birds. You may also see two native butterflies (pulelehua): the Kamehameha and Blackburn butterflies, which feed on the nettle (māmaki) and 'a'ali'i plants by the lava flow. The Kamehameha is easy to identify. With a 3-inch wingspan and upper wings that are a bold orange-red with black and white markings, this beautiful velvet-winged traveler was named for one of Hawai'i's famous kings. Females often lay their eggs on the māmaki, which grows along the roadside in Kīpuka Kī and Kīpuka Puaulu. Though hard to find, the small Blackburn butterfly may be spotted near the Mauna Loa Road. Look for the iridescent purplish blue on the tops of their wings

The trail can be windy early in the afternoon, so time the trip for morning or late afternoon. If it's cloudy, do some other sightseeing and return when the clouds lift.

Site Notes You really need at least two days to explore the Park and could easily spend much more time here. It is a good idea to spend the night in Hilo or in the Park. There are numerous accommodations in Volcano, as well as cabins and campgrounds in the Park. Call (808) 985-6000 anytime to get an eruption update or check http://hvo.wr.usgs.gov/.

Hours Hawai'i Volcanoes National Park is open 24 hours a day all year. Kīlauea Visitor Center is open daily from 7:45 AM–5 PM; Jaggar Museum is open daily from 8:30 AM–5 PM.

Nearby Services Gas, food and lodging are available at Volcano. For more information contact the Big Island Visitors Bureau, (808) 961-5797 (Hilo Office), (808) 886-1655 (West Hawai'i Office), www.bigisland.org.

Special Tips Use caution when driving the Park's winding roads. Wear closed-toe shoes that protect your feet if you plan to hike. Be sure to read the Park's brochure about safe lava viewing. Bring a flashlight for evening lava viewing. Air quality can be poor in some areas of the Park, depending on eruption activity and winds. Real time air quality information is available at the Kīlauea Visitor Center.

Contact Information Hawai'i Volcanoes National Park, PO Box 52, Hawai'i National Park, HI 96718, (808) 985-6000, www.nps.gov/havo

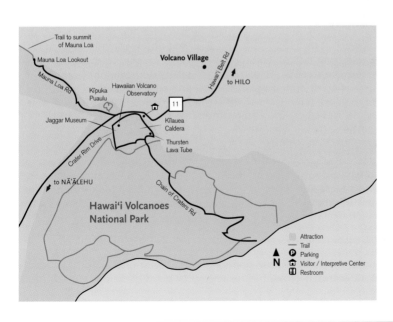

Trail to summit of Mauna Loa

Mauna Loa Lookout

Mauna Loa Rd

Kīpuka Puaulu

Hawaiian Volcano Observatory

Volcano Village

Hawai'i Belt Rd

to HILO

11

Jaggar Museum

Crater Rim Drive

Kīlauea Caldera

Thursten Lava Tube

to NĀ'ĀLEHU

Chain of Craters Rd

Hawai'i Volcanoes National Park

Attraction
Trail
Parking
Visitor / Interpretive Center
Restroom

N

wandering tattler

DESCRIPTION

Good birding in a downtown park? Yes, during winter Wailoa River State Recreation Area in the heart of Hilo town offers terrific birding by Hawaiian standards. This 131-acre site is located along Hilo Bay and embraces the lower portion of the Wailoa River. At one time, this lower portion of the river was developed into fishponds and today, the river here still looks like a large pond. When you're not watching for birds, there are walking paths, picnic tables and the Wailoa Center with information and art displays. The setting is very tranquil, with picturesque views of Mauna Kea and Hilo Bay. The Park includes a statue of Kamehameha I and a memorial recognizing the tsunami that devastated Hilo on April 1, 1946.

WILDLIFE TO WATCH

In addition to the typical non-native **mynas**, **cardinals**, **house sparrows** and **zebra doves** that are permanent, year-round residents, you can see **Canada geese**, **wandering tattlers** ('ūlili) and **Pacific golden-plovers** (kōlea) from fall through spring. Mixed among the migrants, you'll undoubtedly see some resident **Hawaiian coots** ('alae ke'oke'o) and a scattering of farm ducks. A surprising variety of migratory waterfowl and shorebirds stop at Wailoa River. **Snow geese** have been seen in the area, as well as **northern pintails** (koloa māpu), **northern shovelers** (koloa mohā), **pied-billed grebes**, **redheads**, **buffleheads** and **teal**. **Cattle egrets**, **great blue herons** and **green herons** sometimes hunt in shallow areas of the river. A high point of your visit may be the chance sighting of the **Hawaiian hawk** ('io). This compact hawk has two color phases: all dark or dark on the back and pale with streaking on the chest. They hold their wings in a V shape in flight, often gliding on updrafts. The hawk has long been a symbol of the Hawaiian ali'i, or chiefs, who named 'Iolani Palace after these graceful soaring birds.

VIEWING TIPS

Make sure you scan all of the open water and shoreline with binoculars to find solitary or small groupings of migratory shorebirds and waterbirds.

Watch for Pacific golden-plovers and Canada geese on the turf. Anglers and other recreationists may drive the birds to quieter portions of the park, so take your time to look throughout the area. The elevated bridges over the river are good vantage points to look for birds and enjoy the scenery.

SITE NOTES

This is a very manicured site without any natural habitats except the ponds of the river. Much of the site is accessible to those with disabilities.

Hours 7 AM to midnight

Nearby Services Gas, food and lodging are available in Hilo. For more information, contact the Big Island Visitors Bureau, (808) 961-5797 (Hilo Office), (808) 886-1655 (West Hawai'i Office), www.bigisland.org.

Special Tips None

Contact Information Department of Land and Natural Resources, Division of State Parks, 75 Aupuni Street, Room 204, Hilo, HI 96720, (808) 974-6200, www.hawaii.gov/dlnr/dsp

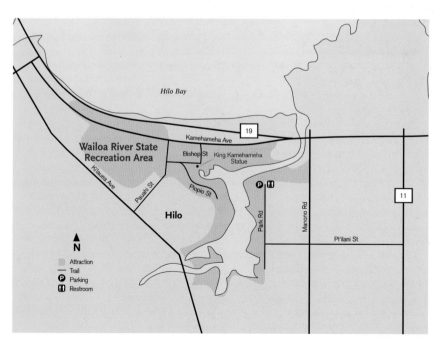

HAWAI'I • *Wailoa River State Recreation Area*

Hawaiian short-eared owl

BACKGROUND

In hues of reds and browns, evidence of old lava flows is everywhere here, on top of the world. The Saddle Road is an extraordinarily scenic, winding road that stretches between Mauna Kea and Mauna Loa. It includes a portion of the road once intended to connect Kona and Hilo, a project that was never completed because the partially built thoroughfare was covered by a river of lava spewed from Mauna Loa. Birders looking for a somewhat rigorous drive that leads to reliable forest bird viewing—either from a short trail or your vehicle—will enjoy this foray into the wilder side of Hawaiʻi. Most of the viewing occurs within a 38-acre kīpuka, an area where lava has threaded around islands of vegetation that survived eruptions in 1843 and 1935 and ensuing outside influences. The remaining patches of ʻōhiʻa, koa, māmane and naio are a few of the once abundant forest trees that now survive in these lava-bordered islands. Their colorful and often pleasant smelling flowers are a vital source of food for native forest birds that are almost always evident, from the ʻiʻiwi, ʻapapane and ʻamakihi to less common Hawaiʻi thrush (ʻōmaʻo) and ʻelepaio.

DESCRIPTION

If you've seen television or movie presentations about volcanism, you've watched as molten streams of lava pour down mountainsides, capriciously parting to spare a swath or island of vegetation. The trip to this native forest tree sanctuary will allow you to not only see the results of such flows, but also to observe the colorful forest birds that have evolved to survive in these small enclaves. You can spot them from your vehicle or by hiking a trail built by the Youth Conservation Corps in the late 1970s. A .6-mile loop trail with side trails traverses the side of the kīpuka up to the summit of two adjoining hilltops. On a clear day the views of Mauna Kea and Mauna Loa can be spectacular. The entire Saddle Road is marked by many kīpuka that are magnets for forest birds, so drive slowly and be prepared to stop to scan the treetops for feeding birds. The grasslands are also home to the Hawaiian short-eared owl (pueo) and the Hawaiian hawk (ʻio). Both can be seen scouring the grasslands for rodents during the day. As you enjoy these native birds, remember their habitat is being actively managed to fence out feral sheep and goats, control weeds and replant native vegetation once present here.

WILDLIFE TO WATCH

This may be one of the best places to see native forest birds anytime of year on the Big Island. These birds are closely tied to 'ōhi'a, koa, māmane and naio ecosystems, which are still plentiful along the Saddle Road. Predators and introduced grazing animals have been fenced out of the sanctuary, helping to protect these unique native birds. You will be able to see the crimson colored 'i'iwi and 'apapane along the koa and 'apapane trails. The bright yellow 'amakihi can be spotted with little effort on the 'amakihi leg of the trail system. Stop long enough to relish the silence and then their calls, and enjoy the magic of their songs. Bring binoculars and scan the open grasslands and you may be rewarded with views of hunting **Hawaiian hawks** or **short-eared owls**. Even **nēnē**, the small relatives of Canadian geese, are occasionally present during the summer in the grasslands, where they feed on grass, seeds and berries. You may also spot the **Hawai'i thrush** and the 'elepaio.

VIEWING TIPS

You can spot some of these birds easily because you will notice a flash of color as they speed past. Bring binoculars to locate the more secretive birds or those that are farther away. Scan the upper canopy for signs of the colorful forest birds. Use your ears to locate birds such as the Hawai'i thrush, a drab bird with a call that has been compared to the sound of tuning a radio between stations. The 'elepaio is not so elusive, often flying very close to people and even following hikers along the trail. If it perches, you may notice its tail cocked at an acute angle. If it calls, you will remember its voice: a squeaky version of its own name, "ele-pa-yo." If you want a sure bet to see Hawaiian hawks, drive up the paved portion of the Mauna Kea Observatory Road, where you can also relish the view of the grasslands. If your interest in forest birds has been piqued, call ahead to visit the Maulua Tract of Hakalau Forest National Wildlife Refuge, a premier sanctuary for endangered forest birds. You must receive permission in advance to visit this site located off of the Saddle Road. A 4WD vehicle is necessary. Call (808) 933-6915.

Site Notes   As you gain elevation, the weather can be variable so bring layers of clothes and a raincoat; expect cool, windy conditions and fog or rain. The site is very rustic with very few visitor amenities. It takes 45 minutes from Hilo or 90 minutes

HAWAI'I • *Kīpuka Pu'u Huluhulu*

from Kona to get here, so plan on spending at least half a day to make this trip.

Hours 7:45 AM–4:30 PM

Nearby Services Gas, food and lodging are available in Hilo. For more information, contact the Big Island Visitors Bureau, (808) 961-5797 (Hilo Office), (808) 886-1655 (West Hawai'i Office), www.bigisland.org.

Special Tips The paved road is very narrow and winding on the Kona side. If you stop, chose an area where you can safely pull off of the road. Rental car companies may not allow you to drive their 2WD vehicles on the Saddle Road, primarily due to the rugged gravel road that leads to the Mauna Kea Observatory just north of the viewing site. Though the sanctuary is fenced, archery hunting for game birds occurs in the environs on weekends from November through the third weekend in January.

Contact Information Department of Land and Natural Resources/Division of Forestry and Wildlife, 19 E. Kawili St., Hilo, HI, (808) 974-4221, www.hawaii.gov/dlnr/dsp or www.dofaw.net

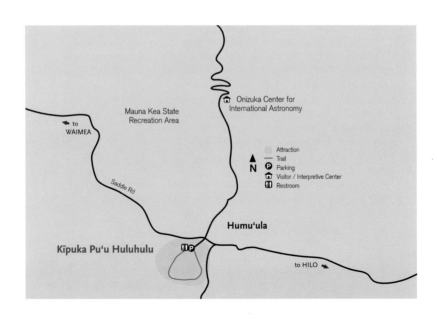

Erckel's francolins

white-browed laughingthrush

BACKGROUND

Hawaiians prize their native resources, and it was the local community that rallied in 1962 to save the Kalōpā tract and other state forests in the Hāmākua district of Hawaiʻi Island. This occurred during an era of continuing loss of native forests, making this native forest's story one of protection and renewal. During the last 30 years, Youth Conservation Corps workers have devoted considerable energy to this forest by building trails, controlling non-native plants and helping with landscaping. As you enter the 100-acre Park, you'll notice many ferns, trees and shrubs that are rare or uncommon, but have been replanted to restore and augment the native ʻōhiʻa forest. The ʻōhiʻa, with shaggy bark and red or yellow flowers, is the most common tree at Kalōpā. Also prevalent is the kōpiko, a member of the coffee family with black bark and yellow-orange fruit. Botanists believe that the planted kōpiko have played a major role in shading out invasive guava; this collection may be the best example of a restored kōpiko grove anywhere on Hawaiʻi.

DESCRIPTION

Kalōpā is the lone remnant of rain forest on a mountainside that was destined for sugarcane cultivation. Trails wind through mossy trees, some of which measure 56 inches in diameter—a testimony to their great longevity. When you enter this ʻōhiʻa forest located at the 2,000-foot elevation, you will leave the sometimes cloudless views of the summit of Mauna Kea and enter a cloistered, shady realm of towering trees. You can begin your visit at the arboretum, a 4-acre parcel with plants brought to Hawaiʻi by the early Polynesians. Though the koa were planted in 1979, some have reached 75 feet in height with a diameter of 14 inches. A .7-mile trail begins at the arboretum and loops through the heart of the ʻōhiʻa rain forest. It is extremely peaceful, the deep silence punctuated only by the light chirping of birds and insects. If it is cool, foggy or misty, the forest takes on a mysterious, almost other-worldly quality. This is largely a pleasant botanical experience with opportunities to see some noteworthy native species.

WILDLIFE TO WATCH

You probably won't see honeycreepers here because there are not enough nectar producing trees; however, the little insect-eating **'elepaio** thrives in the Park. The 'elepaio's coloring differs from island to island, and even on the same island. Those in rain forests like Kalōpā have darker heads and breasts than their dryland cousins. Compared with other forest birds, these birds are quite bold, sometimes approaching people who are near. You may see them sitting with their tail cocked or moving from branch to branch in search of insects. They are enthusiastic singers so you may hear them before you see them. In Hawaiian lore, the 'elepaio is the guardian spirit for canoe builders. When they felled a koa tree, they knew the wood was good if the 'elepaio sang and that the wood was bad (full of insects) if the bird pecked at it for a meal. **Hawaiian hawks** ('io) and **Hawaiian hoary bats** ('ōpe'ape'a) make occasional appearances. A pair of Hawaiian hawks nests in the Park, sometimes in trees next to the arboretum lawn. There are many non-native birds, such as the **cardinal**, **linnet**, **melodious laughing-thrush** and, most conspicuous, the **Kalij pheasant**. As you drive in, watch for **wild turkeys**, which are plentiful in the area. Also, take time to appreciate less charismatic and unusual creatures that the Park sustains, including such oddities as **flightless crickets**. You may also spot **black-crowned night-herons** ('auku'u). There are many wildlife species.

black francolin

VIEWING TIPS

You may have to work to see wildlife here, in part because the heavy growth makes them difficult to see, and because the range of species is limited. Consider investing in audio tapes so you can learn to identify them by their calls. Come at dusk to catch a glimpse of the Hawaiian hoary bat, which sometimes catches insects in flight near the arboretum. Look for night-herons in pothole ponds near the gulch, where they hunt for crayfish.

Site Notes The Park is adjacent to the Kalōpā Gulch Trail System, where you will find additional wooded and very steep trails to explore. Hakalau Forest, one of the finest native forests on the island, is also on the Park's border. If you have children with energy to burn, they can take a nice downhill jog through a chamber-like forest and across a ridgetop on a .8-mile trail. In addition to campsites, the Park offers cabins for rent. Contact the Park to make reservations for a cabin.

Hours No posted hours, though the Park is considered a day use park. It is considered closed at night, from one-half hour before sunset to one-half hour before sunrise.

Nearby Services Gas and food are available at Honoka'a. Lodging is available at Kalōpā State Park, Waimea and Hilo. For more information about nearby accommodations, contact Big Island Visitors Bureau, (808) 961-5797 (Hilo Office), (808) 886-1655 (West Hawai'i Office), www.bigisland.org.

Special Tips The road is narrow. Avoid standing near old trees during high wind as branches may fall. Be aware that pig hunting is allowed on weekends and state holidays. If you visit the gulch rim, the terrain is very steep and slippery when wet.

Contact Information Department of Natural Resources, Division of State Parks, 75 Aupuni St., Hilo, HI, 96720, (808) 974-6200, www.hawaii.gov/dlnr/dsp

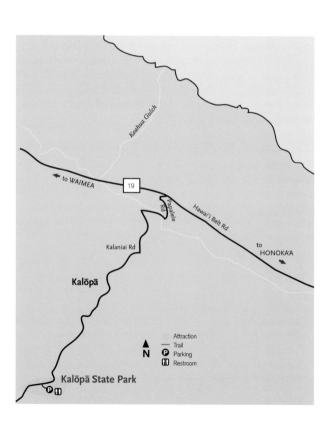

Kalij pheasant

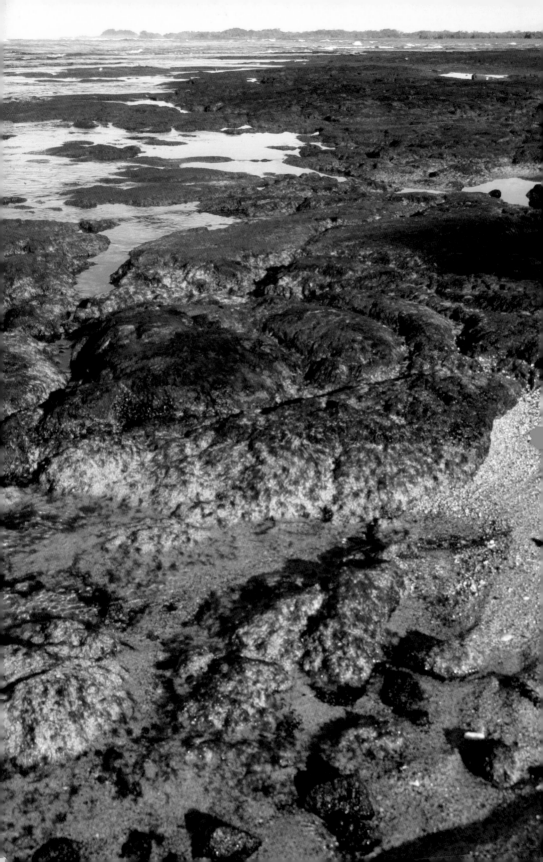

Hawaiian stilts

BACKGROUND

Evidence of Kailua-Kona's developed shoreline seems to fade away as you are caught up with the beauty and bounty of this nearly urban site. The 1,161-acre Park was once the site of a thriving Hawaiian village built on lava flows from the imposing Hualalai volcano. Thousands of archeological and cultural features have been discovered throughout the site. These finds are so significant that Kaloko-Honokōhau is protected as a National Historic Park. This helps preserve the relationship between the people who resided here, their regard for the area's natural resources and their connection with Hawai'i's early culture. The massive seawall that defines Kaloko fishpond, the fish trap at 'Ai'ōpio, several shrines (heiau) and even a stone slide are tangible reminders of the ancient Hawaiians' engineering skills. The sand enclosure at 'Aimakapā Pond was used for fish aquaculture.

DESCRIPTION

In addition to the rich cultural features preserved at this Park, Kaloko-Honokōhau is also perhaps the Big Island's best natural wetland. The ponds, wetlands and tidal areas support a rich array of wildlife and offer a bonanza of viewing opportunities just a stone's throw from town. The 'Aimakapā and Kaloko fishponds provide essential resting, feeding and breeding habitat for the endangered Hawaiian stilt (ae'o) and the Hawaiian coot ('alae ke'oke'o). The ponds and tidal areas are an important sanctuary for numerous migratory shorebirds and waterfowl between September and April. Serious birders will especially find it rewarding to visit the 'Aimakapā Pond because it functions as a migrant bird magnet, attracting a range of unusual and rare birds. Such oddities as canvasback or greater scaup can be mixed in with the more common northern pintail (koloa māpu) and American wigeon. Clusters of small ponds scattered throughout the lava flows are filled with brackish water and sustain many interesting aquatic species, including the Hawaiian red shrimp ('ōpae 'ula) and orange-black damselfly (pinao). The Park is located on a very scenic, crescent-shaped bay with shallow lava shelves. You can often see green sea turtles (honu) basking on the sun-drenched sands or grazing on sea lettuce that grows profusely on these shelves. Offshore waters may produce views of spinner dolphins (nai'a) and during winter, passing humpback whales (koholā).

WILDLIFE TO WATCH

As you walk to the ponds on the trail or lava flows, watch the shrubs and brush for **yellow-billed cardinals**, **saffron finches**, **African silverbills**, **lavender waxbills** and other non-native birds that are present year-round. At the ponds you should have excellent views of resident **Hawaiian stilts** and **Hawaiian coots**. If you don't see the stilts immediately, listen for them calling from the weedy areas of the ponds and follow the sound to find these statuesque black-and-white shorebirds.

From fall through spring they are joined by a wide range of migratory ducks. You'll have reliable views of **northern pintail**, **northern shoveler** (koloa moha), **American wigeon**, **green-winged teal** and other waterfowl. You might also see such rarities as the **canvasback**, **greater scaup**, **Eurasian wigeon**, **garganey** and **tufted duck**.

The rocky shoreline and pond mudflats are popular with many shorebirds. You can identify some of the common ones by their feeding habits. For example, the **Pacific golden-plover** (kōlea) usually runs a short distance and then stops to peck at an insect or invertebrates. The **wandering tattler** ('ūlili) probes deeply in mud or under rocks and has a habit of bobbing its head up and down. It may suddenly crouch if it feels threatened. There is also the chance to make rare sightings of **spotted sandpipers** (upupā), **rufous-necked stints** or numerous other species finding a temporary respite at the Park. The rocky shoreline attracts **black-crowned night-herons** ('auku'u) that hunt for small fish hiding in the sea lettuce.

While you're at the ponds shift your perspective in close to observe the aerial ballet of feeding **damselflies** (pinao). Propelled by long lacy wings, the damselflies can often be seen hovering just above the water's surface or resting lightly on pond vegetation. Under the pond surface, watch for **Hawaiian red shrimp**. Look for **whales** during winter and **turtles** all year. You may also spot **spinner dolphins**.

VIEWING TIPS

Arrive at low tide to see shorebirds on the exposed rocky shelves. Time a visit for high tide to watch sea turtles feeding on sea lettuce in the bay or basking on the warm, sandy beach. Approach the ponds quietly so you don't flush the birds.

HAWAI'I • Kaloko-Honokōhau National Historic Park

Premier
— SITE —

Green Sea Turtle

In a Hawaiian myth, a goddess rides on the back of a green sea turtle. The association of turtles (honu) with Hawaiian mythology underscores the longevity of these reptiles, which are descended from ancestors born 150 million years ago. Over time, the green sea turtle has also become an especially important 'aumakua, or family god or guardian, for many Hawaiians. Hawaiians have lived closely with the honu, hunting it for food and using its shell to make fish hooks, ornaments and other useful items.

Of the five species of sea turtles that occur in Hawai'i, the green sea turtle is most common. It is not unusual to see them in bays and off-shore waters throughout the main Hawaiian Islands. A few nest on Moloka'i and Maui (along the coast near Lahaina and Waihe'e); however, most swim 800 miles to mate and nest at French Frigate Shoals in the remote Hawaiian Islands.

On these isolated islands the female uses her flippers to dig a pit nest, where she may deposit about 100 plum-sized eggs. After two months the eggs hatch all at once, normally under the cover of darkness. Together, tiny hatchlings—each weighing barely an ounce—dig through the heavy sand encasing the nest. When it is cool, indicating that it is evening, they leave the nest. If they are not distracted by shoreline lighting or eaten by predators, they will find the ocean and swim furiously for 36 to 48 hours. If they survive this perilous trip, they will then spend several years at sea before they return to the breeding grounds.

Six of seven of the world's sea turtle species are threatened or endangered. There were once tens of millions of green sea turtles in the world. Today they are threatened, with perhaps only 200,000 females surviving to reach sexual maturity at age 35 to 50 years.

The green sea turtle population in Hawai'i, while threatened, has steadily exhibited signs of recovery following three decades of research, conservation and management directed at restoring the once depleted population. Some viewing sites, such as Kaloko-Honokōhau National Historic Park, offer reliable turtle viewing in a setting that does not adversely affect the animals.

See pages 21–25 for ethical viewing tips.

HAWAI'I • Kaloko-Honokōhau National Historic Park

Site Notes The Visitor Contact Station is a half mile north of the Honokōhau Harbor entrance. It offers information, maps and a bookstore.

Hours Kaloko Road gate is open from 8 AM–5 PM daily. Visitors are welcome in the Park after 5 PM, but vehicles must be outside of Visitor Contact Station parking area and Kaloko area before the gates are closed. Visitor Contact Station hours are 8:30 AM–4 PM daily. Before and after hours, the best access to the Park is located on the north edge of Honokōhau Small Boat Harbor. Follow the harbor road to the right around the harbor and look for the gravel parking area and pipe gate bearing a National Park boundary sign.

Nearby Services A gas station is located across the highway. Food and lodging are available in Kailua-Kona. For more information, contact the Big Island Visitors Bureau, (808) 961-5797 (Hilo Office), (808) 886-1655 (West Hawaiʻi Office), www.bigisland.org.

Special Tips Keep a distance from resting turtles. Wear sturdy, closed-toe shoes to protect your feet from the lava.

Contact Information Kaloko-Honokōhau National Historic Park, 73-4786 Kanalani St. #14, Kailua-Kona, HI 96740, (808) 329-6881, www.nps.gov/kaho

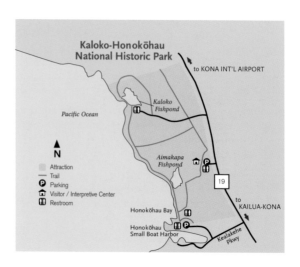

black-crowned night-heron